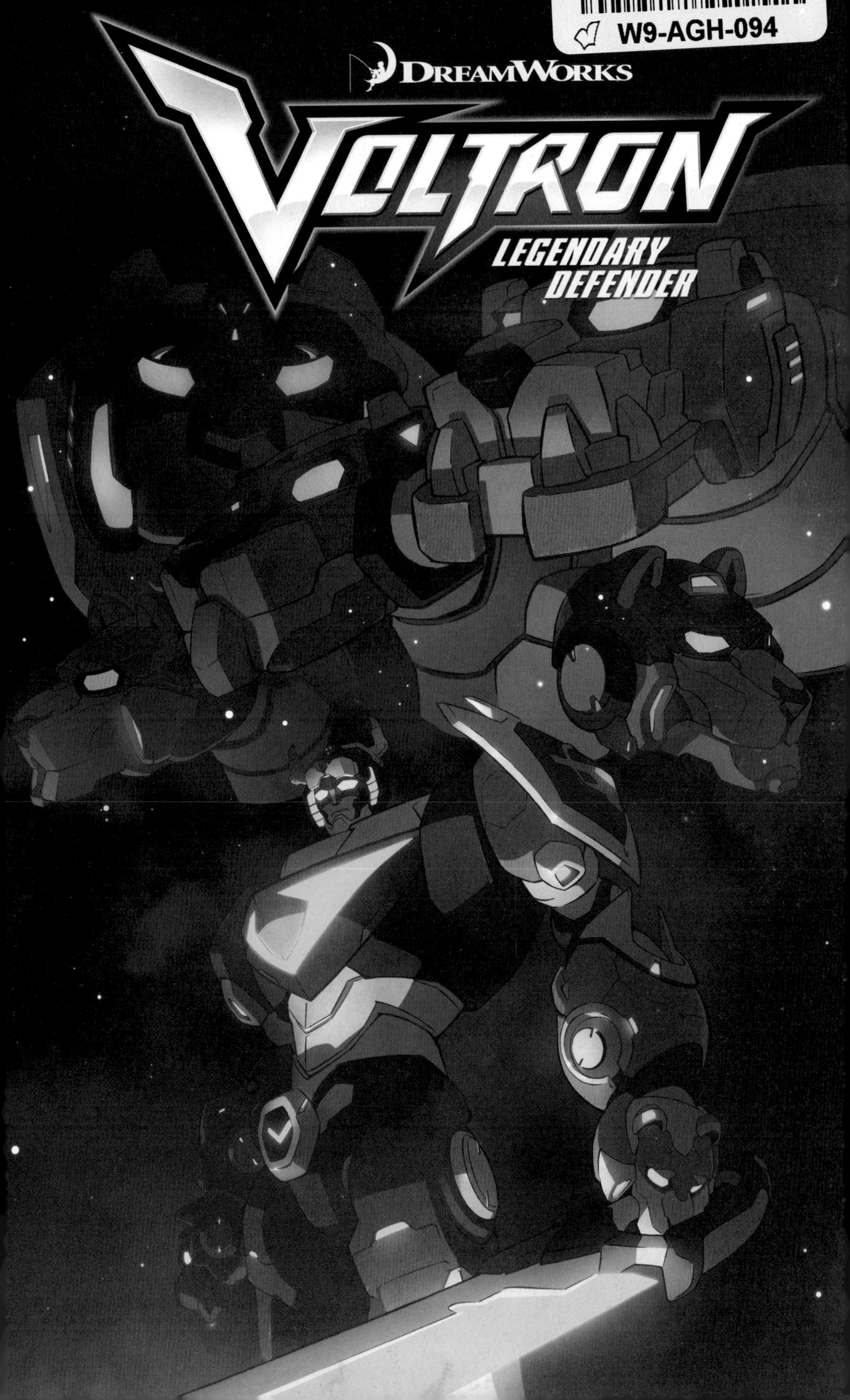
DreamWorks
Voltron
Legendary Defender

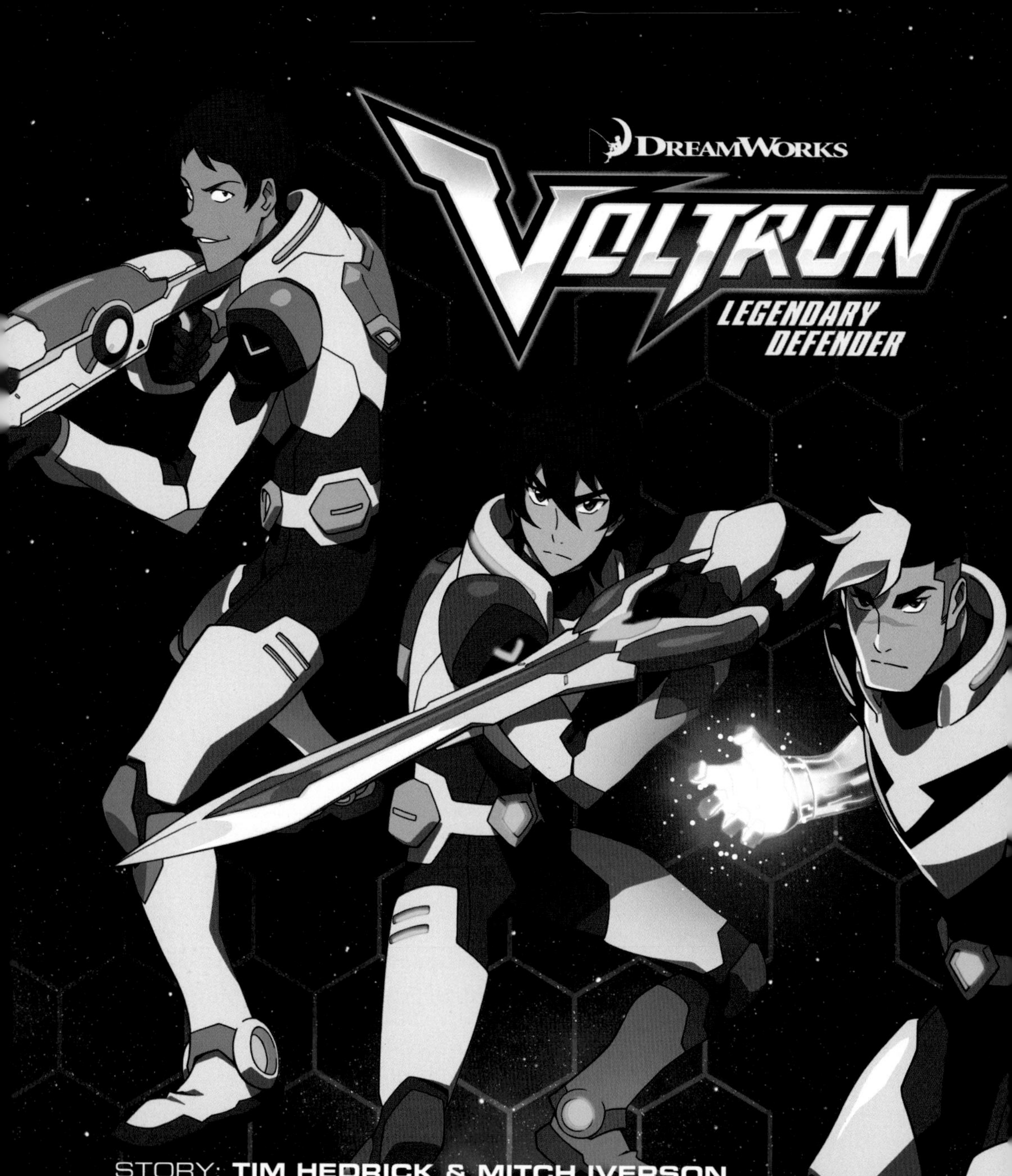
DREAMWORKS
VOLTRON
LEGENDARY DEFENDER

STORY: **TIM HEDRICK & MITCH IVERSON**
ART: **DIGITAL ART CHEFS**
LETTERING:: **ANDWORLD DESIGN**
COVER: **MARIKO YAMASHIN**
EDITOR: **IAN BRILL**

ADDITONAL ART
EUGENE LEE, CHRIS PALMER, STEVE AHN, & ANTHONY WU (PAGE 30
CHRISTIE TSENG & KIRK SHINMOTO (PAGE 56
KIHYUN RYU & ARTHUR LOFTIS (PAGE 82
JOAQUIM DOS SANTOS & DREW BERRY (PAGE 108
JON CHAD (PAGE 133
KHARY RANDOLPH & JOHN RAUCH (PAGE 134

LION FORGE

10 9 8 7 6 5 4 3

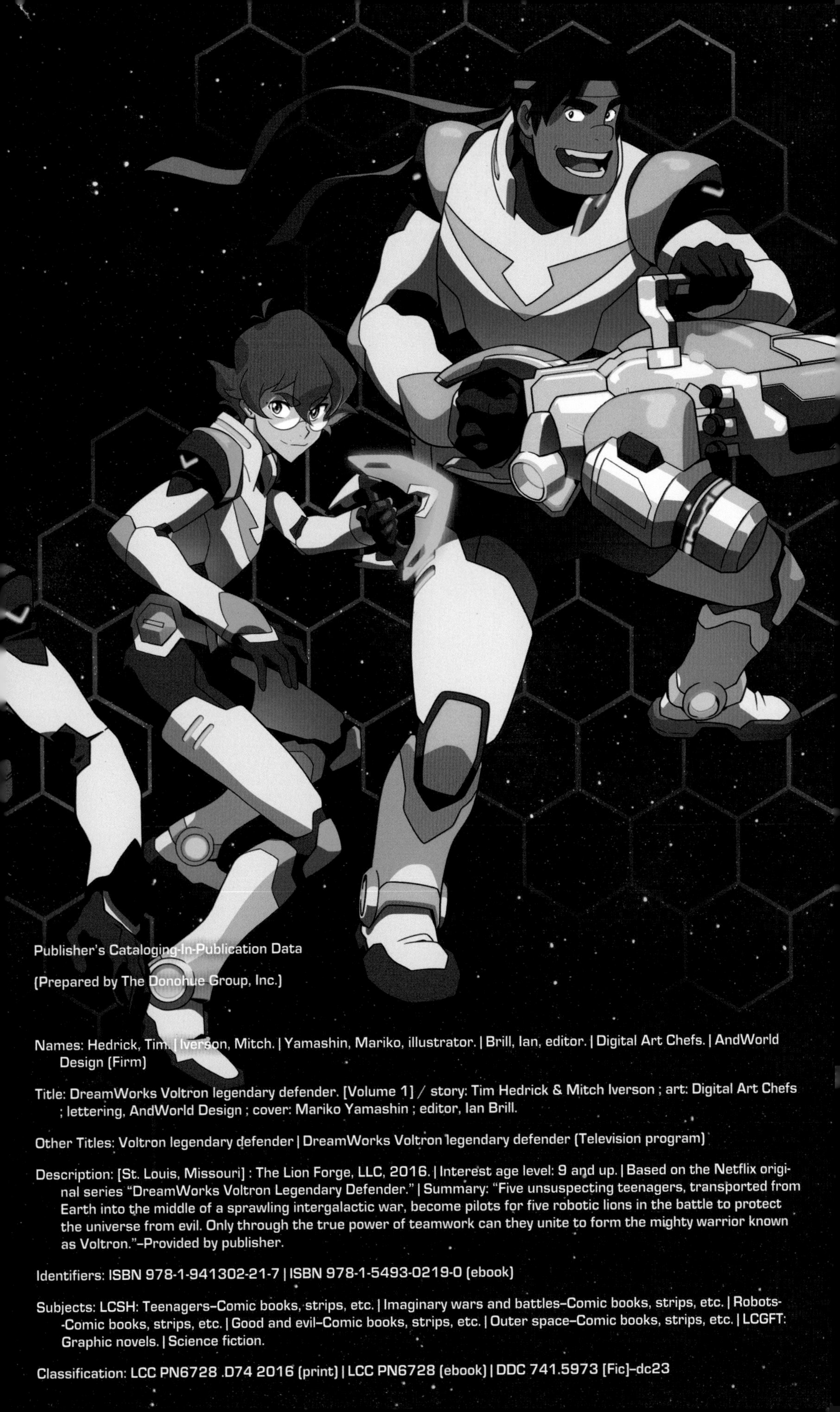

Publisher's Cataloging-In-Publication Data

(Prepared by The Donohue Group, Inc.)

Names: Hedrick, Tim. | Iverson, Mitch. | Yamashin, Mariko, illustrator. | Brill, Ian, editor. | Digital Art Chefs. | AndWorld Design (Firm)

Title: DreamWorks Voltron legendary defender. [Volume 1] / story: Tim Hedrick & Mitch Iverson ; art: Digital Art Chefs ; lettering, AndWorld Design ; cover: Mariko Yamashin ; editor, Ian Brill.

Other Titles: Voltron legendary defender | DreamWorks Voltron legendary defender (Television program)

Description: [St. Louis, Missouri] : The Lion Forge, LLC, 2016. | Interest age level: 9 and up. | Based on the Netflix original series "DreamWorks Voltron Legendary Defender." | Summary: "Five unsuspecting teenagers, transported from Earth into the middle of a sprawling intergalactic war, become pilots for five robotic lions in the battle to protect the universe from evil. Only through the true power of teamwork can they unite to form the mighty warrior known as Voltron."–Provided by publisher.

Identifiers: ISBN 978-1-941302-21-7 | ISBN 978-1-5493-0219-0 (ebook)

Subjects: LCSH: Teenagers–Comic books, strips, etc. | Imaginary wars and battles–Comic books, strips, etc. | Robots–Comic books, strips, etc. | Good and evil–Comic books, strips, etc. | Outer space–Comic books, strips, etc. | LCGFT: Graphic novels. | Science fiction.

Classification: LCC PN6728 .D74 2016 (print) | LCC PN6728 (ebook) | DDC 741.5973 [Fic]–dc23

CHAPTER ONE:
SHAKEDOWN AT THE FRIPPING BULGOGIAN

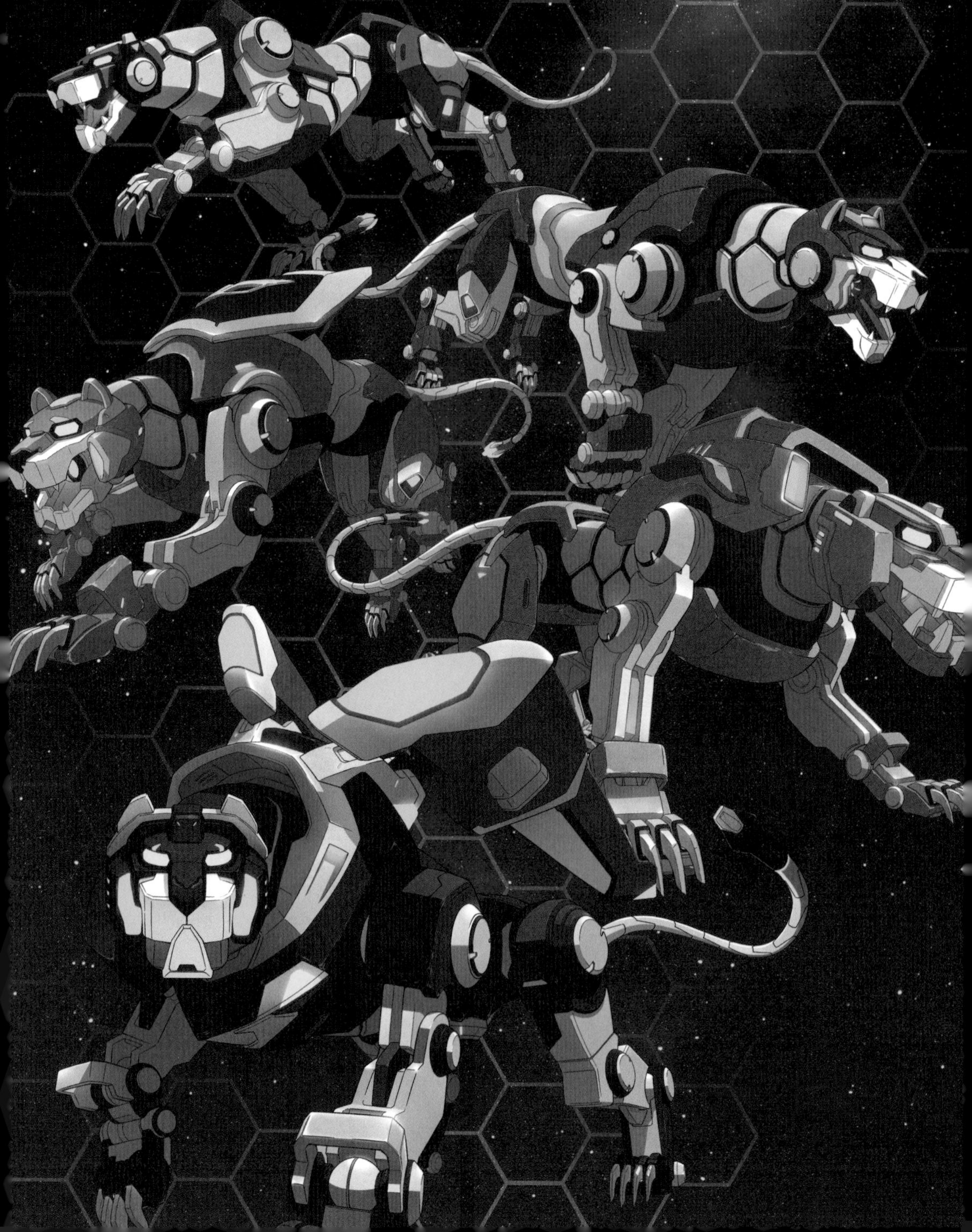

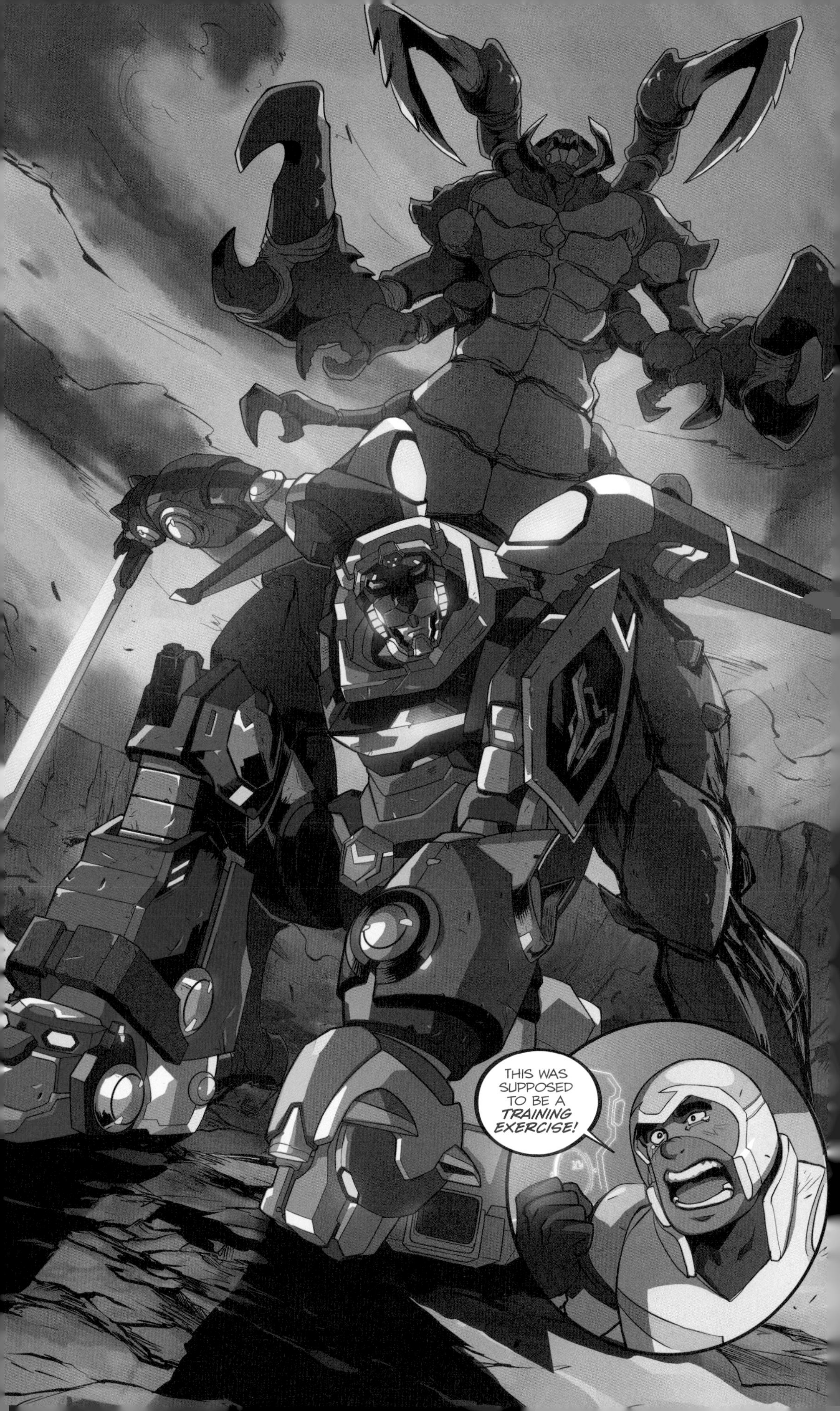
THIS WAS SUPPOSED TO BE A ***TRAINING EXERCISE!***

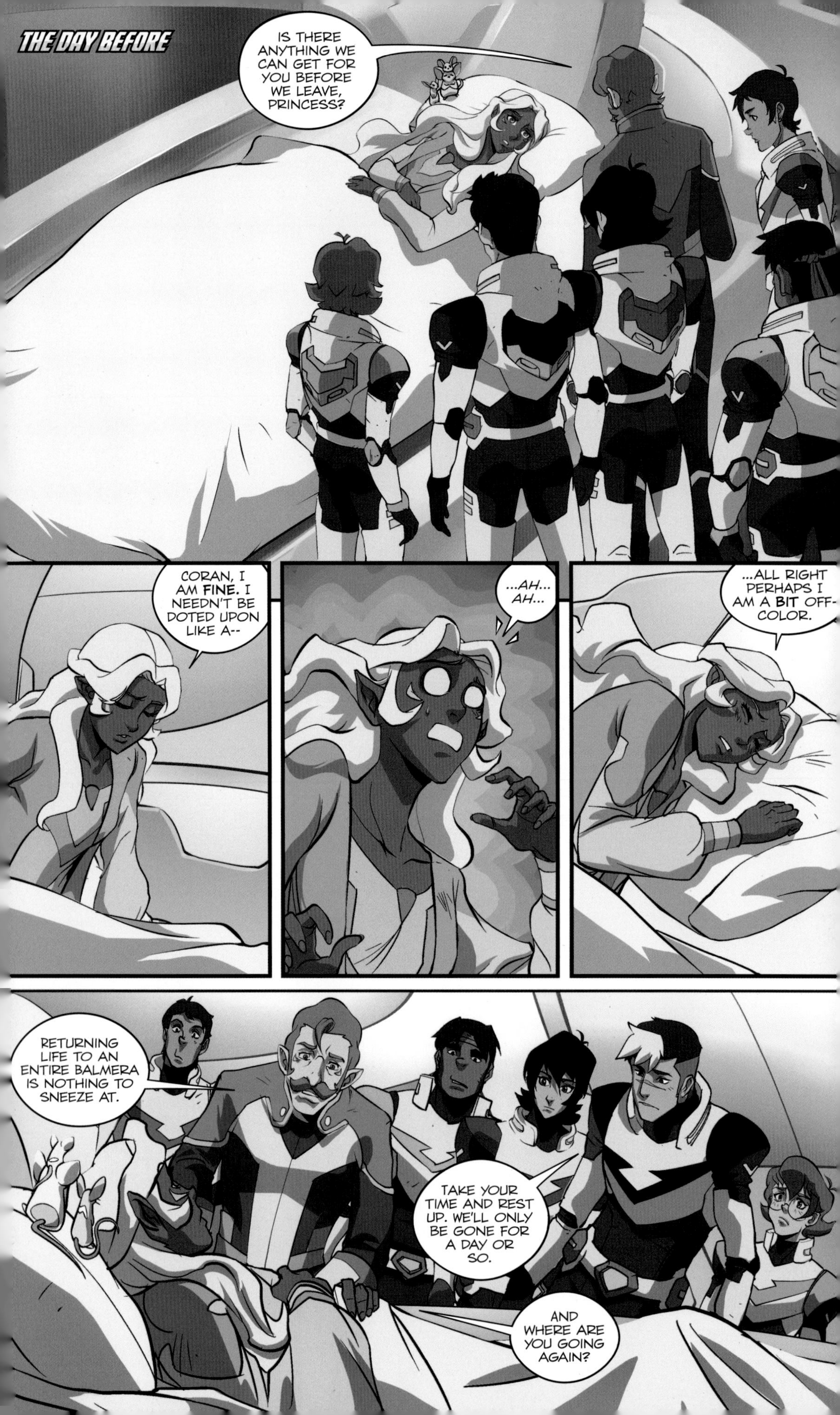
THE DAY BEFORE
IS THERE ANYTHING WE CAN GET FOR YOU BEFORE WE LEAVE, PRINCESS?
CORAN, I AM FINE. I NEEDN'T BE DOTED UPON LIKE A--
...AH... AH...
...ALL RIGHT PERHAPS I AM A BIT OFF-COLOR.
RETURNING LIFE TO AN ENTIRE BALMERA IS NOTHING TO SNEEZE AT.
TAKE YOUR TIME AND REST UP. WE'LL ONLY BE GONE FOR A DAY OR SO.
AND WHERE ARE YOU GOING AGAIN?

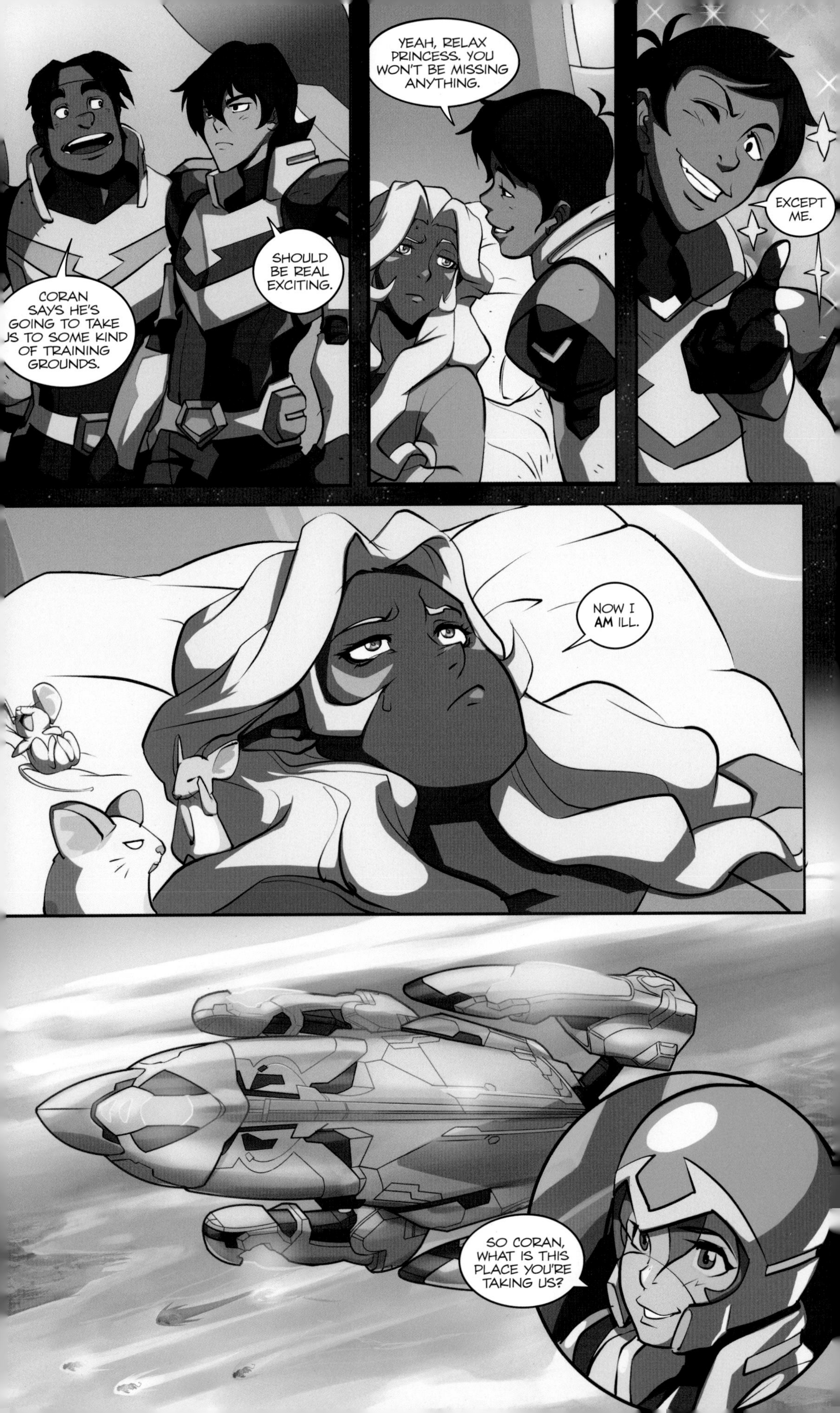
CORAN SAYS HE'S GOING TO TAKE US TO SOME KIND OF TRAINING GROUNDS.
SHOULD BE REAL EXCITING.
YEAH, RELAX PRINCESS. YOU WON'T BE MISSING ANYTHING.
EXCEPT ME.
NOW I **AM** ILL.
SO CORAN, WHAT IS THIS PLACE YOU'RE TAKING US?

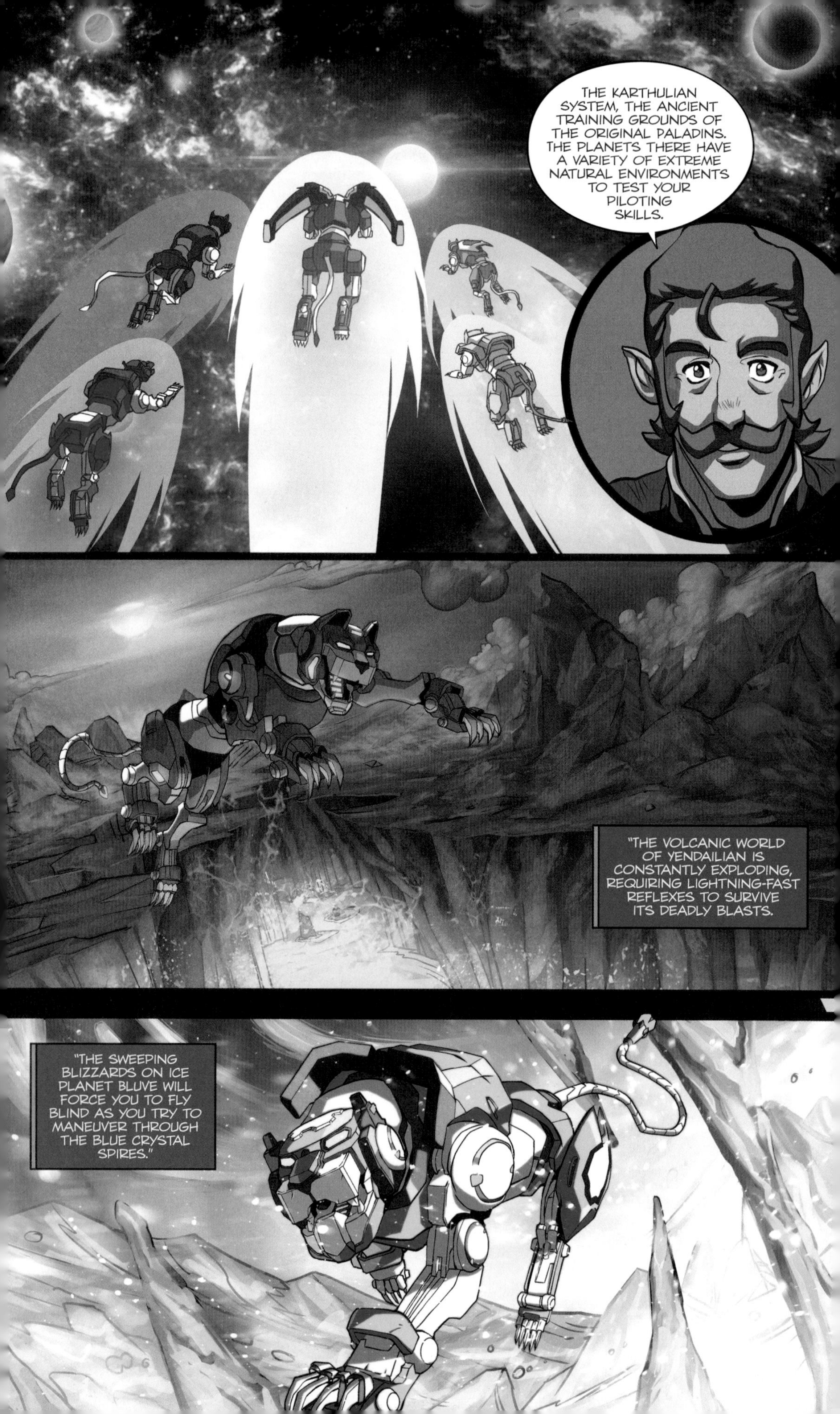
THE KARTHULIAN SYSTEM, THE ANCIENT TRAINING GROUNDS OF THE ORIGINAL PALADINS. THE PLANETS THERE HAVE A VARIETY OF EXTREME NATURAL ENVIRONMENTS TO TEST YOUR PILOTING SKILLS.
"THE VOLCANIC WORLD OF YENDAILIAN IS CONSTANTLY EXPLODING, REQUIRING LIGHTNING-FAST REFLEXES TO SURVIVE ITS DEADLY BLASTS.
"THE SWEEPING BLIZZARDS ON ICE PLANET BLUVE WILL FORCE YOU TO FLY BLIND AS YOU TRY TO MANEUVER THROUGH THE BLUE CRYSTAL SPIRES."

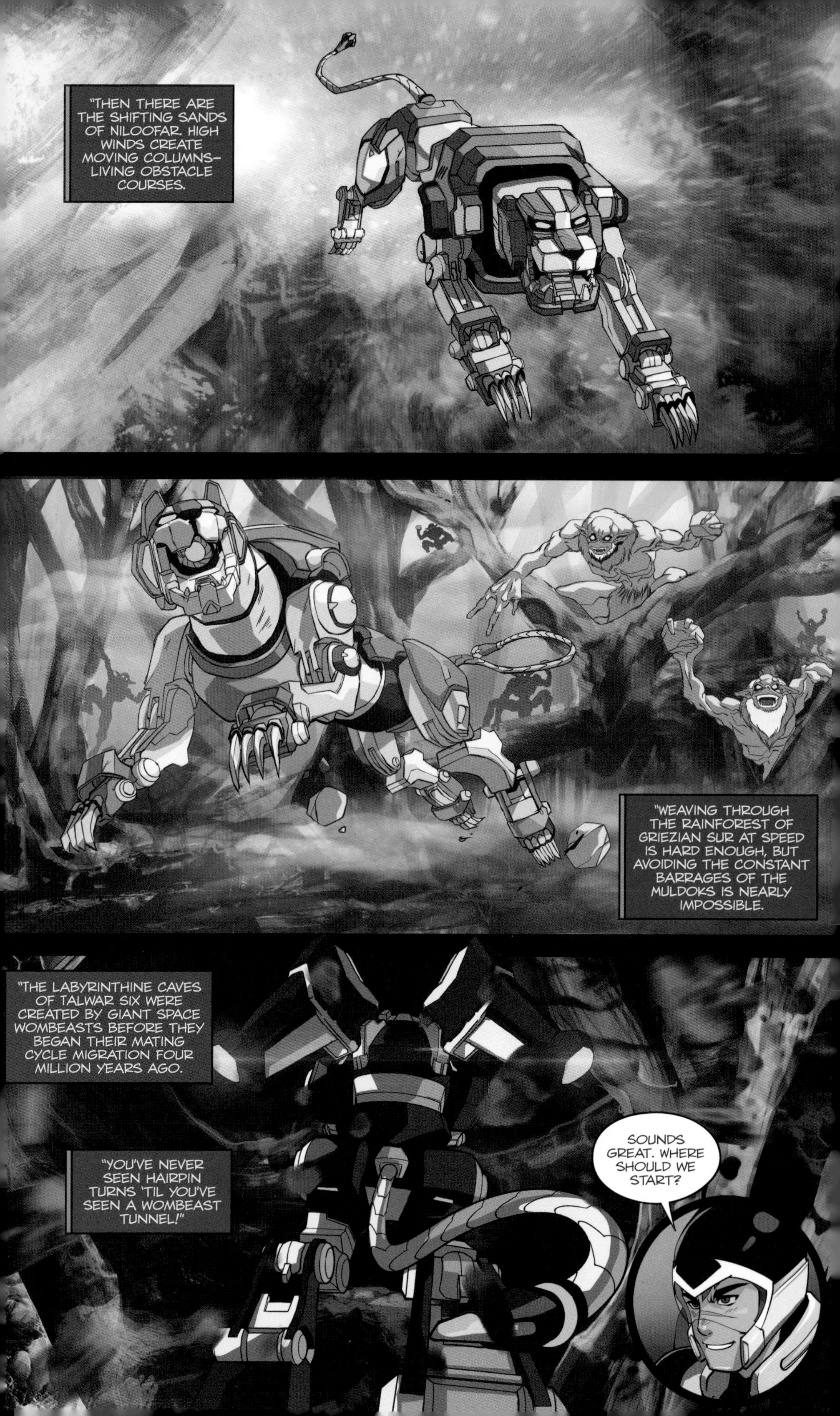
"THEN THERE ARE THE SHIFTING SANDS OF NILOOFAR. HIGH WINDS CREATE MOVING COLUMNS—LIVING OBSTACLE COURSES.
"WEAVING THROUGH THE RAINFOREST OF GRIEZIAN SUR AT SPEED IS HARD ENOUGH, BUT AVOIDING THE CONSTANT BARRAGES OF THE MULDOKS IS NEARLY IMPOSSIBLE.
"THE LABYRINTHINE CAVES OF TALWAR SIX WERE CREATED BY GIANT SPACE WOMBEASTS BEFORE THEY BEGAN THEIR MATING CYCLE MIGRATION FOUR MILLION YEARS AGO.
"YOU'VE NEVER SEEN HAIRPIN TURNS 'TIL YOU'VE SEEN A WOMBEAST TUNNEL!"
SOUNDS GREAT. WHERE SHOULD WE START?

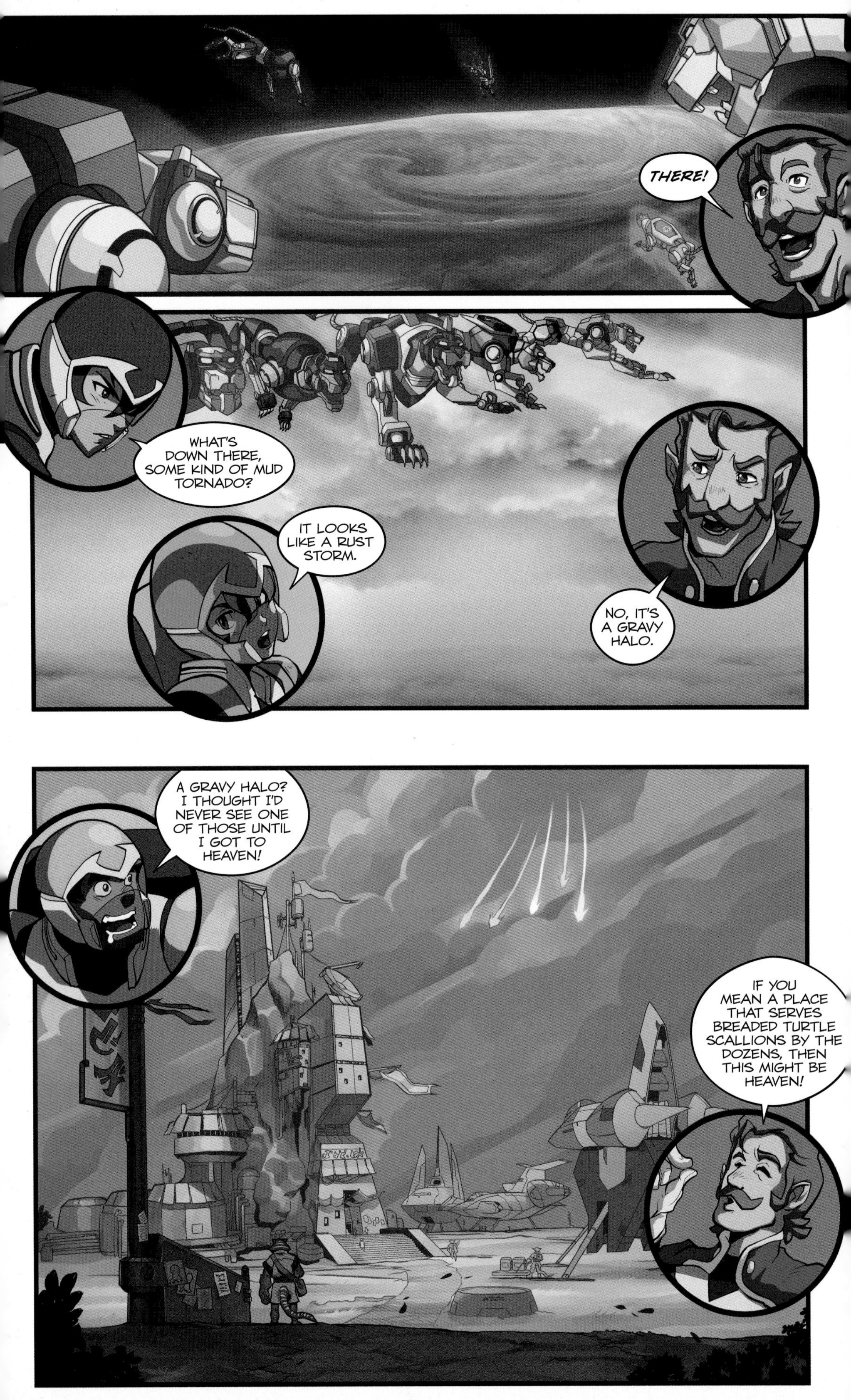
THERE!
WHAT'S DOWN THERE, SOME KIND OF MUD TORNADO?
IT LOOKS LIKE A RUST STORM.
NO, IT'S A GRAVY HALO.
A GRAVY HALO? I THOUGHT I'D NEVER SEE ONE OF THOSE UNTIL I GOT TO HEAVEN!
IF YOU MEAN A PLACE THAT SERVES BREADED TURTLE SCALLIONS BY THE DOZENS, THEN THIS MIGHT BE HEAVEN!

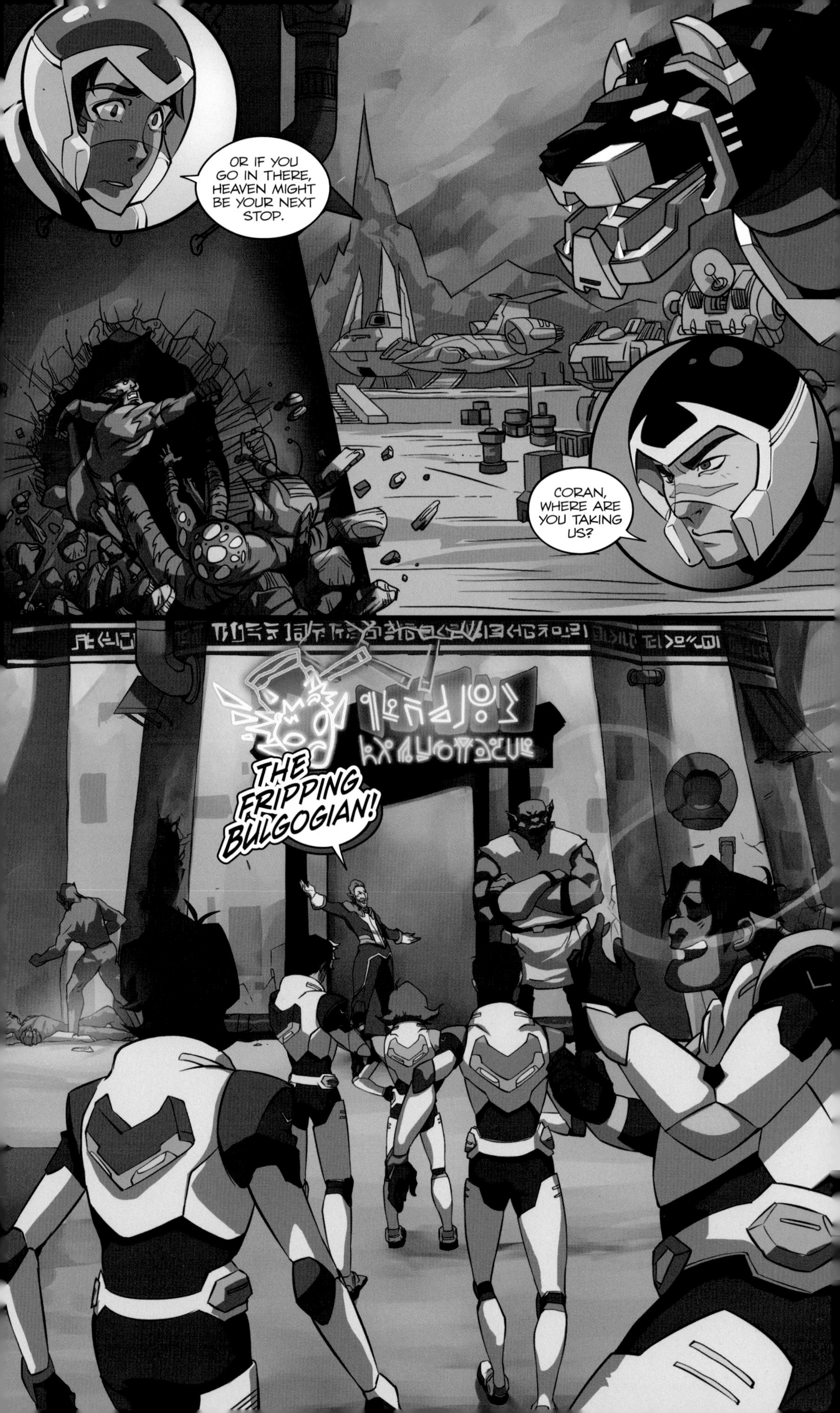
OR IF YOU GO IN THERE, HEAVEN MIGHT BE YOUR NEXT STOP.
CORAN, WHERE ARE YOU TAKING US?
THE FRIPPING BULGOGIAN!

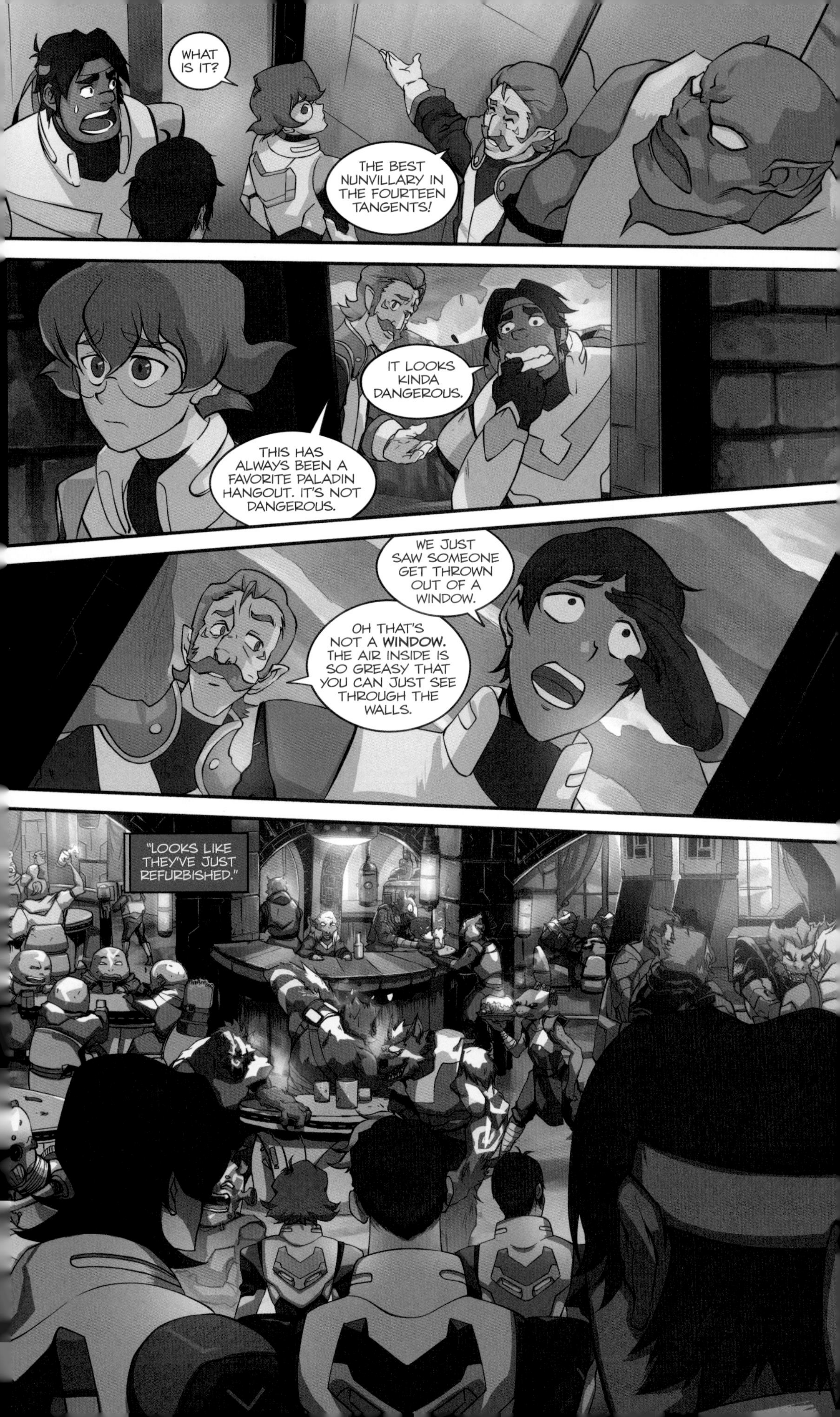

WHAT IS IT?
THE BEST NUNVILLARY IN THE FOURTEEN TANGENTS!
IT LOOKS KINDA DANGEROUS.
THIS HAS ALWAYS BEEN A FAVORITE PALADIN HANGOUT. IT'S NOT DANGEROUS.
WE JUST SAW SOMEONE GET THROWN OUT OF A WINDOW.
OH THAT'S NOT A **WINDOW.** THE AIR INSIDE IS SO GREASY THAT YOU CAN JUST SEE THROUGH THE WALLS.
"LOOKS LIKE THEY'VE JUST REFURBISHED."

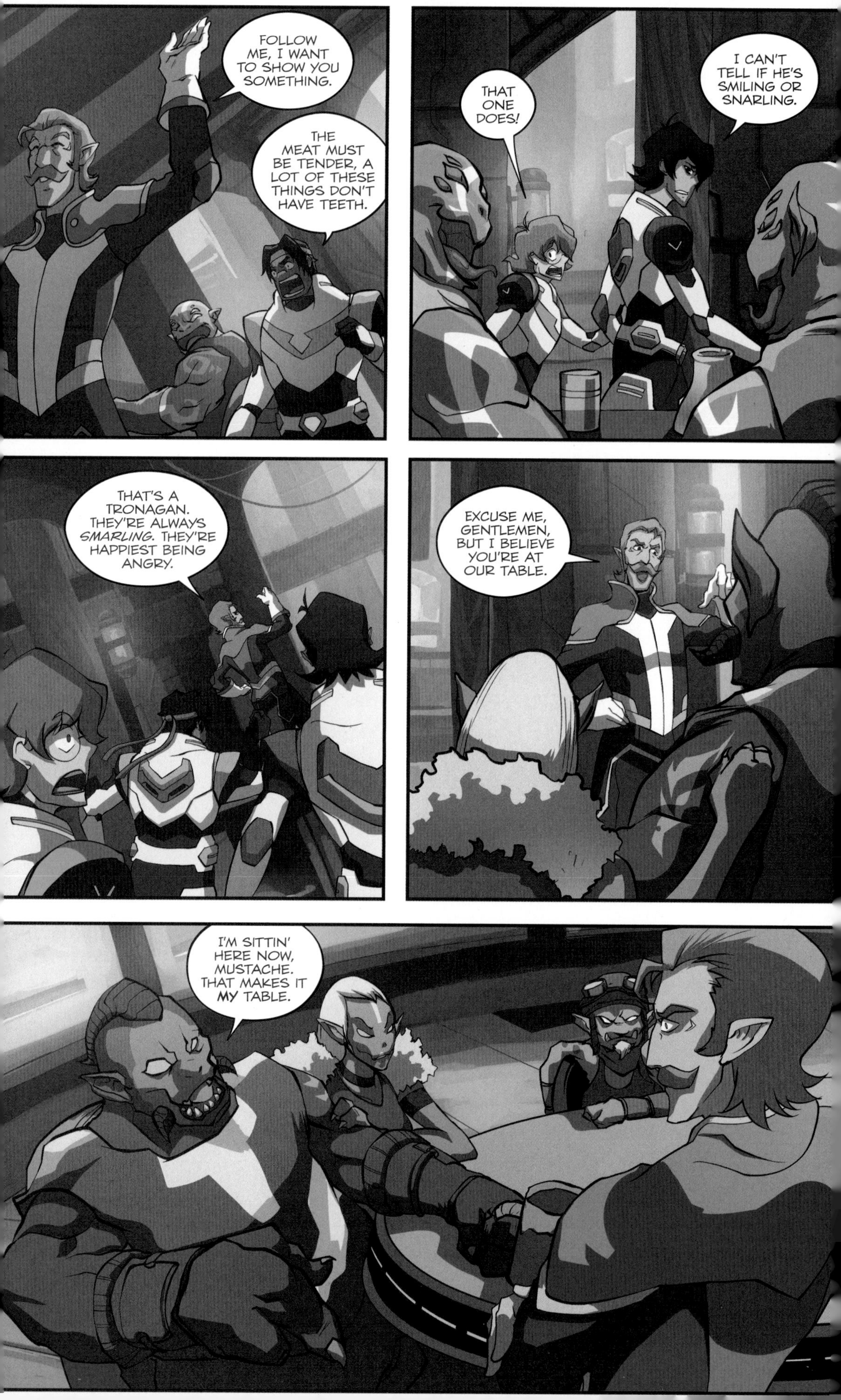
FOLLOW ME, I WANT TO SHOW YOU SOMETHING.
THE MEAT MUST BE TENDER, A LOT OF THESE THINGS DON'T HAVE TEETH.
THAT ONE DOES!
I CAN'T TELL IF HE'S SMILING OR SNARLING.
THAT'S A TRONAGAN. THEY'RE ALWAYS *SMARLING*. THEY'RE HAPPIEST BEING ANGRY.
EXCUSE ME, GENTLEMEN, BUT I BELIEVE YOU'RE AT OUR TABLE.
I'M SITTIN' HERE NOW, MUSTACHE. THAT MAKES IT **MY** TABLE.

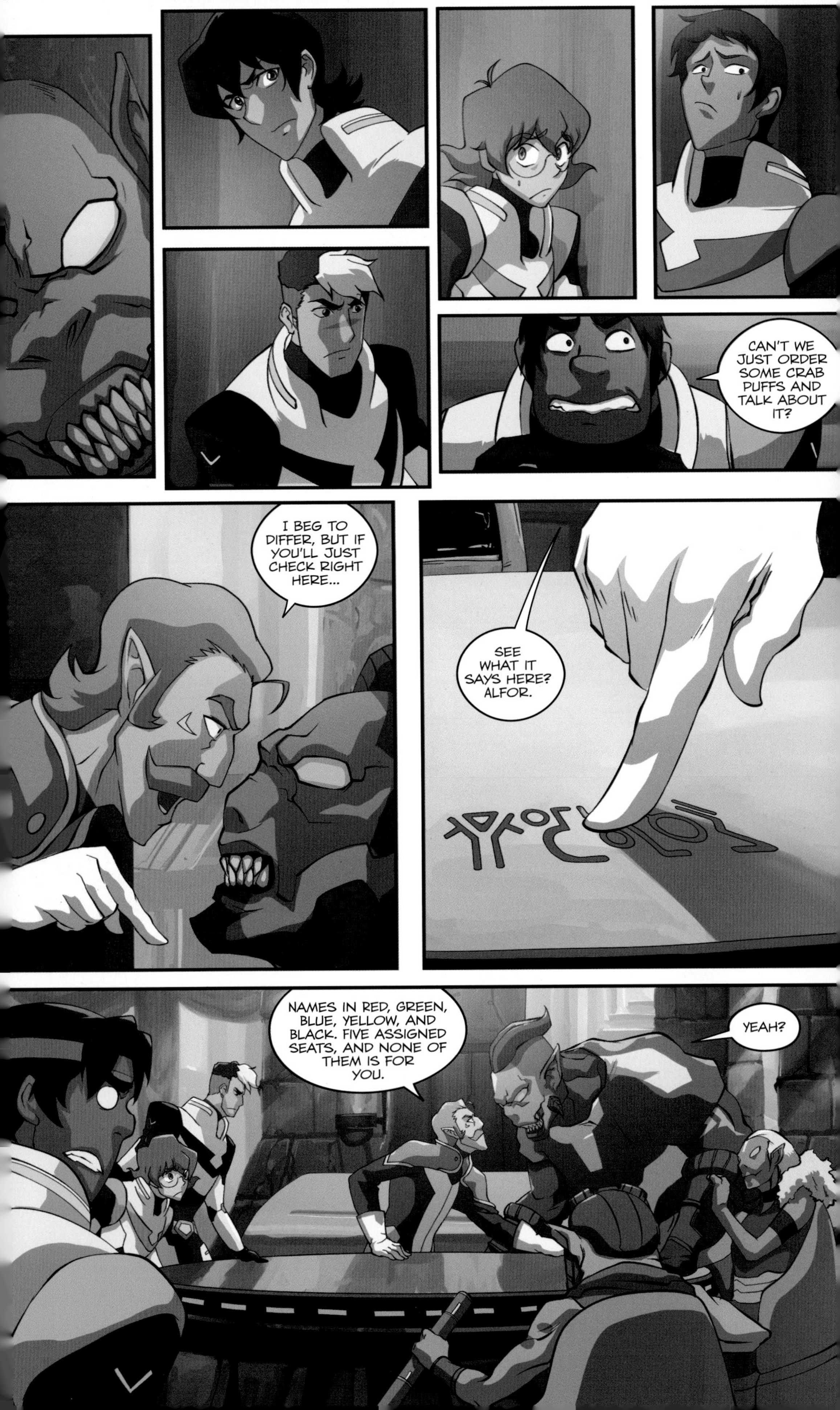
CAN'T WE JUST ORDER SOME CRAB PUFFS AND TALK ABOUT IT?
I BEG TO DIFFER, BUT IF YOU'LL JUST CHECK RIGHT HERE...
SEE WHAT IT SAYS HERE? ALFOR.
NAMES IN RED, GREEN, BLUE, YELLOW, AND BLACK. FIVE ASSIGNED SEATS, AND NONE OF THEM IS FOR YOU.
YEAH?

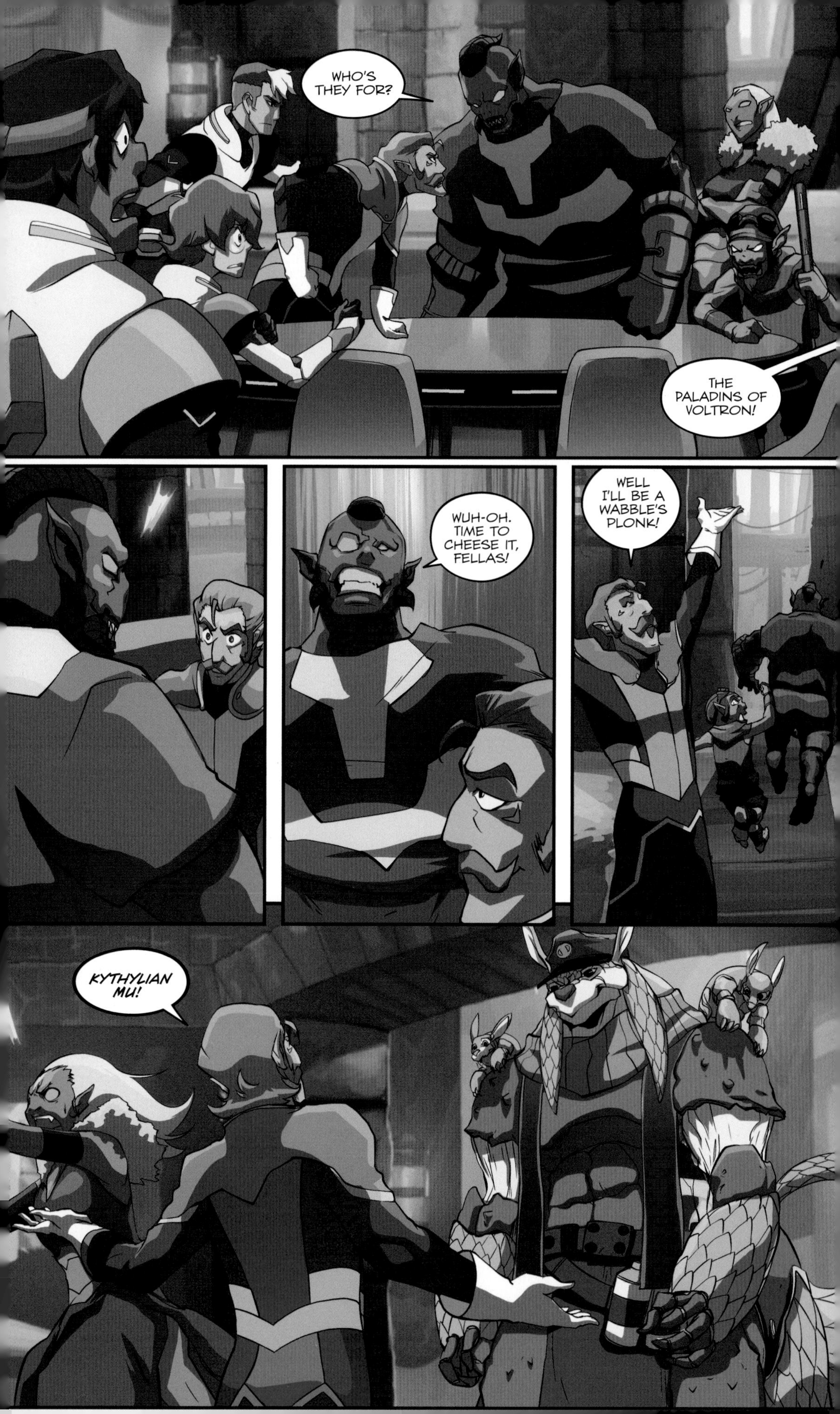
WHO'S THEY FOR?
THE PALADINS OF VOLTRON!
WUH-OH. TIME TO CHEESE IT, FELLAS!
WELL I'LL BE A WABBLE'S PLONK!
KYTHYLIAN MU!

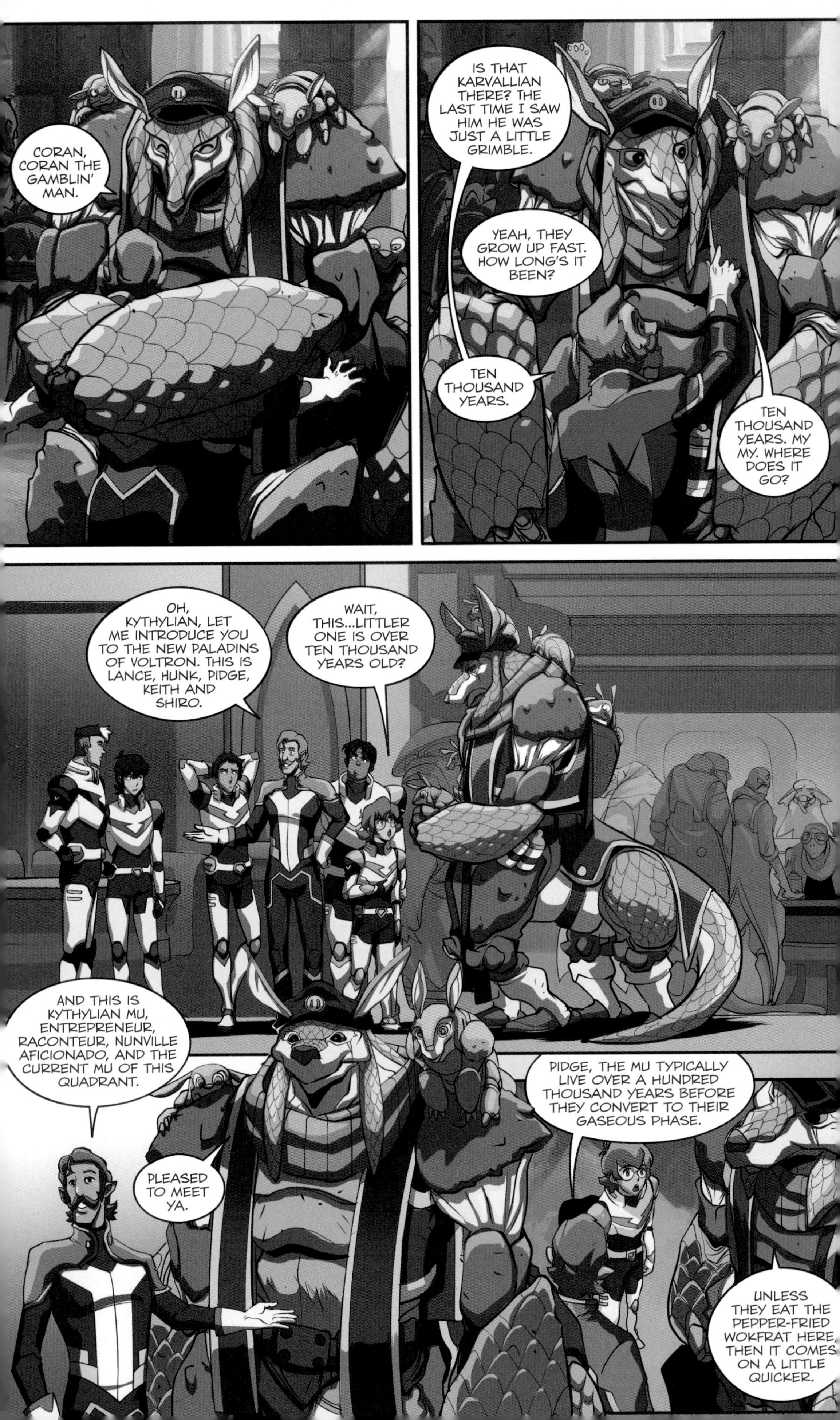
CORAN, CORAN THE GAMBLIN' MAN.
IS THAT KARVALLIAN THERE? THE LAST TIME I SAW HIM HE WAS JUST A LITTLE GRIMBLE.
YEAH, THEY GROW UP FAST. HOW LONG'S IT BEEN?
TEN THOUSAND YEARS.
TEN THOUSAND YEARS. MY MY. WHERE DOES IT GO?
OH, KYTHYLIAN, LET ME INTRODUCE YOU TO THE NEW PALADINS OF VOLTRON. THIS IS LANCE, HUNK, PIDGE, KEITH AND SHIRO.
WAIT, THIS...LITTLER ONE IS OVER TEN THOUSAND YEARS OLD?
AND THIS IS KYTHYLIAN MU, ENTREPRENEUR, RACONTEUR, NUNVILLE AFICIONADO, AND THE CURRENT MU OF THIS QUADRANT.
PLEASED TO MEET YA.
PIDGE, THE MU TYPICALLY LIVE OVER A HUNDRED THOUSAND YEARS BEFORE THEY CONVERT TO THEIR GASEOUS PHASE.
UNLESS THEY EAT THE PEPPER-FRIED WOKFRAT HERE, THEN IT COMES ON A LITTLE QUICKER.

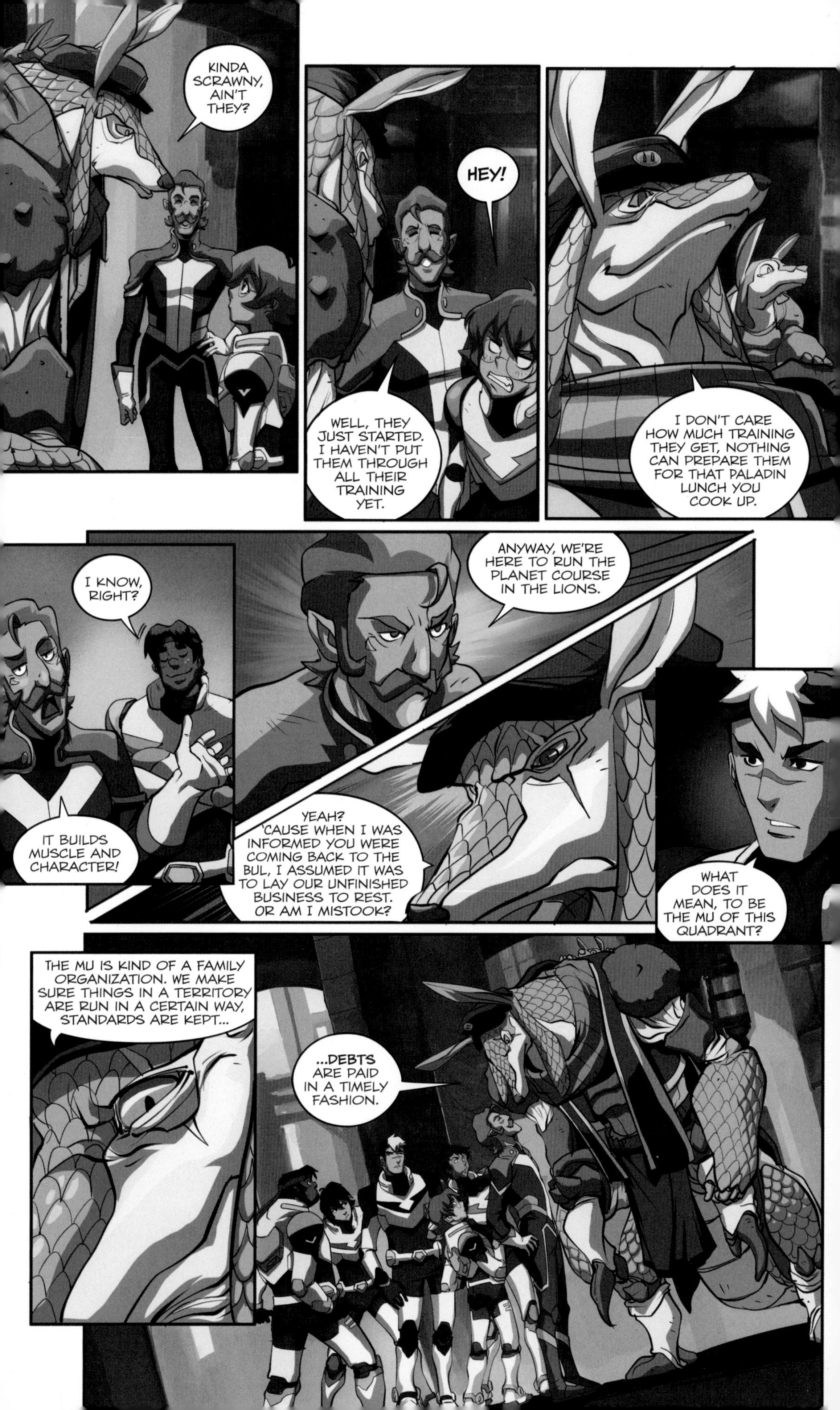
KINDA SCRAWNY, AIN'T THEY?
HEY!
WELL, THEY JUST STARTED. I HAVEN'T PUT THEM THROUGH ALL THEIR TRAINING YET.
I DON'T CARE HOW MUCH TRAINING THEY GET, NOTHING CAN PREPARE THEM FOR THAT PALADIN LUNCH YOU COOK UP.
I KNOW, RIGHT?
IT BUILDS MUSCLE AND CHARACTER!
ANYWAY, WE'RE HERE TO RUN THE PLANET COURSE IN THE LIONS.
YEAH? 'CAUSE WHEN I WAS INFORMED YOU WERE COMING BACK TO THE BUL, I ASSUMED IT WAS TO LAY OUR UNFINISHED BUSINESS TO REST. OR AM I MISTOOK?
WHAT DOES IT MEAN, TO BE THE MU OF THIS QUADRANT?
THE MU IS KIND OF A FAMILY ORGANIZATION. WE MAKE SURE THINGS IN A TERRITORY ARE RUN IN A CERTAIN WAY, STANDARDS ARE KEPT...
...DEBTS ARE PAID IN A TIMELY FASHION.

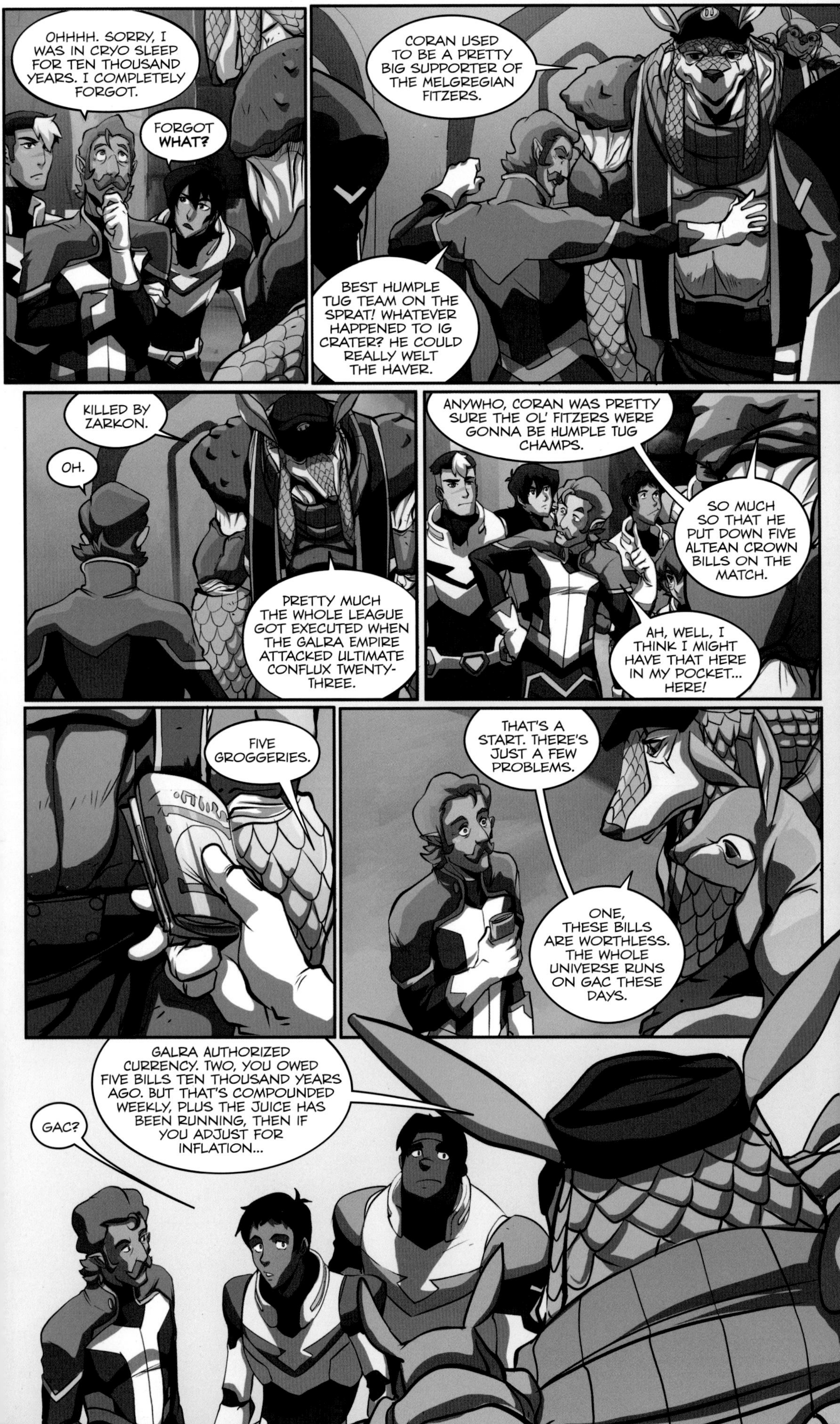
OHHHH. SORRY, I WAS IN CRYO SLEEP FOR TEN THOUSAND YEARS. I COMPLETELY FORGOT.
FORGOT WHAT?
CORAN USED TO BE A PRETTY BIG SUPPORTER OF THE MELGREGIAN FITZERS.
BEST HUMPLE TUG TEAM ON THE SPRAT! WHATEVER HAPPENED TO IG CRATER? HE COULD REALLY WELT THE HAVER.
KILLED BY ZARKON.
OH.
PRETTY MUCH THE WHOLE LEAGUE GOT EXECUTED WHEN THE GALRA EMPIRE ATTACKED ULTIMATE CONFLUX TWENTY-THREE.
ANYWHO, CORAN WAS PRETTY SURE THE OL' FITZERS WERE GONNA BE HUMPLE TUG CHAMPS.
SO MUCH SO THAT HE PUT DOWN FIVE ALTEAN CROWN BILLS ON THE MATCH.
AH, WELL, I THINK I MIGHT HAVE THAT HERE IN MY POCKET... HERE!
FIVE GROGGERIES.
THAT'S A START. THERE'S JUST A FEW PROBLEMS.
ONE, THESE BILLS ARE WORTHLESS. THE WHOLE UNIVERSE RUNS ON GAC THESE DAYS.
GAC?
GALRA AUTHORIZED CURRENCY. TWO, YOU OWED FIVE BILLS TEN THOUSAND YEARS AGO. BUT THAT'S COMPOUNDED WEEKLY, PLUS THE JUICE HAS BEEN RUNNING, THEN IF YOU ADJUST FOR INFLATION...

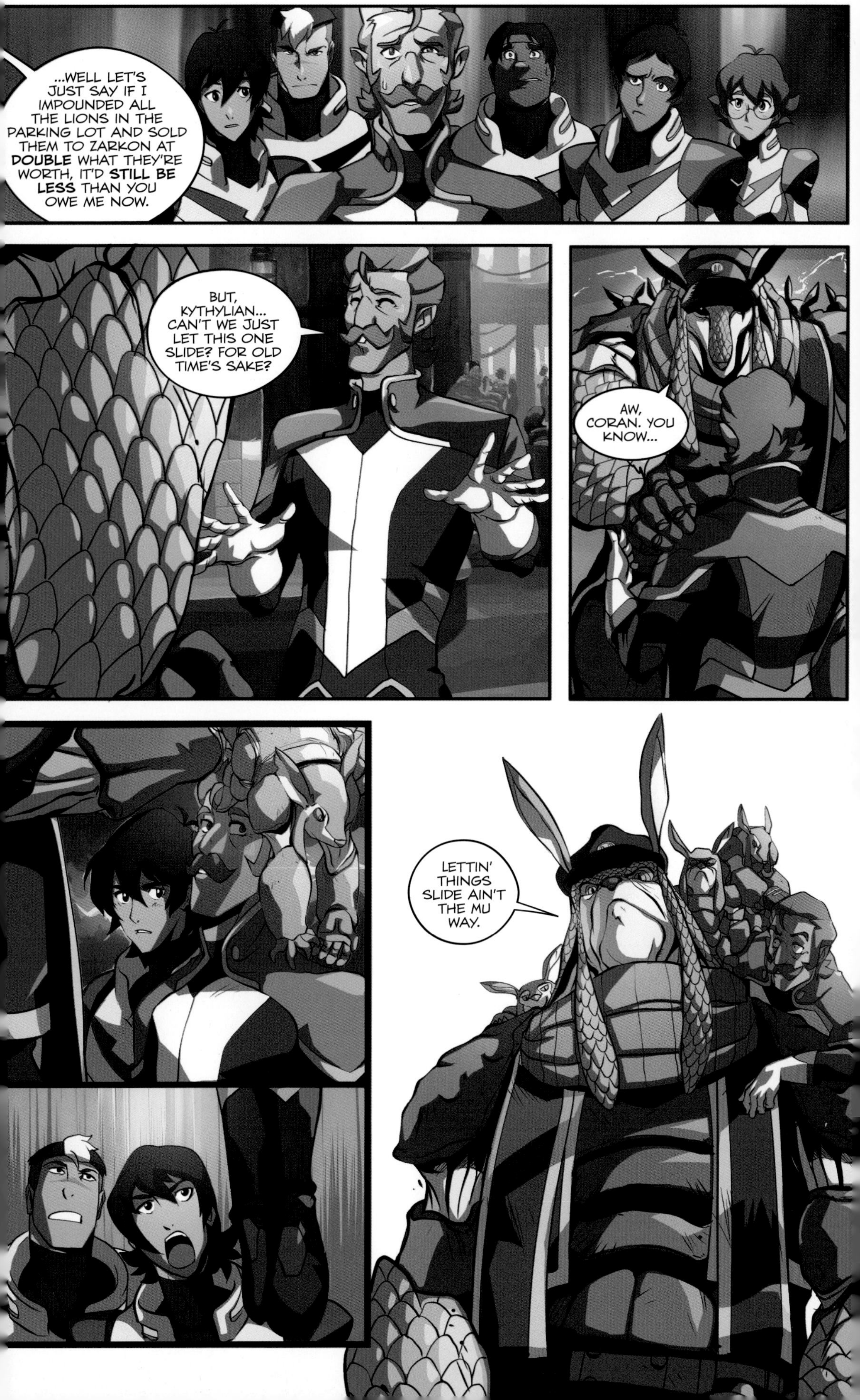
...WELL LET'S JUST SAY IF I IMPOUNDED ALL THE LIONS IN THE PARKING LOT AND SOLD THEM TO ZARKON AT **DOUBLE** WHAT THEY'RE WORTH, IT'D **STILL BE LESS** THAN YOU OWE ME NOW.
BUT, KYTHYLIAN... CAN'T WE JUST LET THIS ONE SLIDE? FOR OLD TIME'S SAKE?
AW, CORAN. YOU KNOW...
LETTIN' THINGS SLIDE AIN'T THE MU WAY.

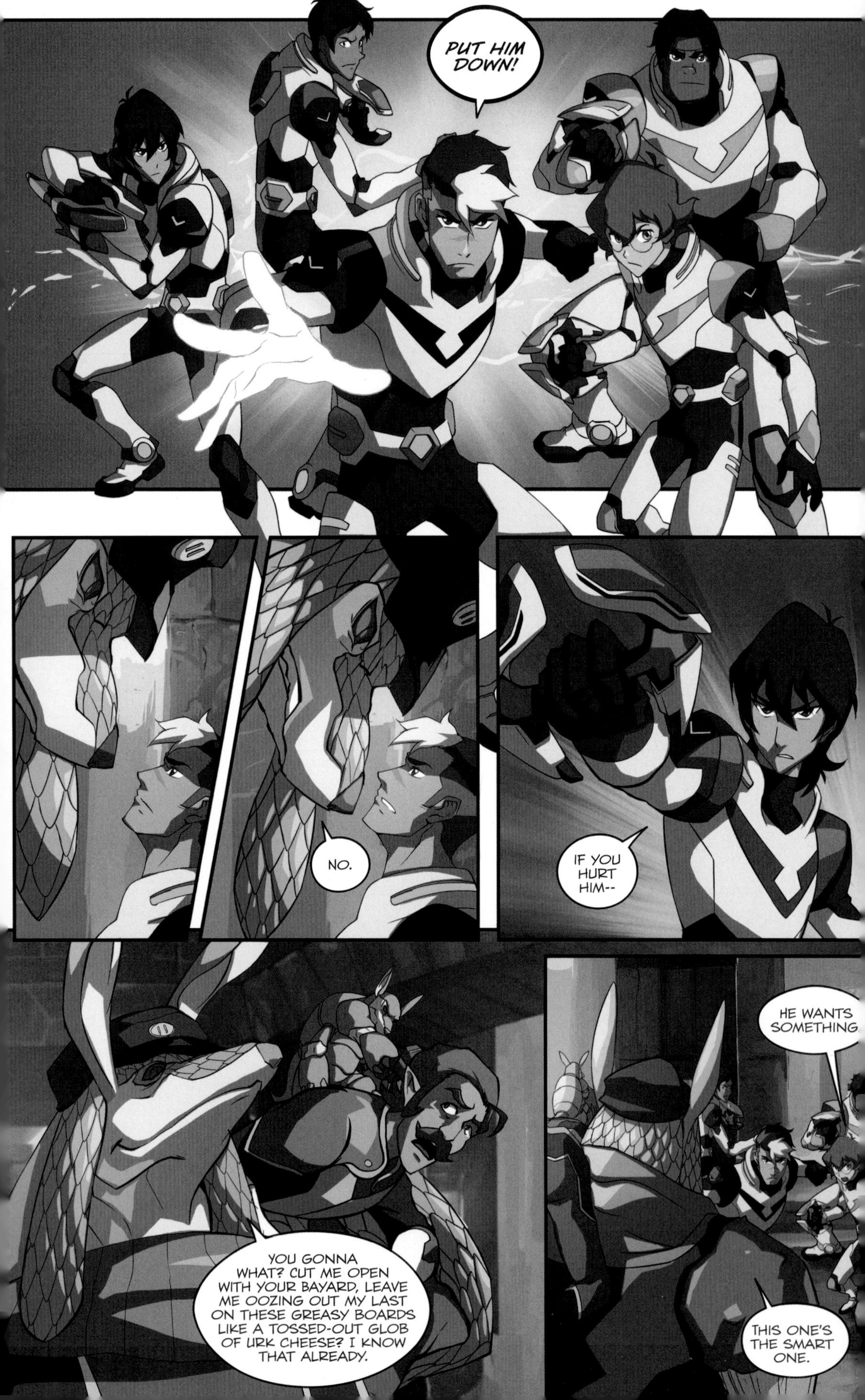
PUT HIM DOWN!
NO.
IF YOU HURT HIM--
YOU GONNA WHAT? CUT ME OPEN WITH YOUR BAYARD, LEAVE ME OOZING OUT MY LAST ON THESE GREASY BOARDS LIKE A TOSSED-OUT GLOB OF URK CHEESE? I KNOW THAT ALREADY.
HE WANTS SOMETHING
THIS ONE'S THE SMART ONE.

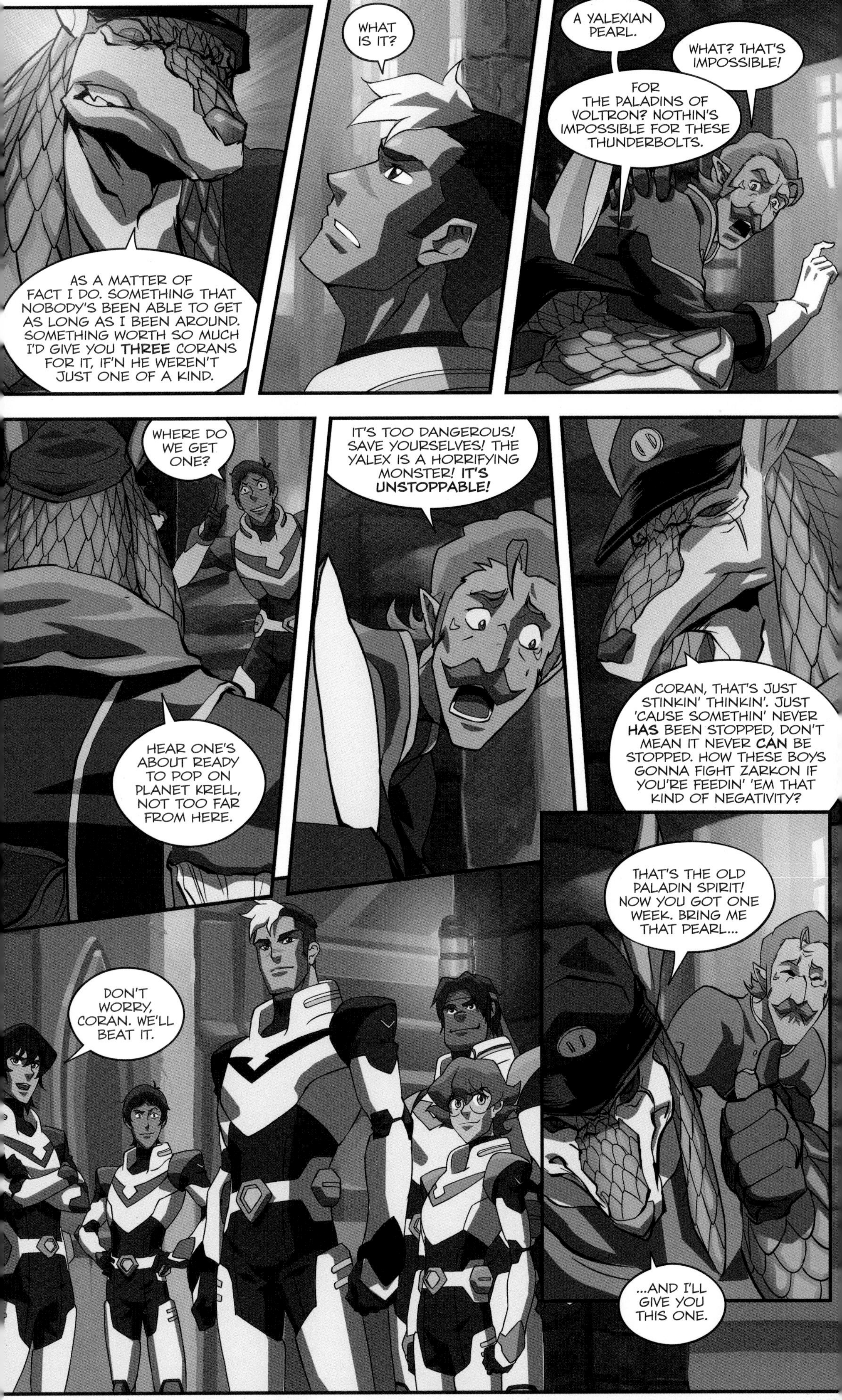

AS A MATTER OF FACT I DO. SOMETHING THAT NOBODY'S BEEN ABLE TO GET AS LONG AS I BEEN AROUND. SOMETHING WORTH SO MUCH I'D GIVE YOU **THREE** CORANS FOR IT, IF'N HE WEREN'T JUST ONE OF A KIND.
WHAT IS IT?
A YALEXIAN PEARL.
WHAT? THAT'S IMPOSSIBLE!
FOR THE PALADINS OF VOLTRON? NOTHIN'S IMPOSSIBLE FOR THESE THUNDERBOLTS.
WHERE DO WE GET ONE?
HEAR ONE'S ABOUT READY TO POP ON PLANET KRELL, NOT TOO FAR FROM HERE.
IT'S TOO DANGEROUS! SAVE YOURSELVES! THE YALEX IS A HORRIFYING MONSTER! **IT'S UNSTOPPABLE!**
CORAN, THAT'S JUST STINKIN' THINKIN'. JUST 'CAUSE SOMETHIN' NEVER **HAS** BEEN STOPPED, DON'T MEAN IT NEVER **CAN** BE STOPPED. HOW THESE BOYS GONNA FIGHT ZARKON IF YOU'RE FEEDIN' 'EM THAT KIND OF NEGATIVITY?
DON'T WORRY, CORAN. WE'LL BEAT IT.
THAT'S THE OLD PALADIN SPIRIT! NOW YOU GOT ONE WEEK. BRING ME THAT PEARL...
...AND I'LL GIVE YOU THIS ONE.

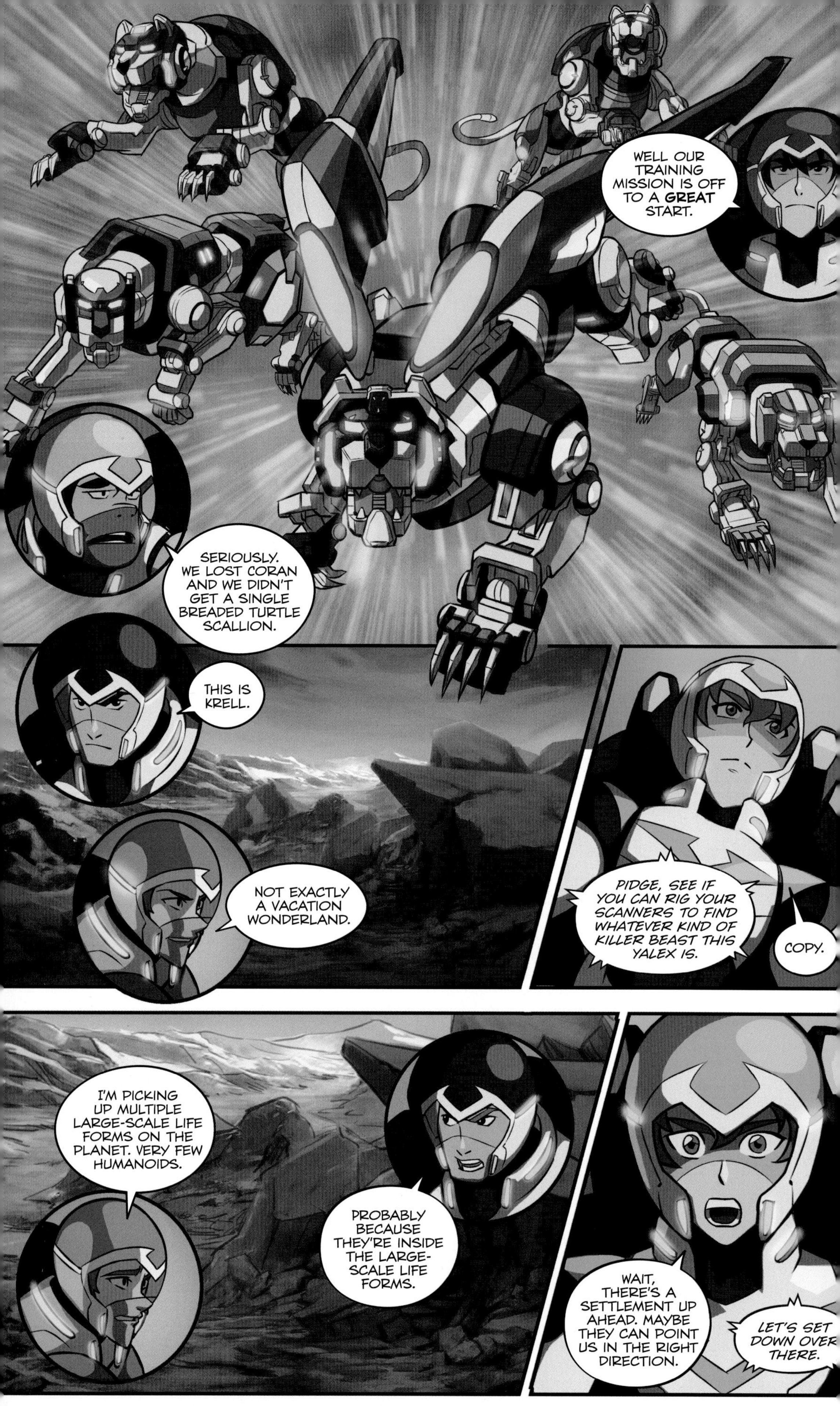

WELL OUR TRAINING MISSION IS OFF TO A **GREAT** START.
SERIOUSLY. WE LOST CORAN AND WE DIDN'T GET A SINGLE BREADED TURTLE SCALLION.
THIS IS KRELL.
NOT EXACTLY A VACATION WONDERLAND.
PIDGE, SEE IF YOU CAN RIG YOUR SCANNERS TO FIND WHATEVER KIND OF KILLER BEAST THIS YALEX IS.
COPY.
I'M PICKING UP MULTIPLE LARGE-SCALE LIFE FORMS ON THE PLANET. VERY FEW HUMANOIDS.
PROBABLY BECAUSE THEY'RE INSIDE THE LARGE-SCALE LIFE FORMS.
WAIT, THERE'S A SETTLEMENT UP AHEAD. MAYBE THEY CAN POINT US IN THE RIGHT DIRECTION.
LET'S SET DOWN OVER THERE.

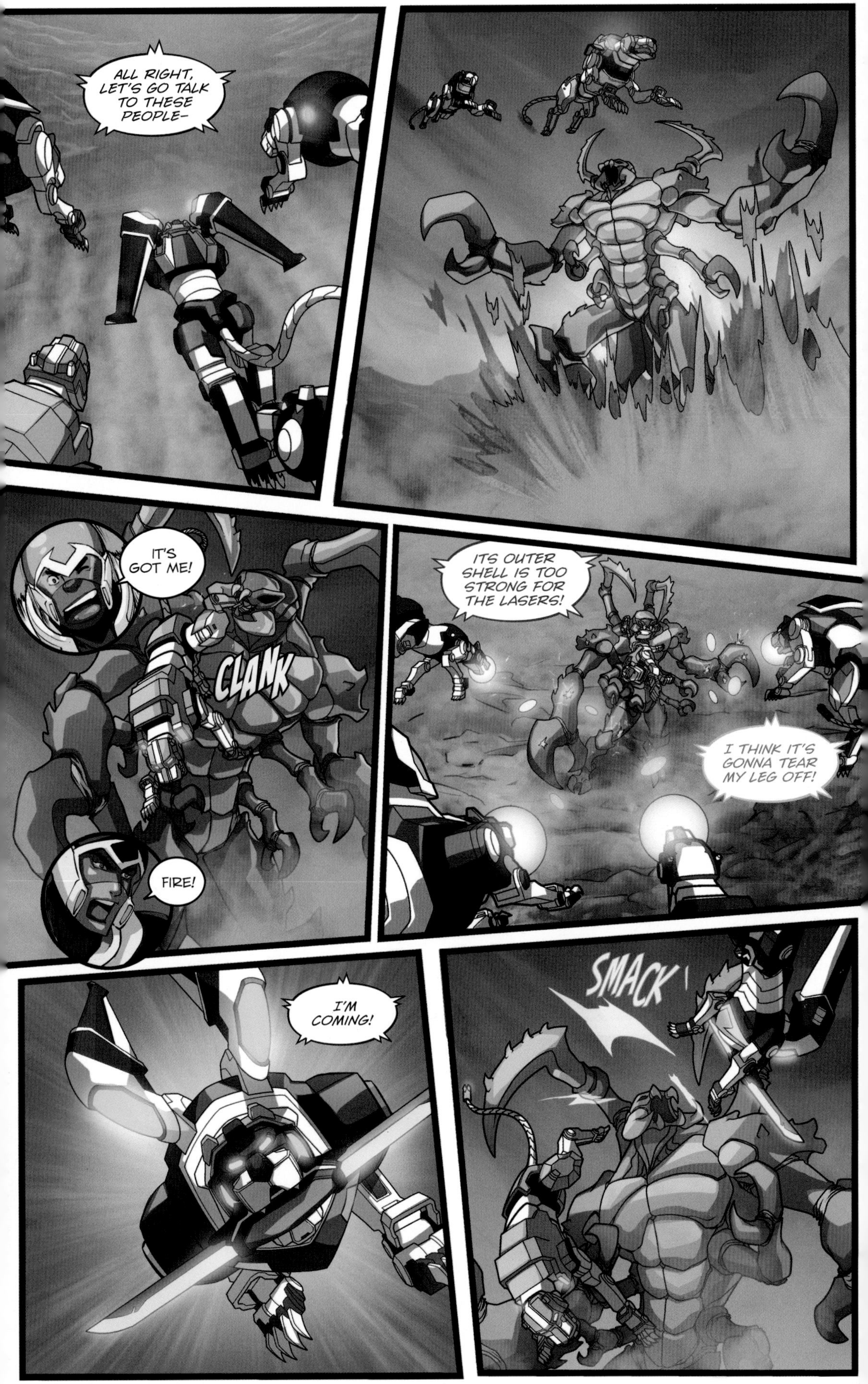
ALL RIGHT, LET'S GO TALK TO THESE PEOPLE-
IT'S GOT ME!
CLANK
FIRE!
ITS OUTER SHELL IS TOO STRONG FOR THE LASERS!
I THINK IT'S GONNA TEAR MY LEG OFF!
I'M COMING!
SMACK

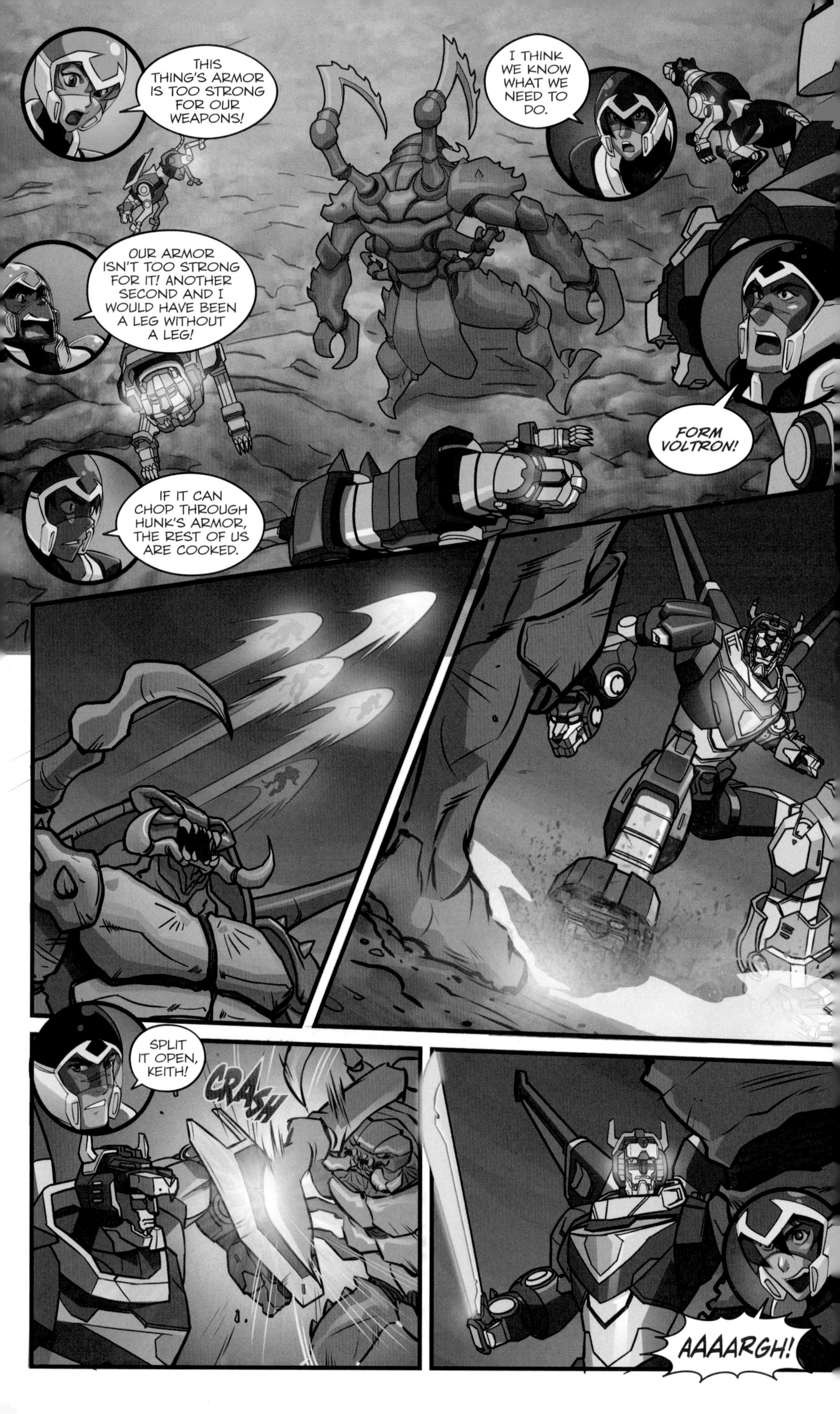
THIS THING'S ARMOR IS TOO STRONG FOR OUR WEAPONS!
I THINK WE KNOW WHAT WE NEED TO DO.
OUR ARMOR ISN'T TOO STRONG FOR IT! ANOTHER SECOND AND I WOULD HAVE BEEN A LEG WITHOUT A LEG!
IF IT CAN CHOP THROUGH HUNK'S ARMOR, THE REST OF US ARE COOKED.
FORM VOLTRON!
SPLIT IT OPEN, KEITH!
CRASH
AAAARGH!

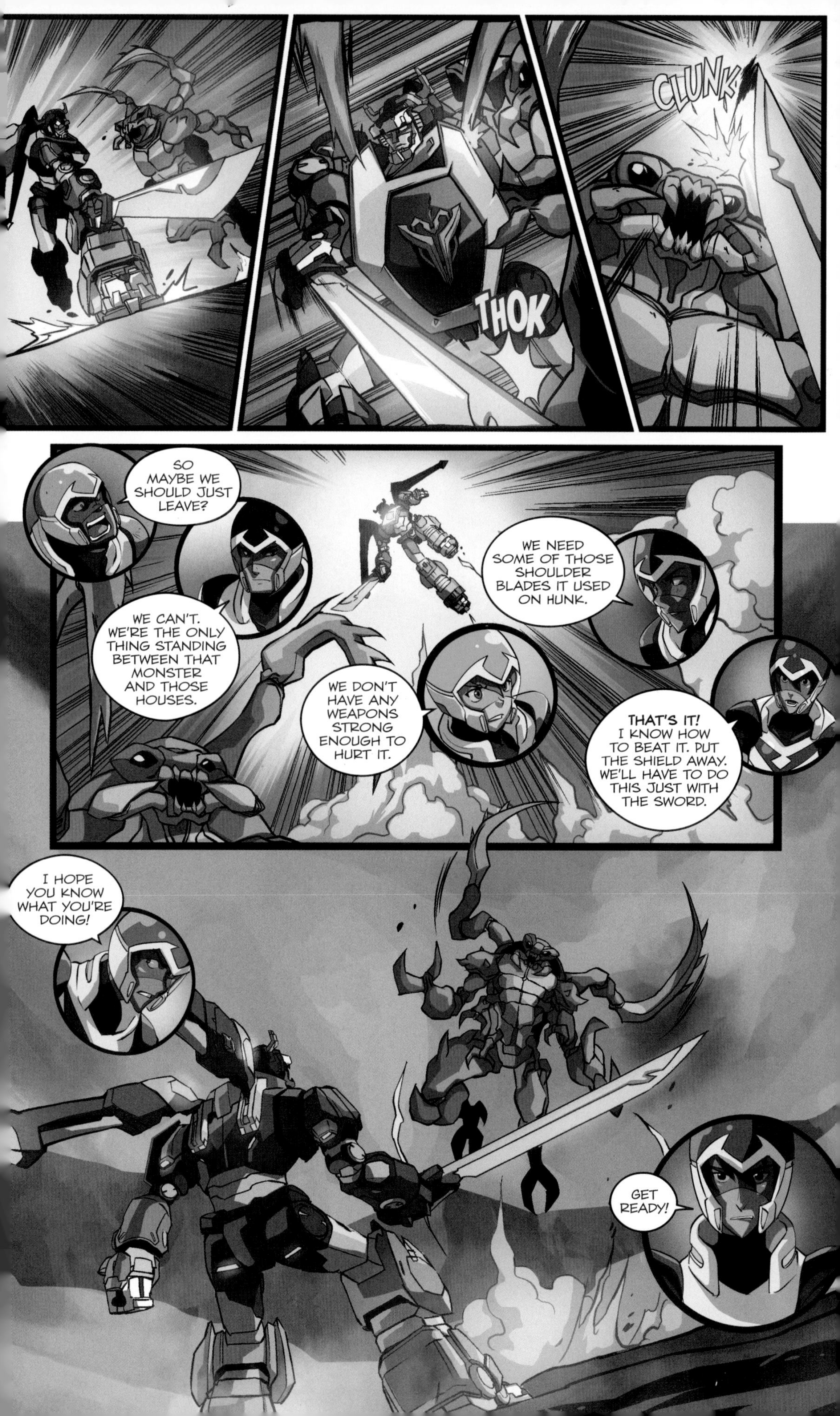
CLUNK
THOK
SO MAYBE WE SHOULD JUST LEAVE?
WE CAN'T. WE'RE THE ONLY THING STANDING BETWEEN THAT MONSTER AND THOSE HOUSES.
WE DON'T HAVE ANY WEAPONS STRONG ENOUGH TO HURT IT.
WE NEED SOME OF THOSE SHOULDER BLADES IT USED ON HUNK.
THAT'S IT! I KNOW HOW TO BEAT IT. PUT THE SHIELD AWAY. WE'LL HAVE TO DO THIS JUST WITH THE SWORD.
I HOPE YOU KNOW WHAT YOU'RE DOING!
GET READY!

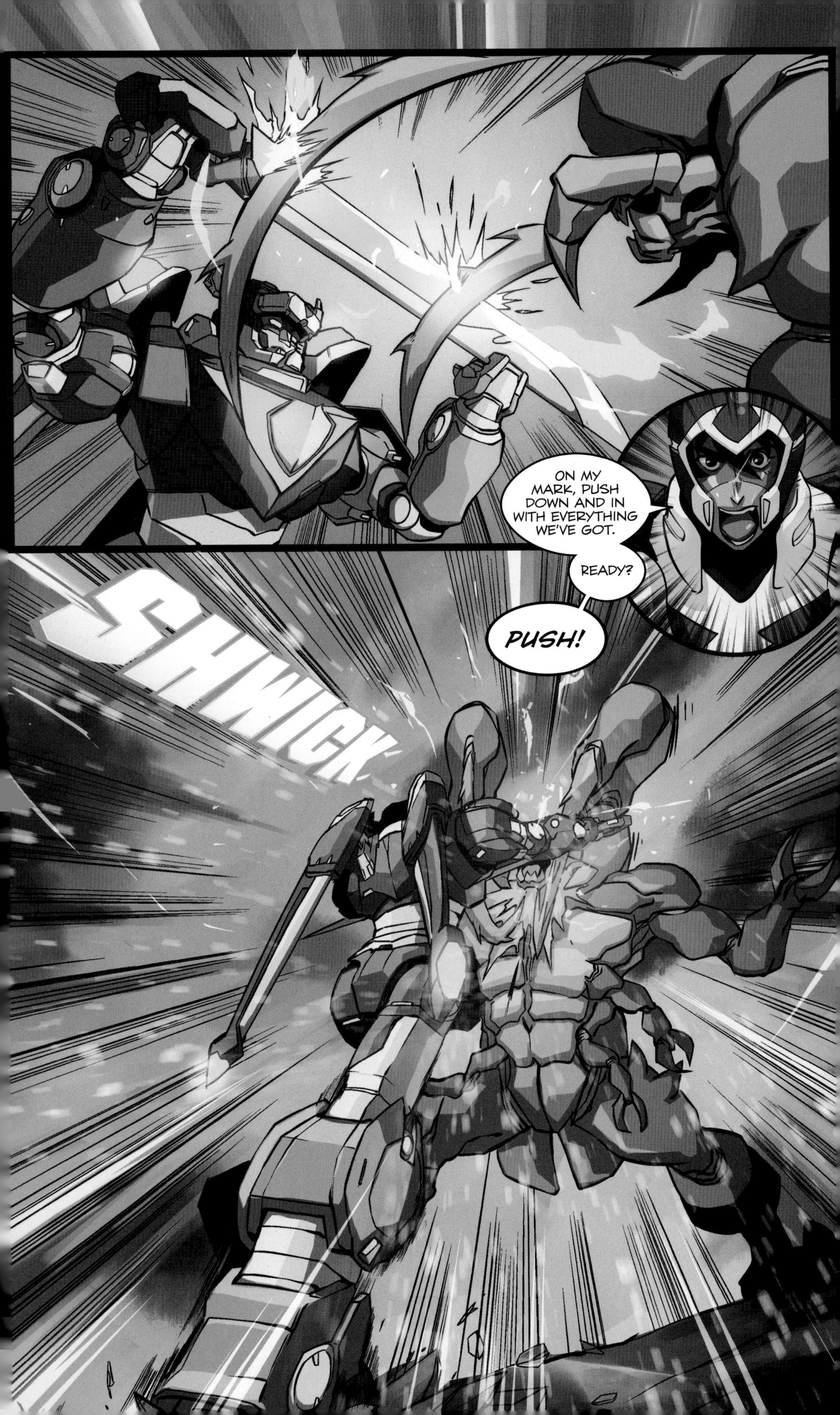
ON MY MARK, PUSH DOWN AND IN WITH EVERYTHING WE'VE GOT.
READY?
PUSH!
SHWICK

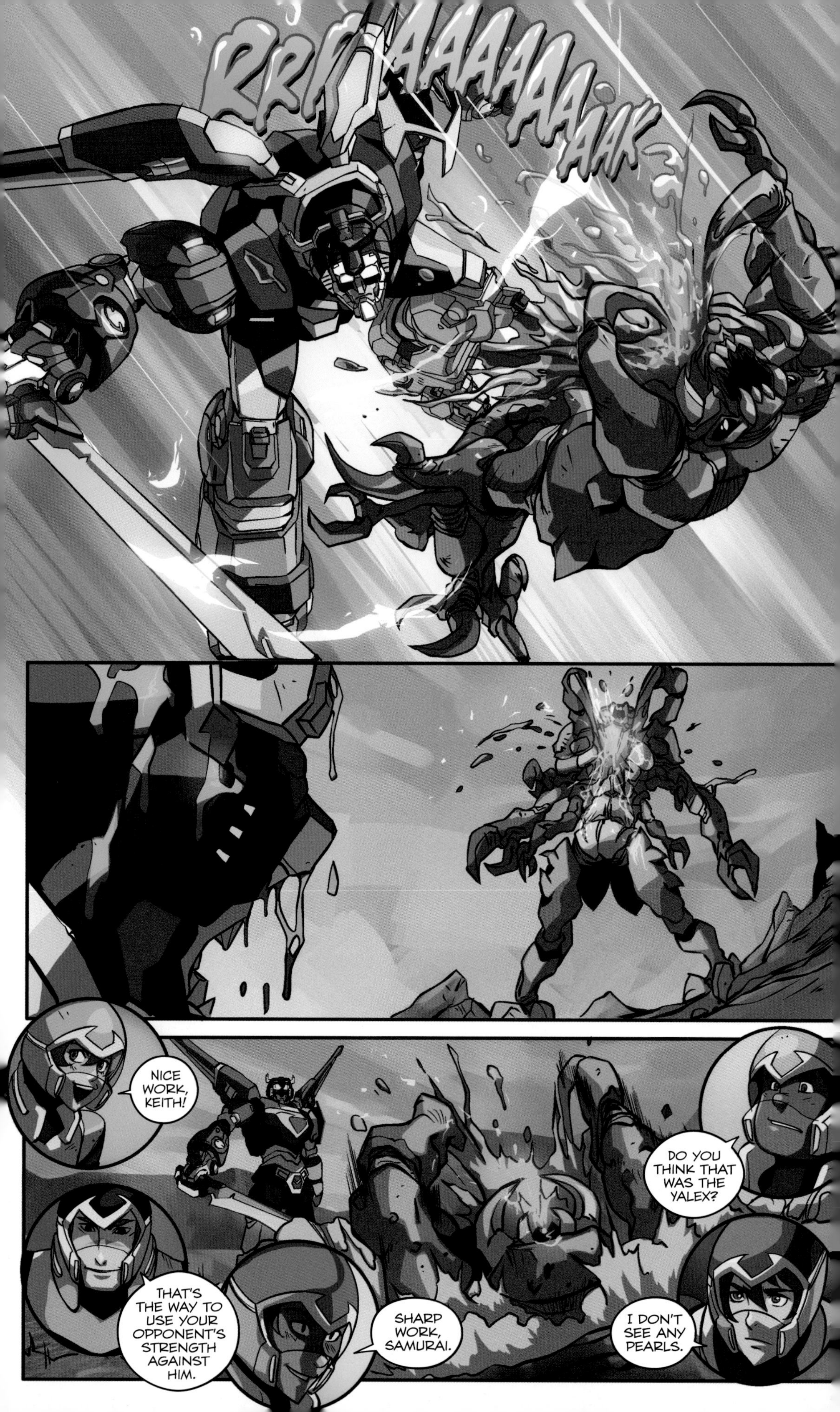
RRRAAAAAAAAAAAK
NICE WORK, KEITH!
DO YOU THINK THAT WAS THE YALEX?
THAT'S THE WAY TO USE YOUR OPPONENT'S STRENGTH AGAINST HIM.
SHARP WORK, SAMURAI.
I DON'T SEE ANY PEARLS.

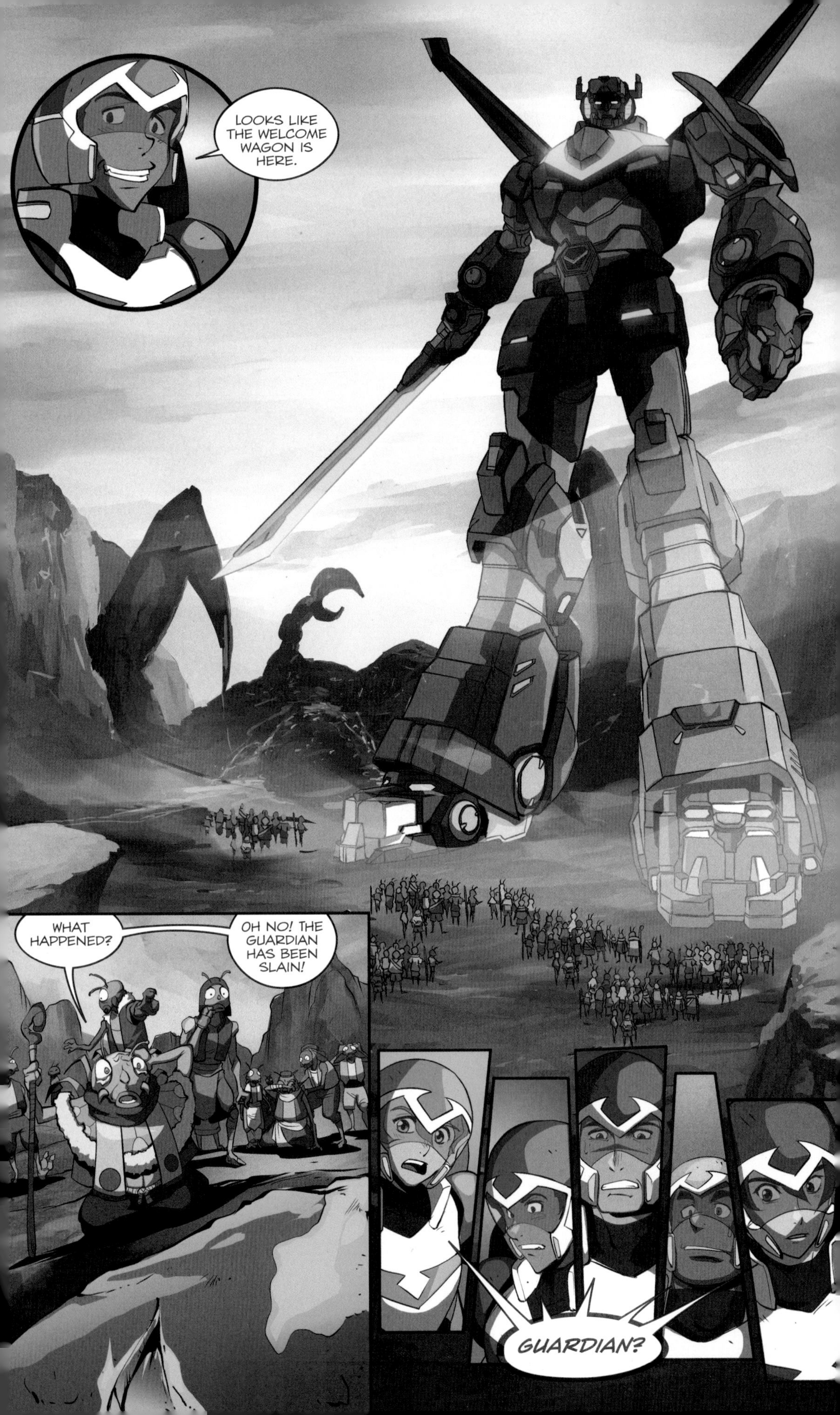
LOOKS LIKE THE WELCOME WAGON IS HERE.
WHAT HAPPENED?
OH NO! THE GUARDIAN HAS BEEN SLAIN!
GUARDIAN?

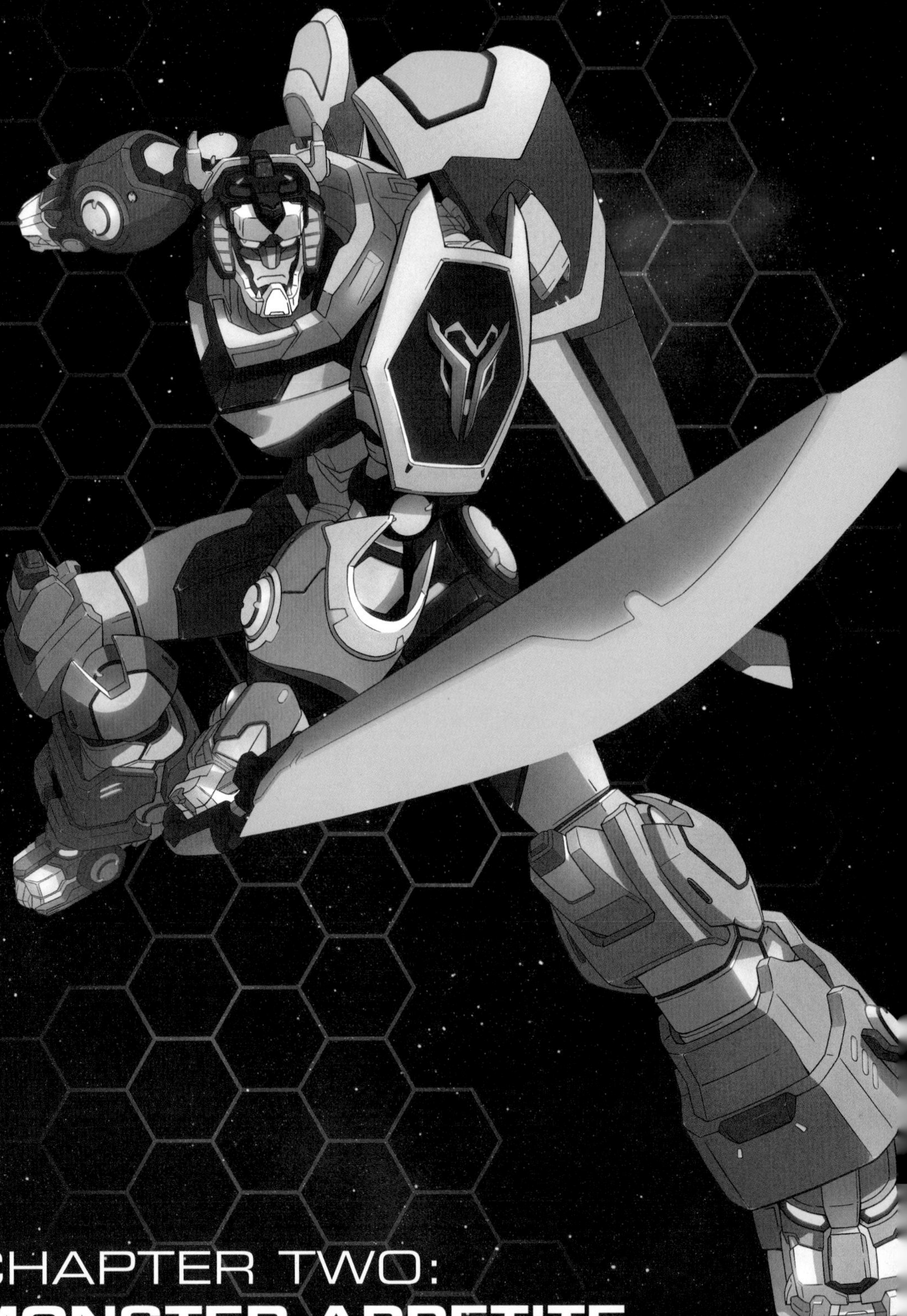

CHAPTER TWO:
MONSTER APPETITE

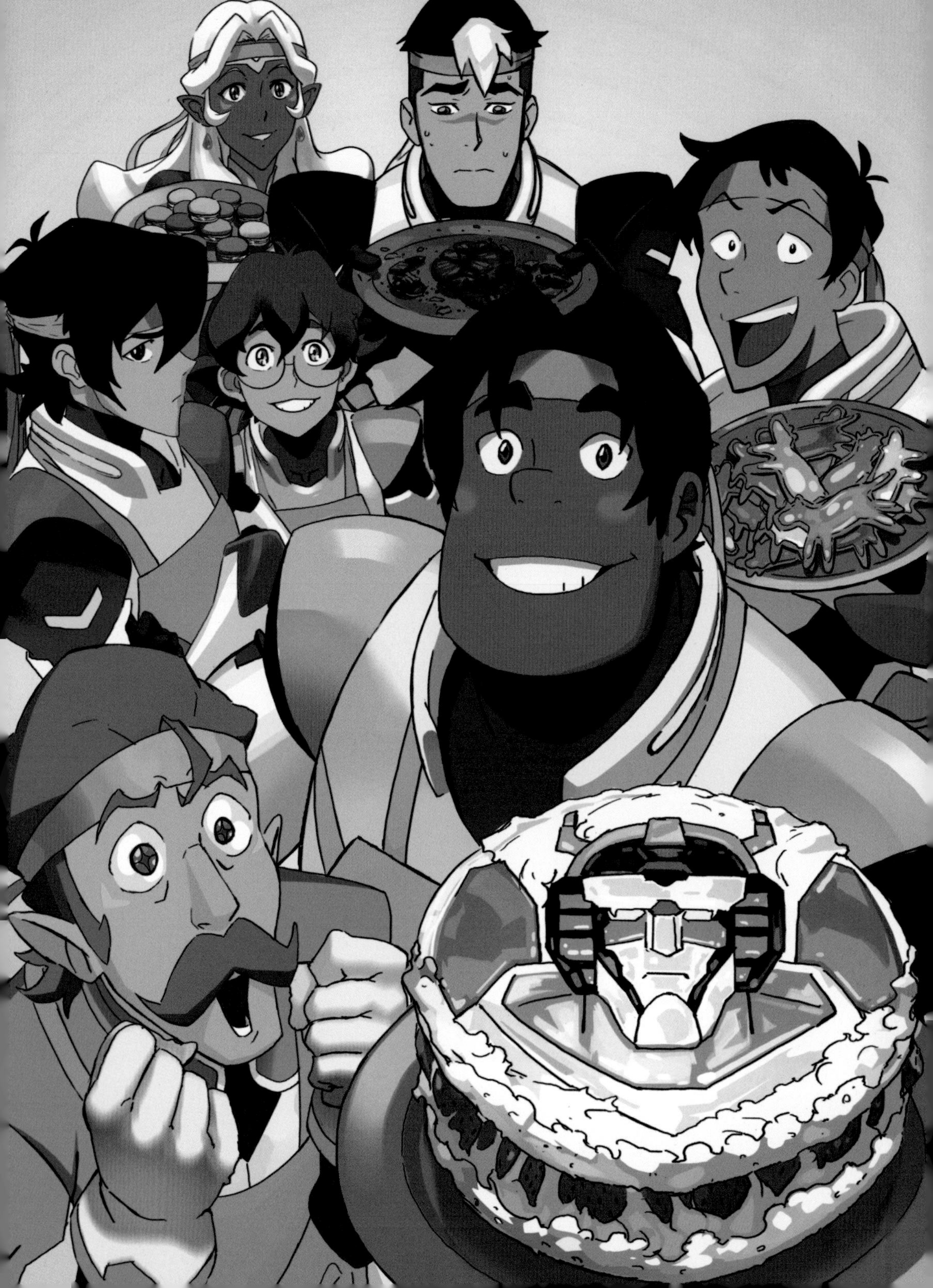

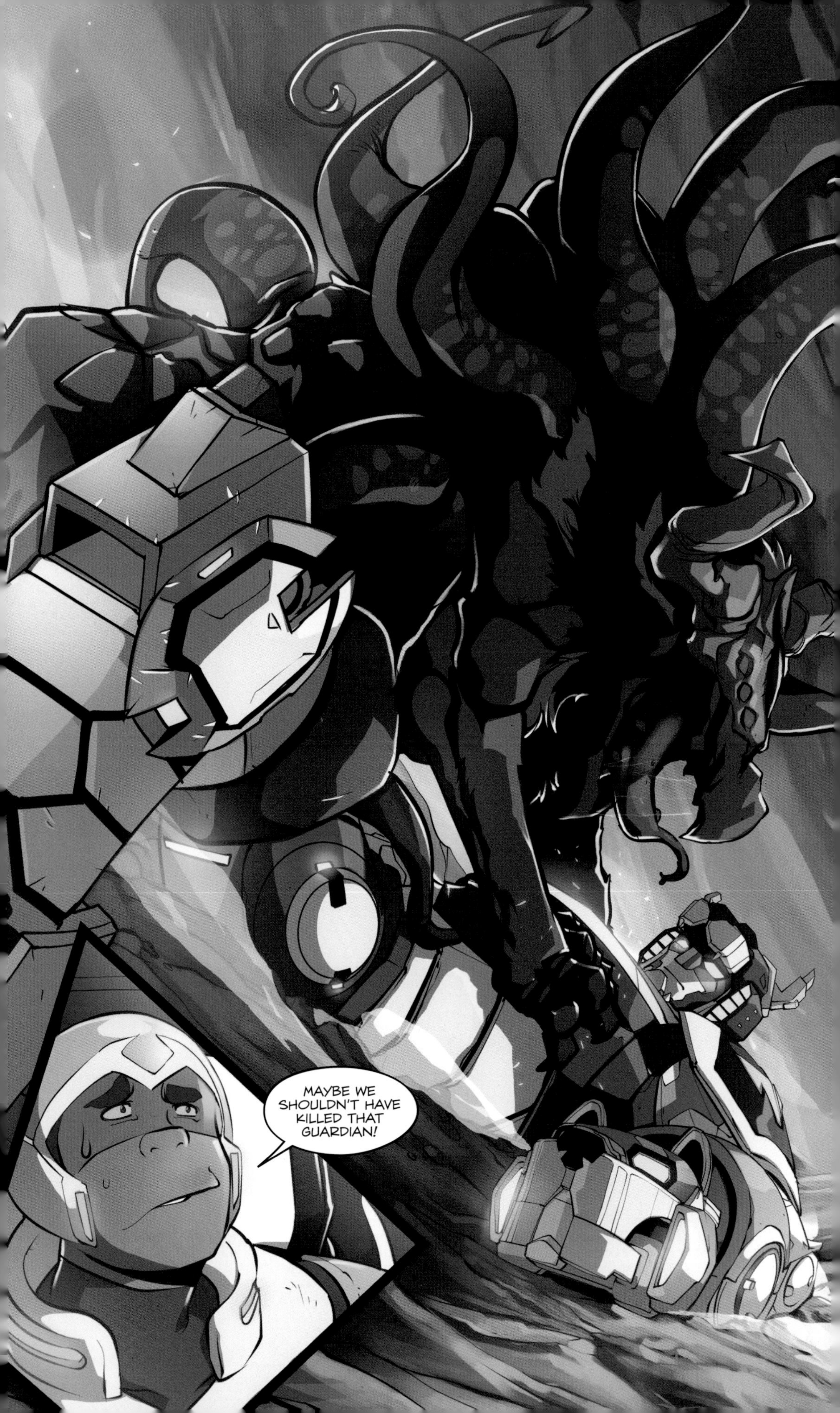
MAYBE WE SHOULDN'T HAVE KILLED THAT GUARDIAN!

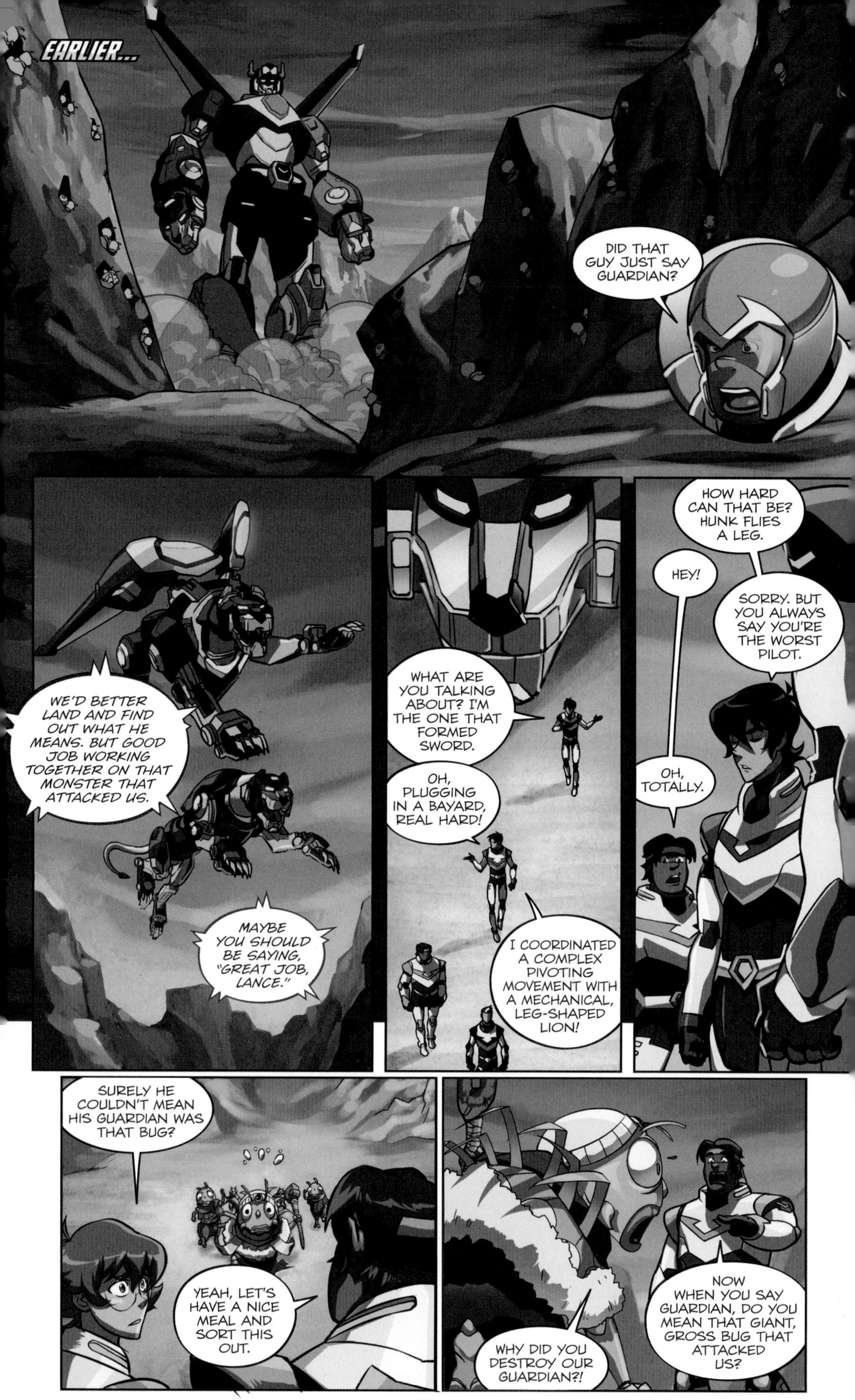
EARLIER...
DID THAT GUY JUST SAY GUARDIAN?
WE'D BETTER LAND AND FIND OUT WHAT HE MEANS. BUT GOOD JOB WORKING TOGETHER ON THAT MONSTER THAT ATTACKED US.
MAYBE YOU SHOULD BE SAYING, "GREAT JOB, LANCE."
WHAT ARE YOU TALKING ABOUT? I'M THE ONE THAT FORMED SWORD.
OH, PLUGGING IN A BAYARD, REAL HARD!
I COORDINATED A COMPLEX PIVOTING MOVEMENT WITH A MECHANICAL, LEG-SHAPED LION!
HOW HARD CAN THAT BE? HUNK FLIES A LEG.
HEY!
SORRY. BUT YOU ALWAYS SAY YOU'RE THE WORST PILOT.
OH, TOTALLY.
SURELY HE COULDN'T MEAN HIS GUARDIAN WAS THAT BUG?
YEAH, LET'S HAVE A NICE MEAL AND SORT THIS OUT.
WHY DID YOU DESTROY OUR GUARDIAN?!
NOW WHEN YOU SAY GUARDIAN, DO YOU MEAN THAT GIANT, GROSS BUG THAT ATTACKED US?

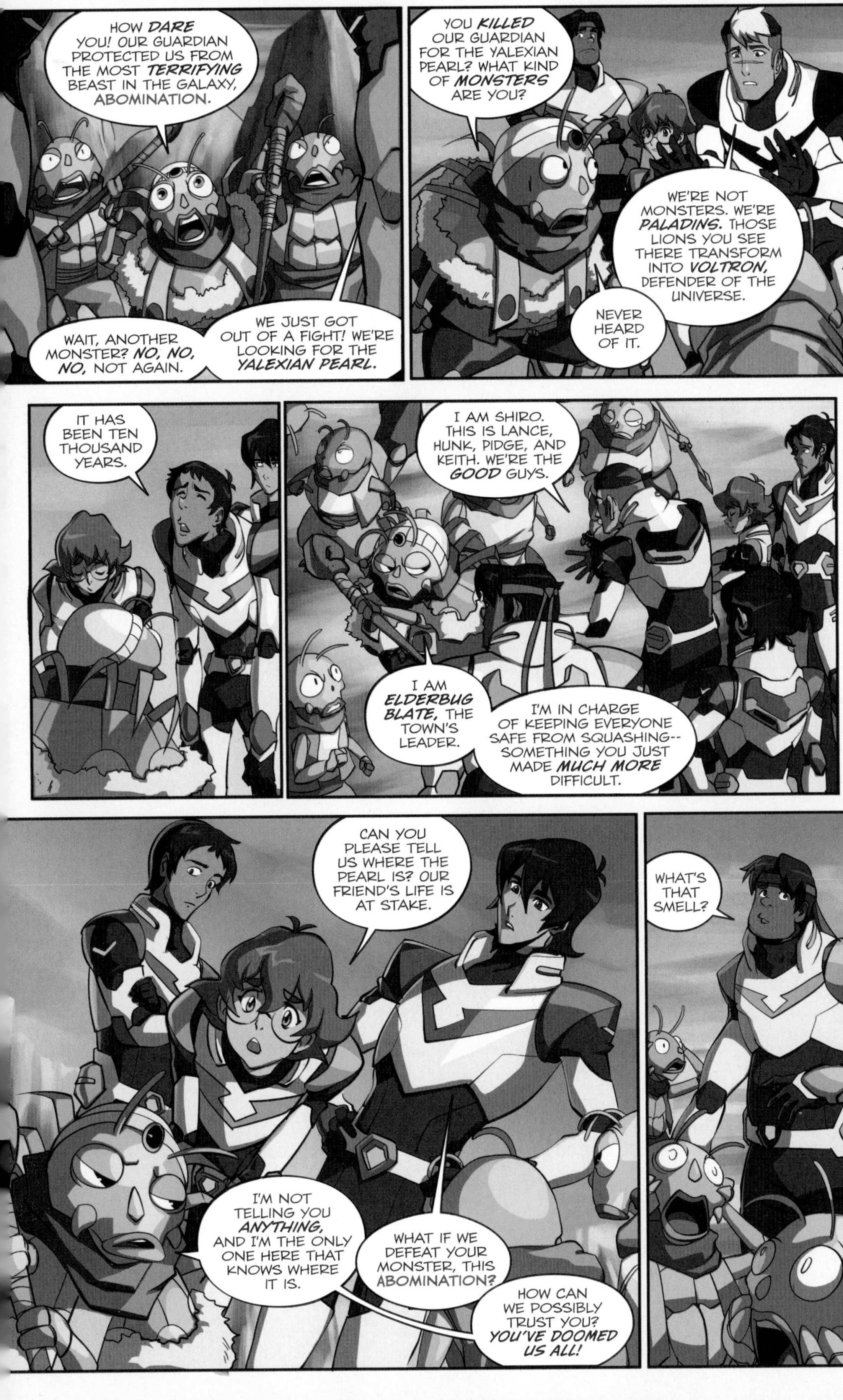
HOW DARE YOU! OUR GUARDIAN PROTECTED US FROM THE MOST TERRIFYING BEAST IN THE GALAXY, ABOMINATION.
WAIT, ANOTHER MONSTER? NO, NO, NO, NOT AGAIN.
WE JUST GOT OUT OF A FIGHT! WE'RE LOOKING FOR THE YALEXIAN PEARL.
YOU KILLED OUR GUARDIAN FOR THE YALEXIAN PEARL? WHAT KIND OF MONSTERS ARE YOU?
WE'RE NOT MONSTERS. WE'RE PALADINS. THOSE LIONS YOU SEE THERE TRANSFORM INTO VOLTRON, DEFENDER OF THE UNIVERSE.
NEVER HEARD OF IT.
IT HAS BEEN TEN THOUSAND YEARS.
I AM SHIRO. THIS IS LANCE, HUNK, PIDGE, AND KEITH. WE'RE THE GOOD GUYS.
I AM ELDERBUG BLATE, THE TOWN'S LEADER.
I'M IN CHARGE OF KEEPING EVERYONE SAFE FROM SQUASHING-- SOMETHING YOU JUST MADE MUCH MORE DIFFICULT.
CAN YOU PLEASE TELL US WHERE THE PEARL IS? OUR FRIEND'S LIFE IS AT STAKE.
I'M NOT TELLING YOU ANYTHING, AND I'M THE ONLY ONE HERE THAT KNOWS WHERE IT IS.
WHAT IF WE DEFEAT YOUR MONSTER, THIS ABOMINATION?
HOW CAN WE POSSIBLY TRUST YOU? YOU'VE DOOMED US ALL!
WHAT'S THAT SMELL?

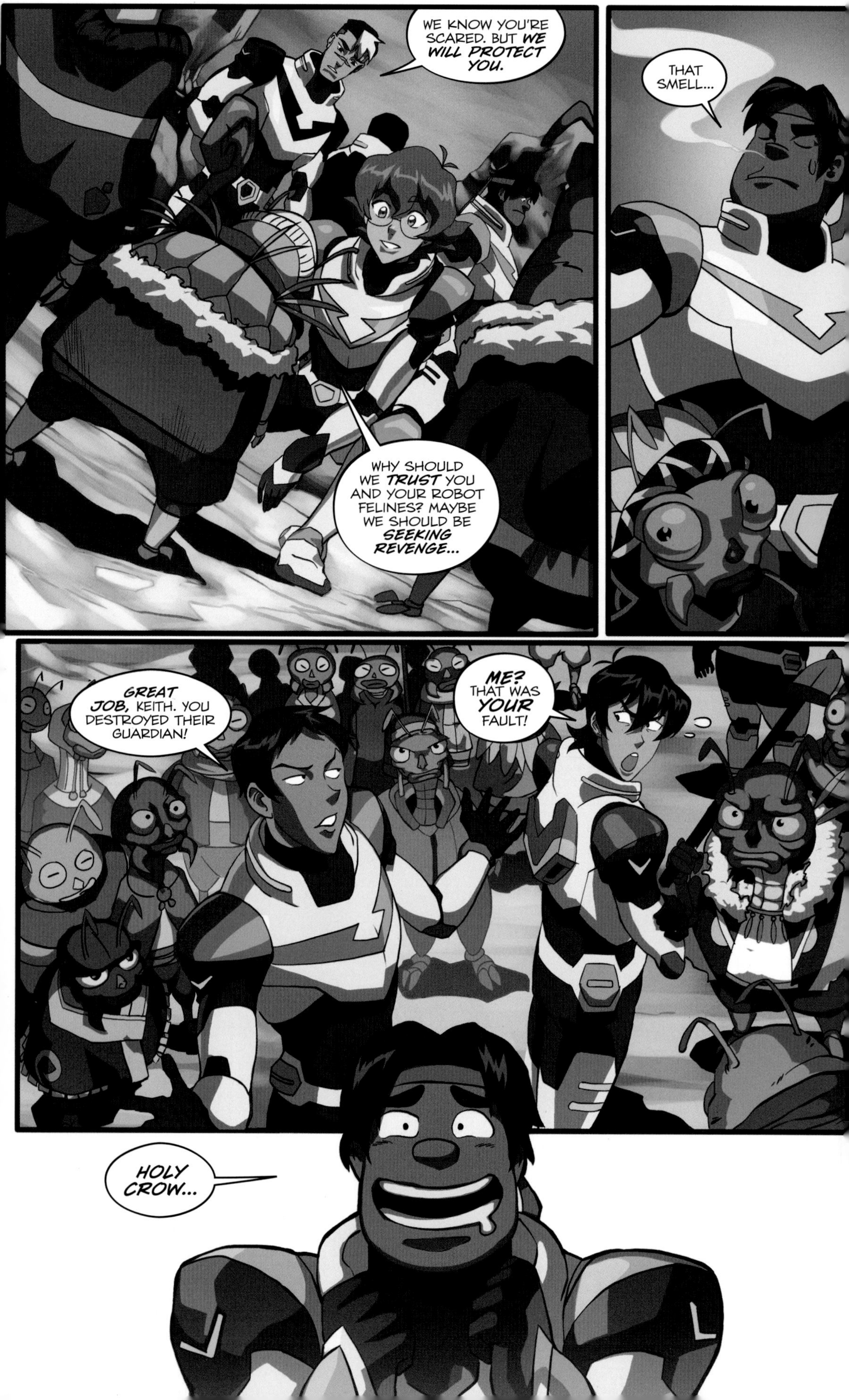

WE KNOW YOU'RE SCARED. BUT WE WILL PROTECT YOU.
WHY SHOULD WE TRUST YOU AND YOUR ROBOT FELINES? MAYBE WE SHOULD BE SEEKING REVENGE...
THAT SMELL...
GREAT JOB, KEITH. YOU DESTROYED THEIR GUARDIAN!
ME? THAT WAS YOUR FAULT!
HOLY CROW...

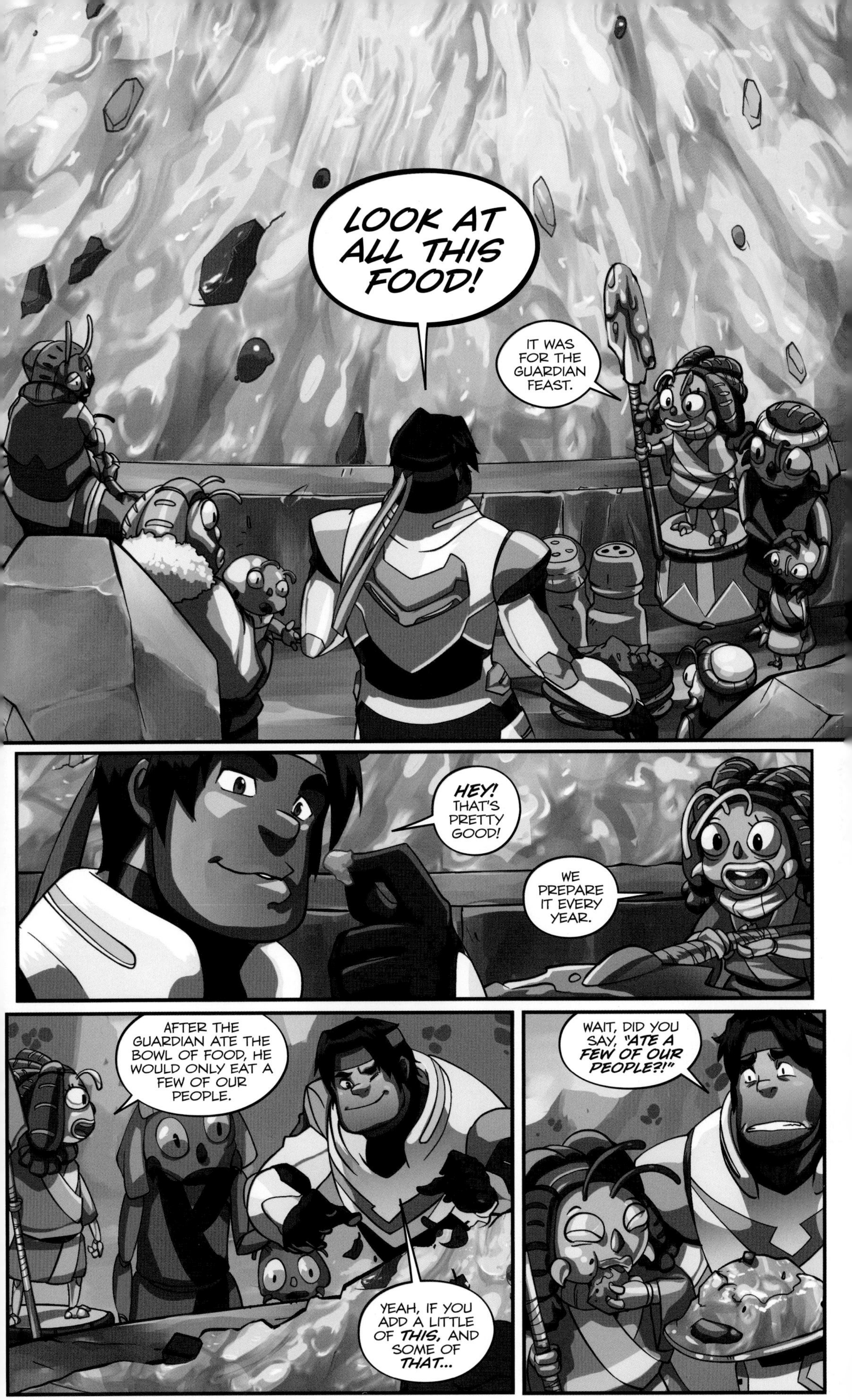
LOOK AT ALL THIS FOOD!
IT WAS FOR THE GUARDIAN FEAST.
HEY! THAT'S PRETTY GOOD!
WE PREPARE IT EVERY YEAR.
AFTER THE GUARDIAN ATE THE BOWL OF FOOD, HE WOULD ONLY EAT A FEW OF OUR PEOPLE.
YEAH, IF YOU ADD A LITTLE OF THIS, AND SOME OF THAT...
WAIT, DID YOU SAY, "ATE A FEW OF OUR PEOPLE?!"

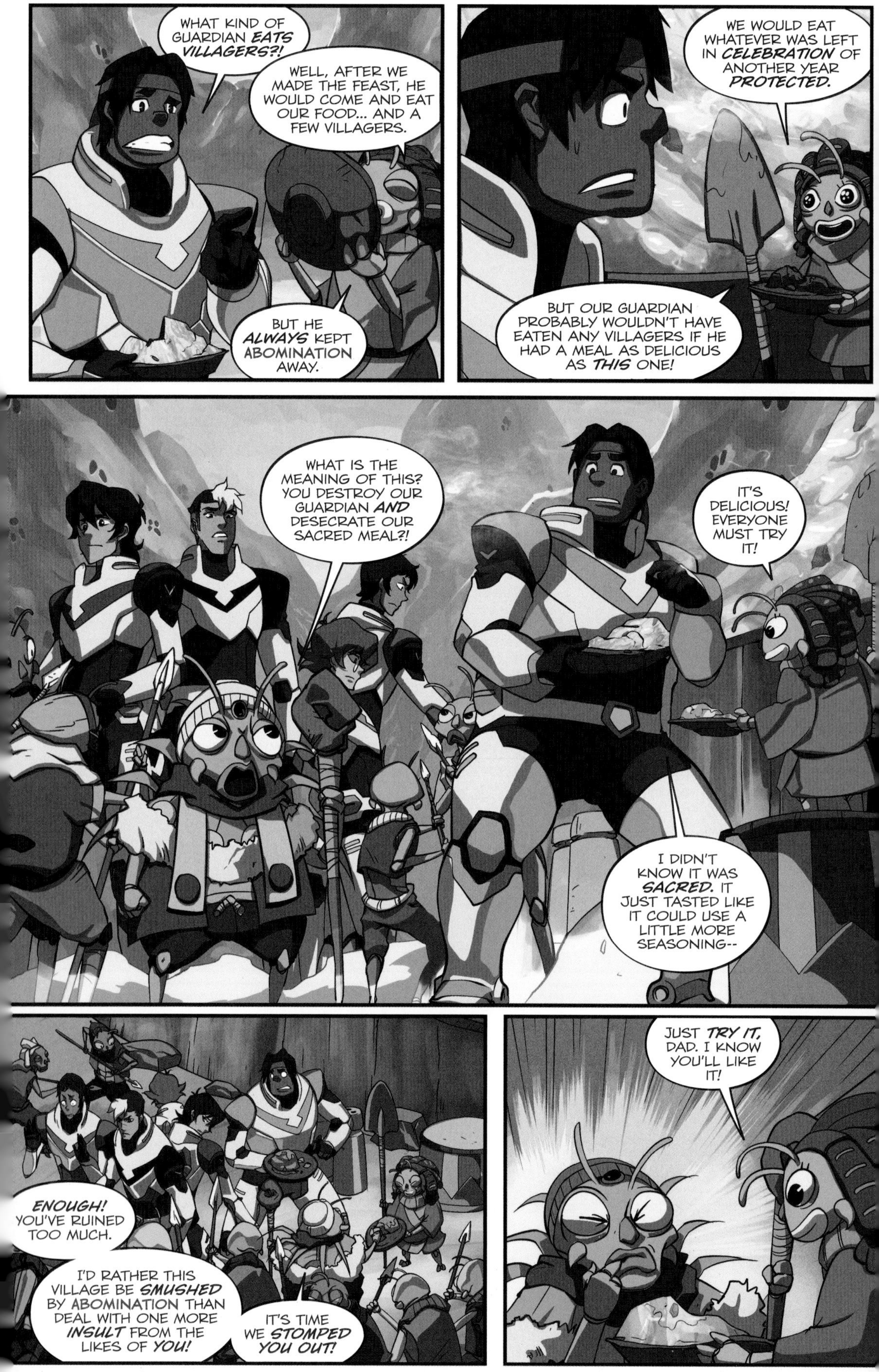

WHAT KIND OF GUARDIAN EATS VILLAGERS?!
WELL, AFTER WE MADE THE FEAST, HE WOULD COME AND EAT OUR FOOD... AND A FEW VILLAGERS.
BUT HE ALWAYS KEPT ABOMINATION AWAY.
WE WOULD EAT WHATEVER WAS LEFT IN CELEBRATION OF ANOTHER YEAR PROTECTED.
BUT OUR GUARDIAN PROBABLY WOULDN'T HAVE EATEN ANY VILLAGERS IF HE HAD A MEAL AS DELICIOUS AS THIS ONE!
WHAT IS THE MEANING OF THIS? YOU DESTROY OUR GUARDIAN AND DESECRATE OUR SACRED MEAL?!
IT'S DELICIOUS! EVERYONE MUST TRY IT!
I DIDN'T KNOW IT WAS SACRED. IT JUST TASTED LIKE IT COULD USE A LITTLE MORE SEASONING--
ENOUGH! YOU'VE RUINED TOO MUCH.
I'D RATHER THIS VILLAGE BE SMUSHED BY ABOMINATION THAN DEAL WITH ONE MORE INSULT FROM THE LIKES OF YOU!
IT'S TIME WE STOMPED YOU OUT!
JUST TRY IT, DAD. I KNOW YOU'LL LIKE IT!

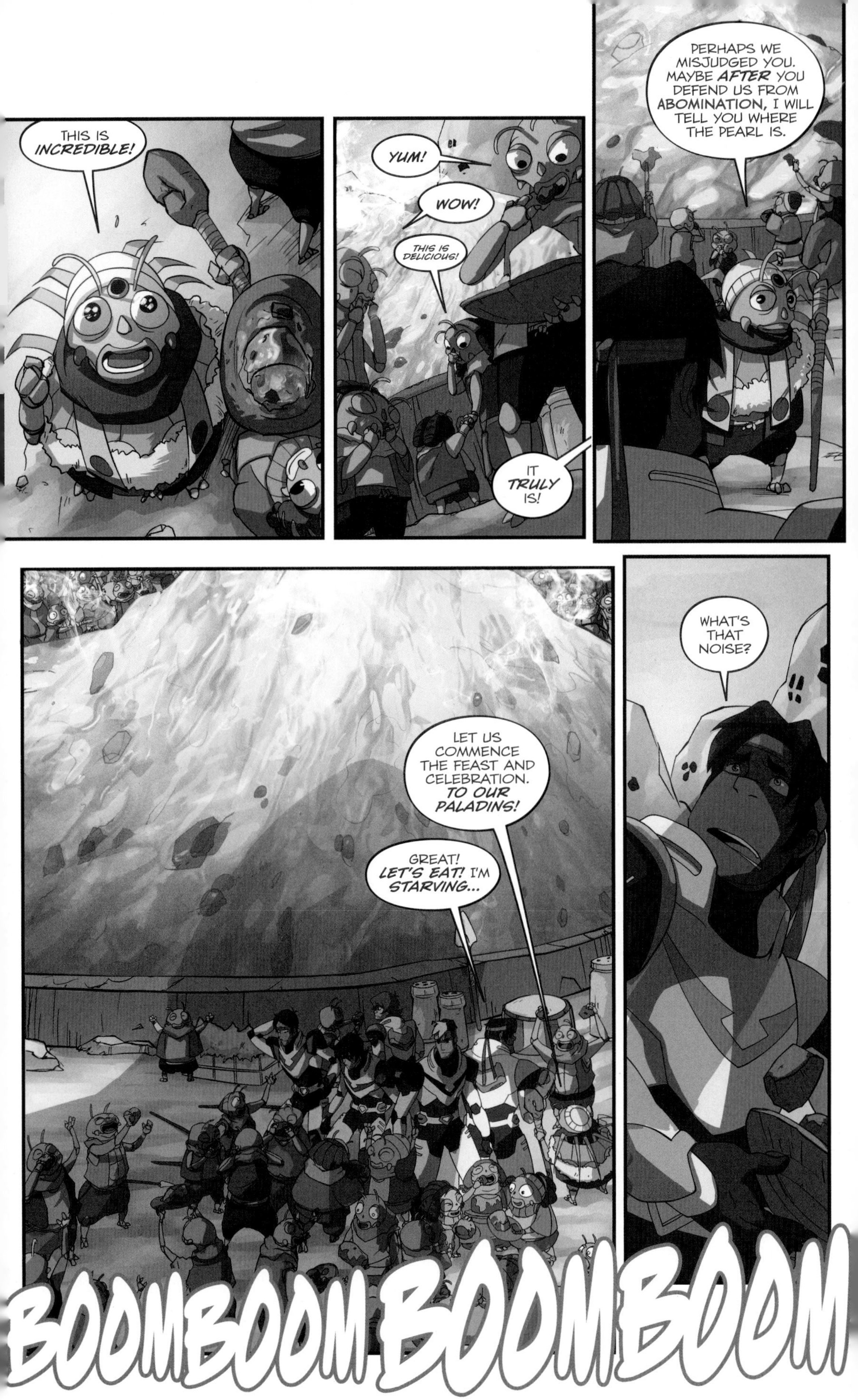
THIS IS INCREDIBLE!
YUM!
WOW!
THIS IS DELICIOUS!
IT TRULY IS!
PERHAPS WE MISJUDGED YOU. MAYBE AFTER YOU DEFEND US FROM ABOMINATION, I WILL TELL YOU WHERE THE PEARL IS.
LET US COMMENCE THE FEAST AND CELEBRATION. TO OUR PALADINS!
GREAT! LET'S EAT! I'M STARVING...
WHAT'S THAT NOISE?
BOOMBOOM BOOMBOOM

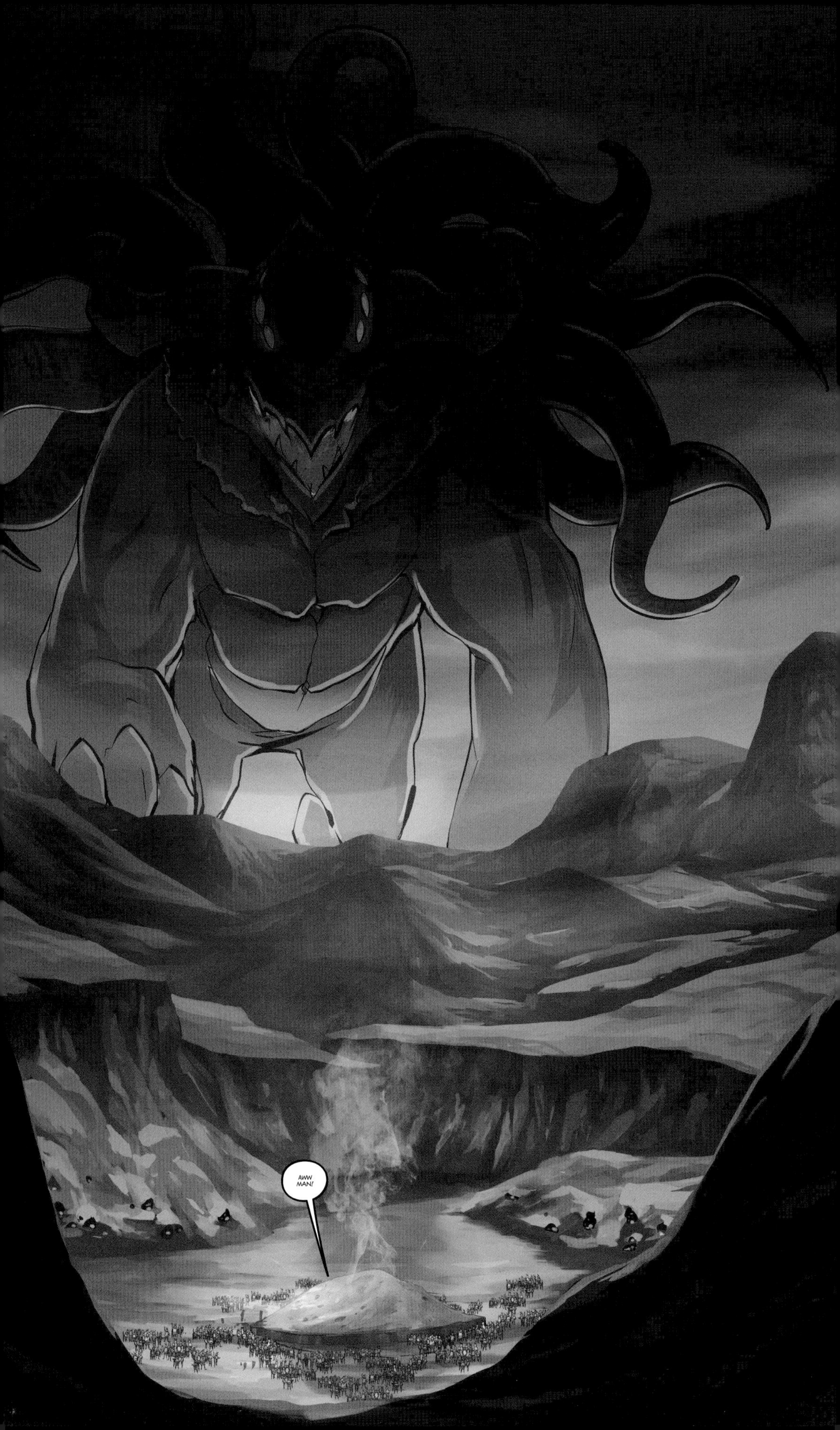
AWW MAN!

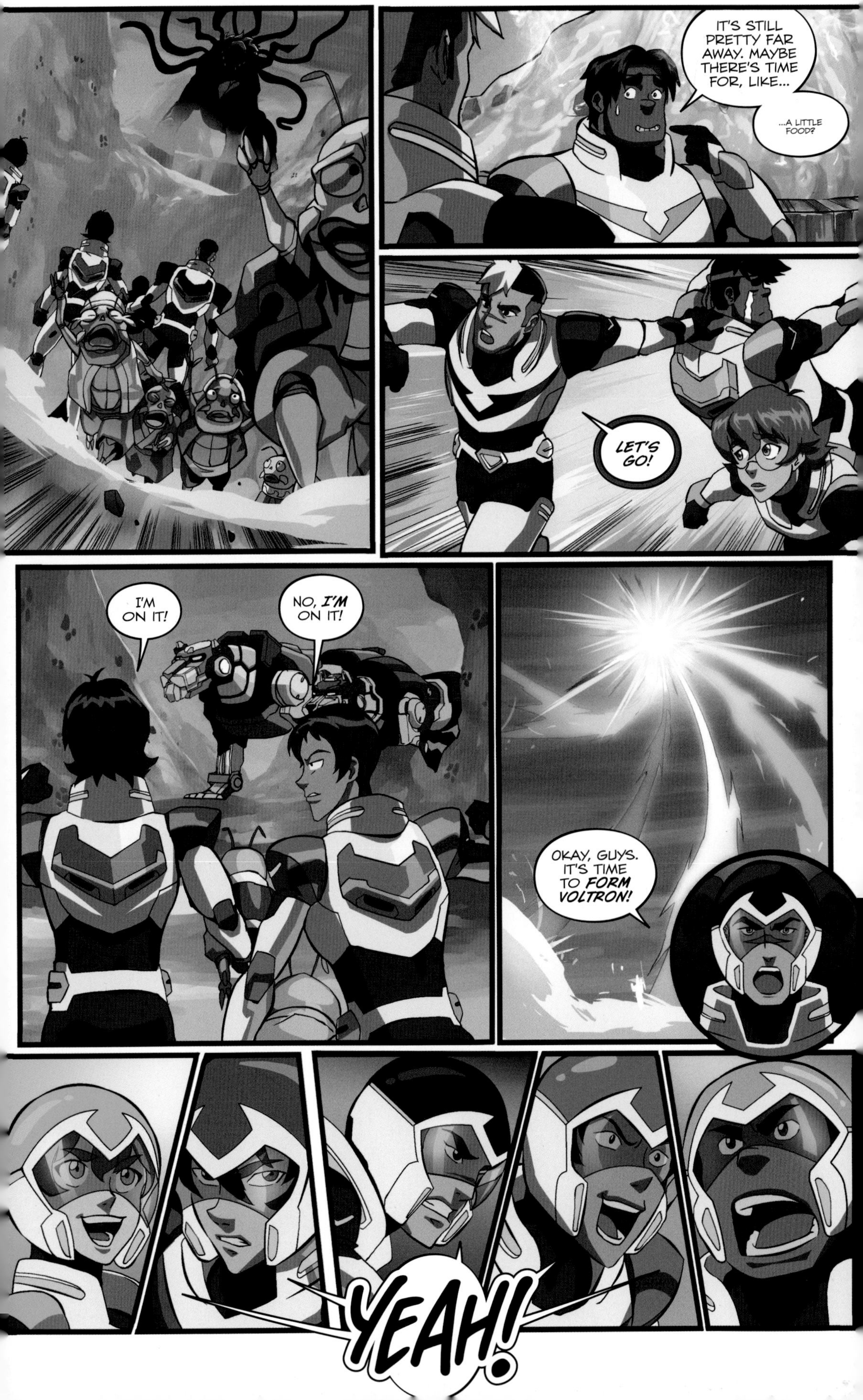
IT'S STILL PRETTY FAR AWAY. MAYBE THERE'S TIME FOR, LIKE...
...A LITTLE FOOD?
LET'S GO!
I'M ON IT!
NO, I'M ON IT!
OKAY, GUYS. IT'S TIME TO FORM VOLTRON!
YEAH!

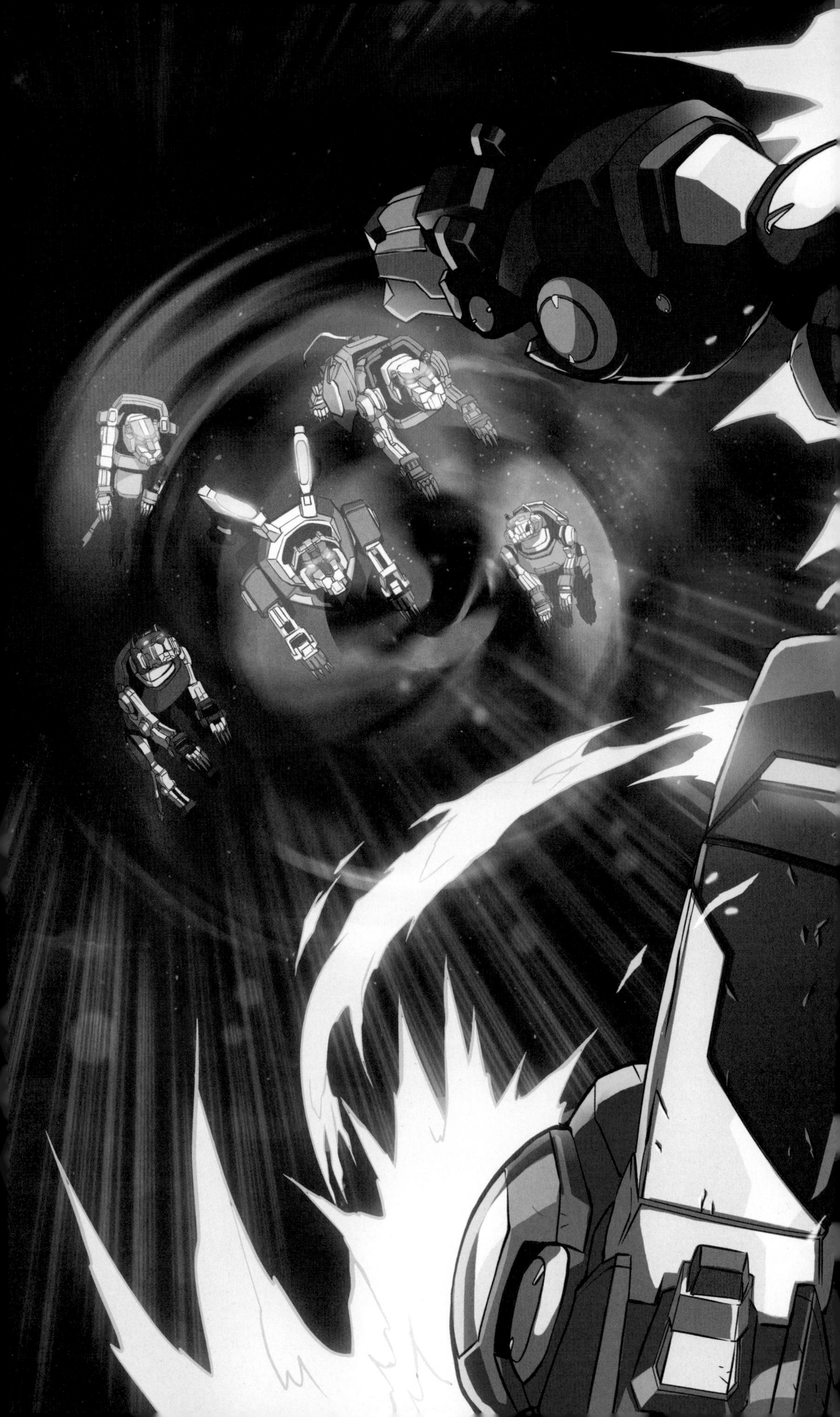

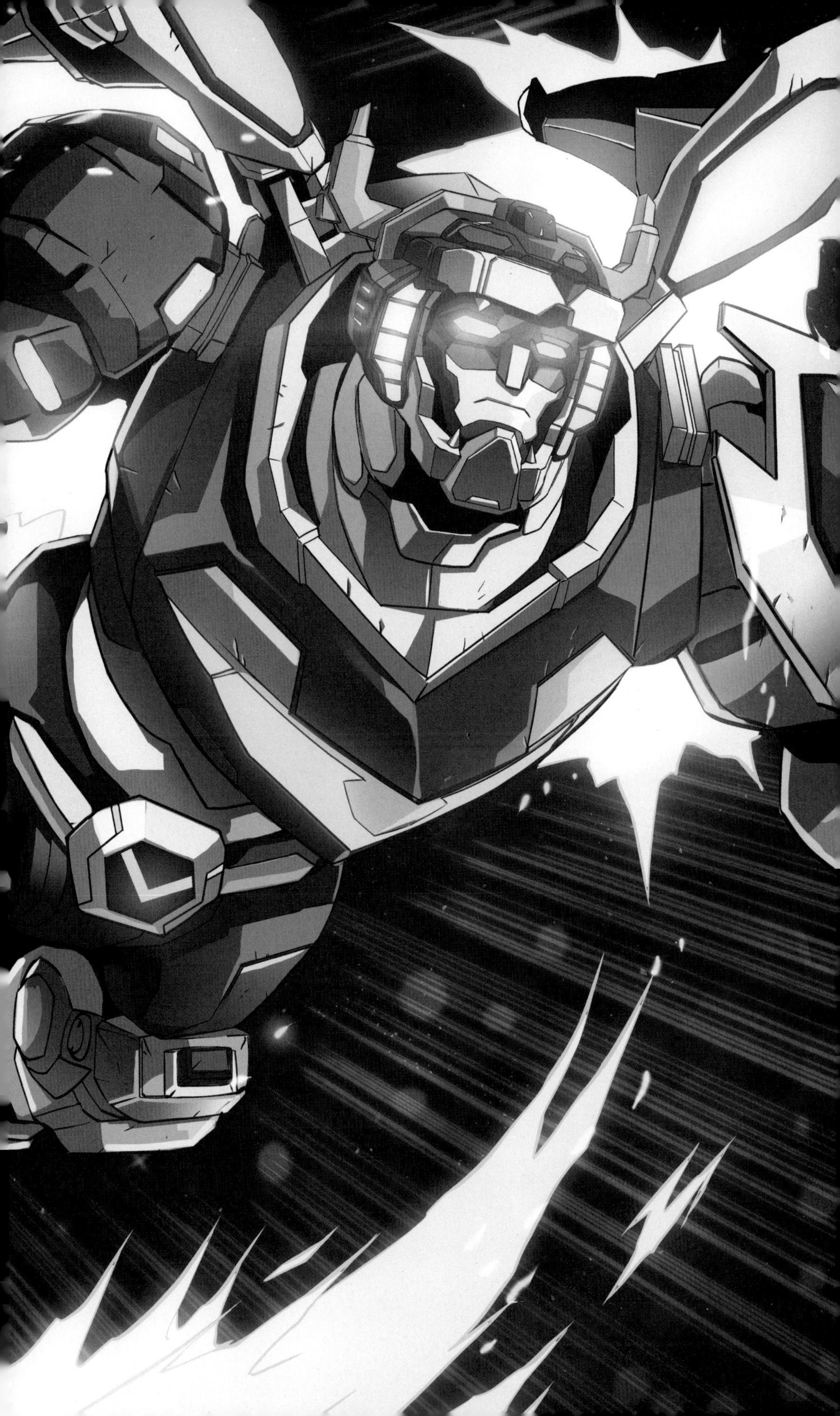

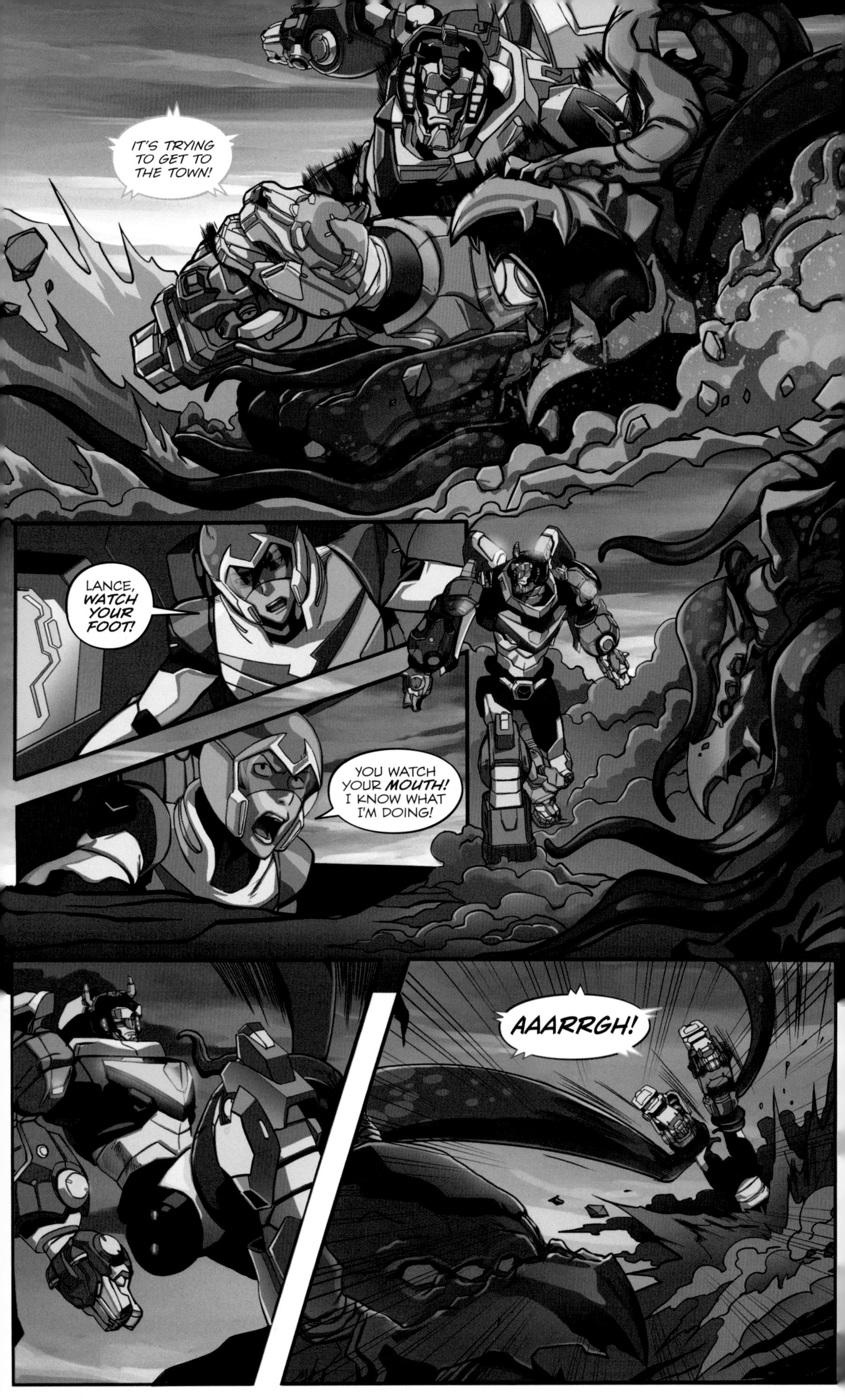
IT'S TRYING TO GET TO THE TOWN!
LANCE, WATCH YOUR FOOT!
YOU WATCH YOUR MOUTH! I KNOW WHAT I'M DOING!
AAARRGH!

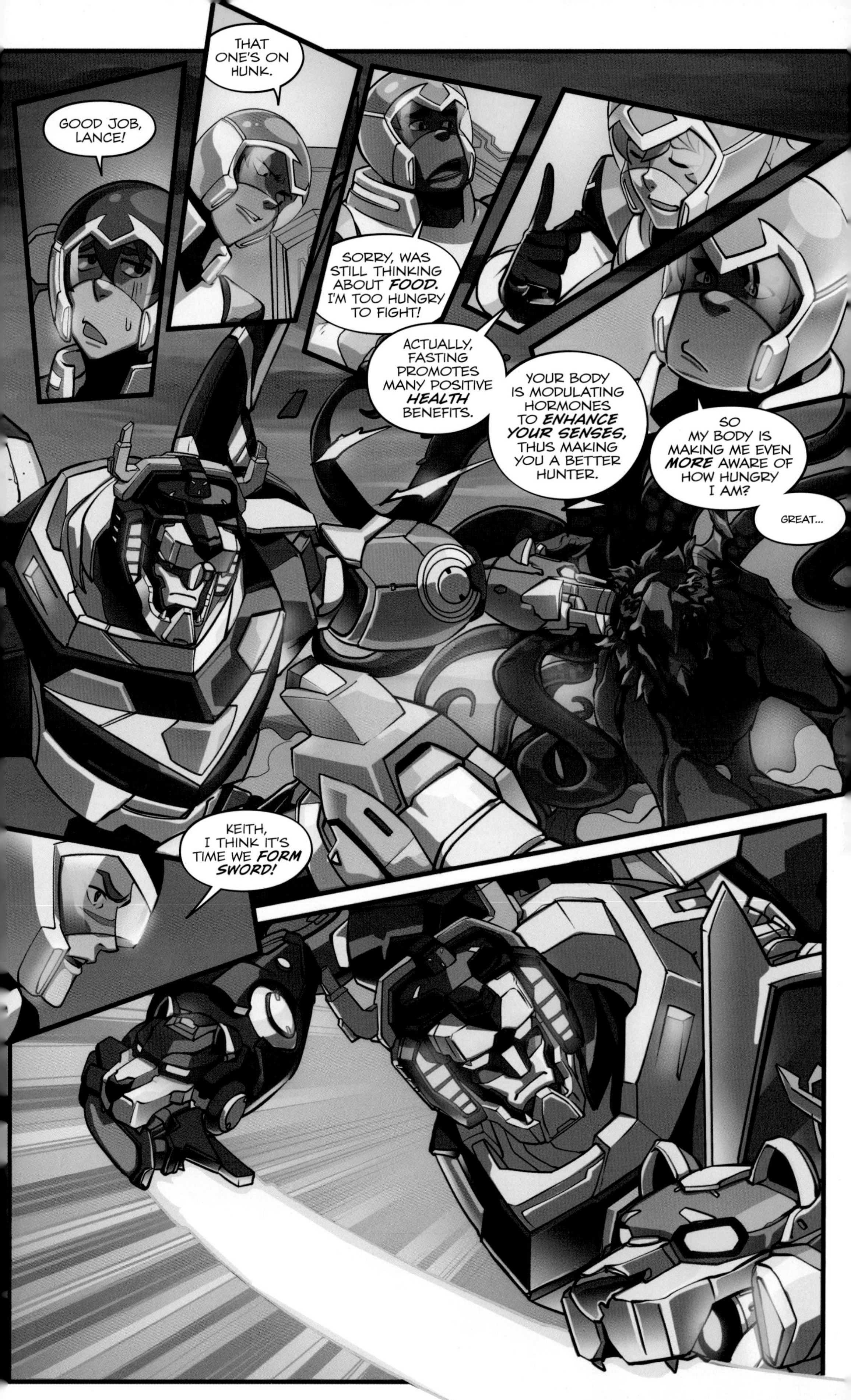
GOOD JOB, LANCE!
THAT ONE'S ON HUNK.
SORRY, WAS STILL THINKING ABOUT FOOD. I'M TOO HUNGRY TO FIGHT!
ACTUALLY, FASTING PROMOTES MANY POSITIVE HEALTH BENEFITS.
YOUR BODY IS MODULATING HORMONES TO ENHANCE YOUR SENSES, THUS MAKING YOU A BETTER HUNTER.
SO MY BODY IS MAKING ME EVEN MORE AWARE OF HOW HUNGRY I AM?
GREAT...
KEITH, I THINK IT'S TIME WE FORM SWORD!

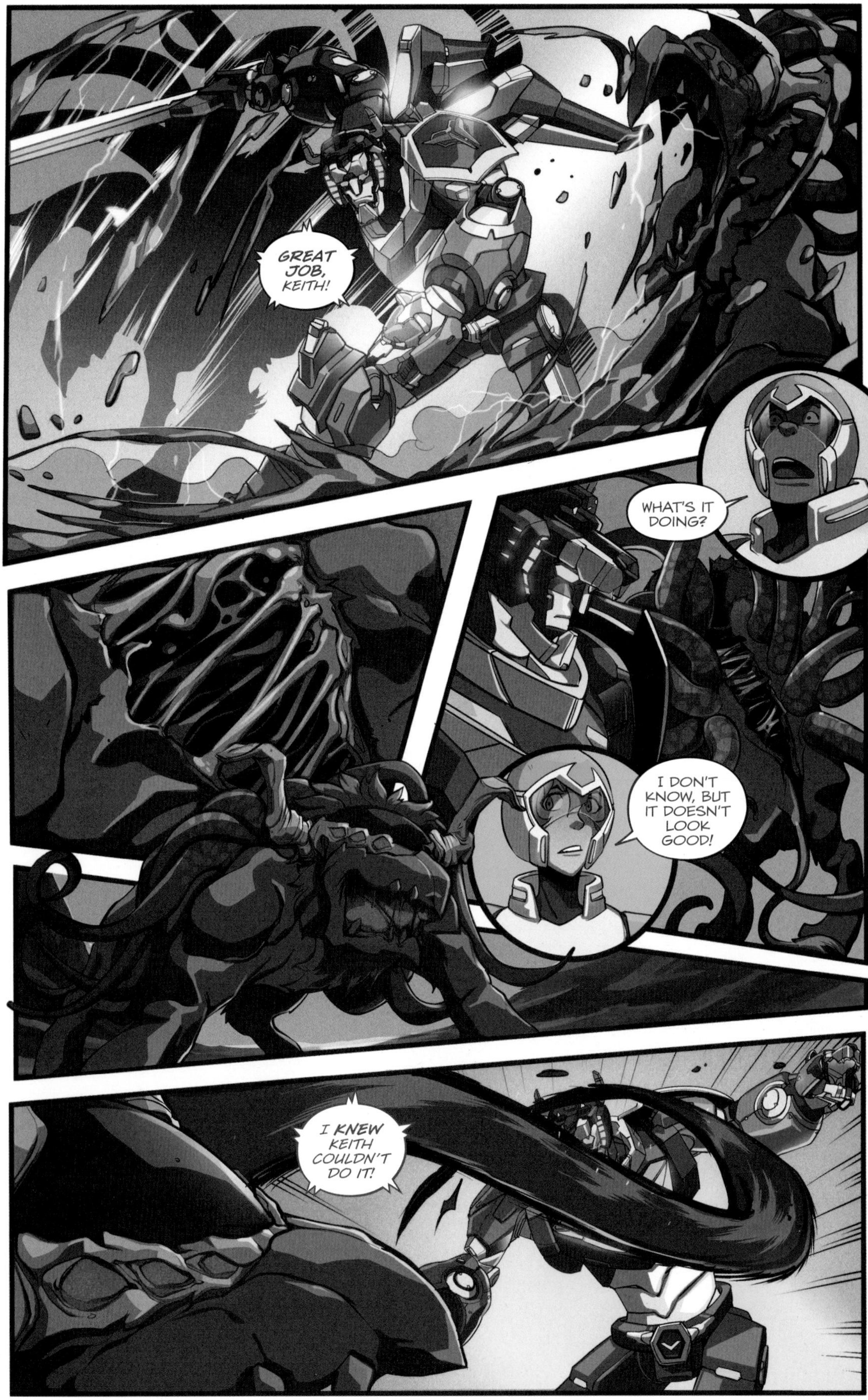
GREAT JOB, KEITH!
WHAT'S IT DOING?
I DON'T KNOW, BUT IT DOESN'T LOOK GOOD!
I KNEW KEITH COULDN'T DO IT!

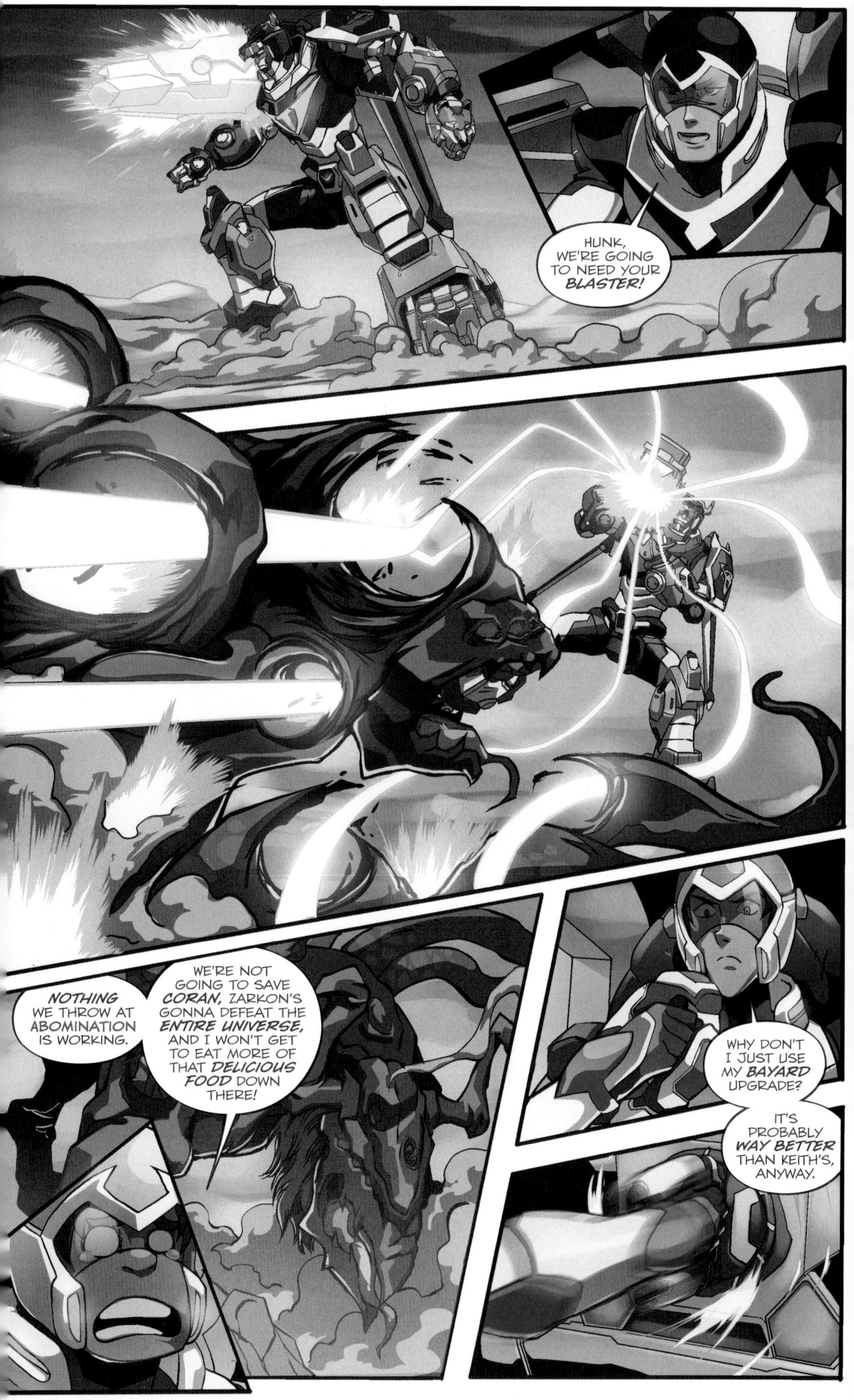
HUNK, WE'RE GOING TO NEED YOUR *BLASTER!*
NOTHING WE THROW AT ABOMINATION IS WORKING.
WE'RE NOT GOING TO SAVE *CORAN,* ZARKON'S GONNA DEFEAT THE *ENTIRE UNIVERSE,* AND I WON'T GET TO EAT MORE OF THAT *DELICIOUS FOOD* DOWN THERE!
WHY DON'T I JUST USE MY *BAYARD* UPGRADE?
IT'S PROBABLY *WAY BETTER* THAN KEITH'S, ANYWAY.

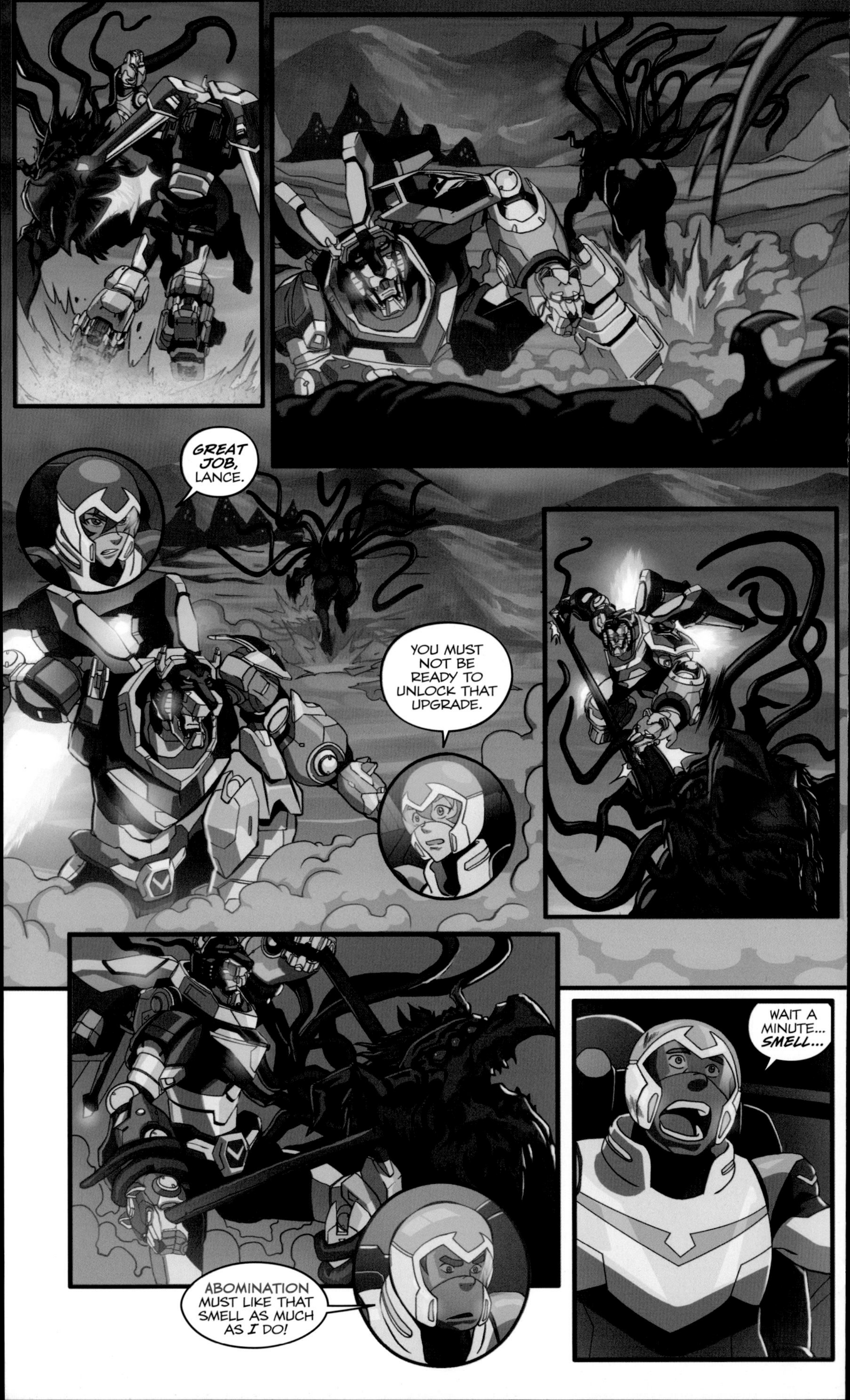
GREAT JOB, LANCE.
YOU MUST NOT BE READY TO UNLOCK THAT UPGRADE.
ABOMINATION MUST LIKE THAT SMELL AS MUCH AS *I* DO!
WAIT A MINUTE... *SMELL*...

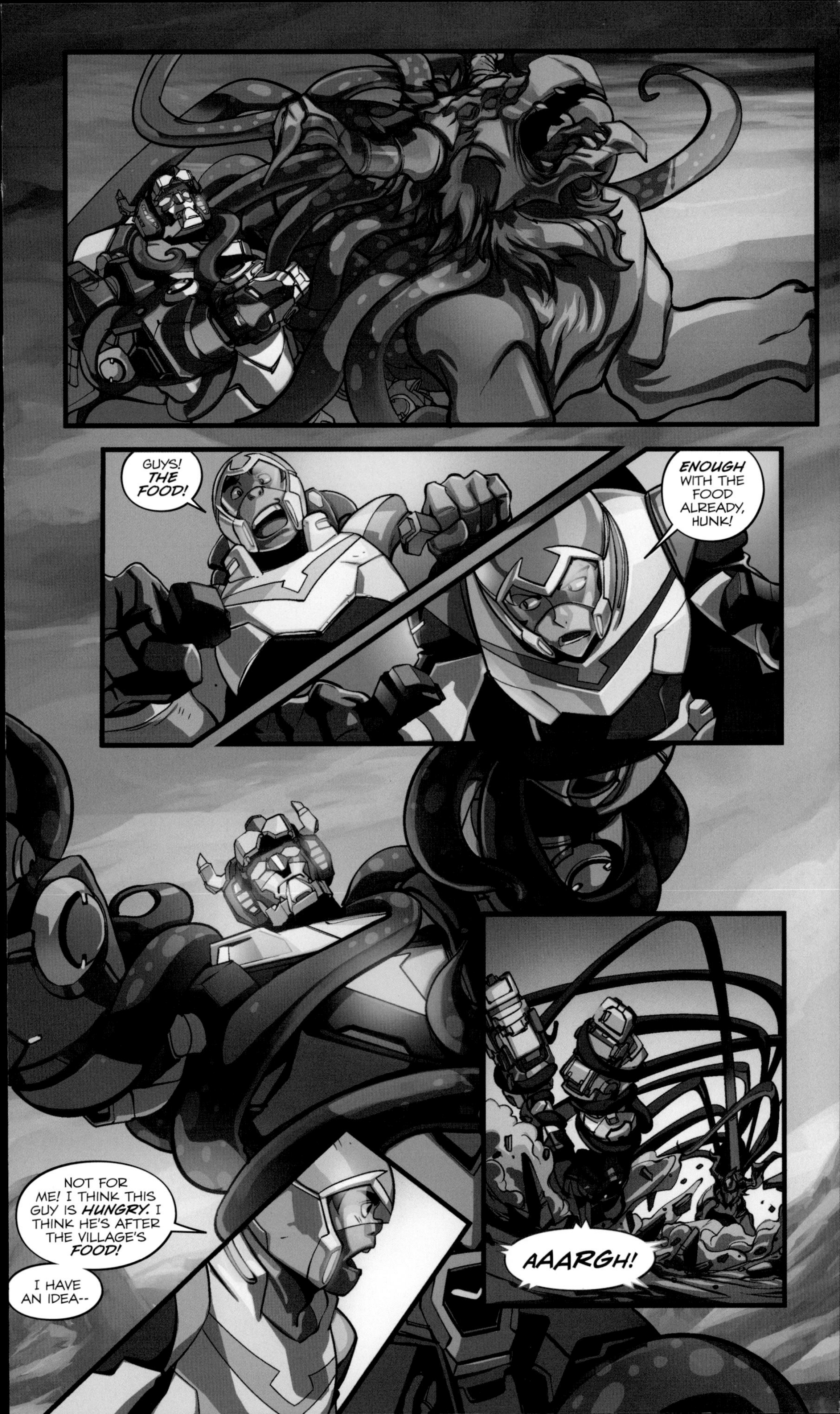
GUYS! THE FOOD!
ENOUGH WITH THE FOOD ALREADY, HUNK!
NOT FOR ME! I THINK THIS GUY IS HUNGRY. I THINK HE'S AFTER THE VILLAGE'S FOOD!
I HAVE AN IDEA--
AAARGH!

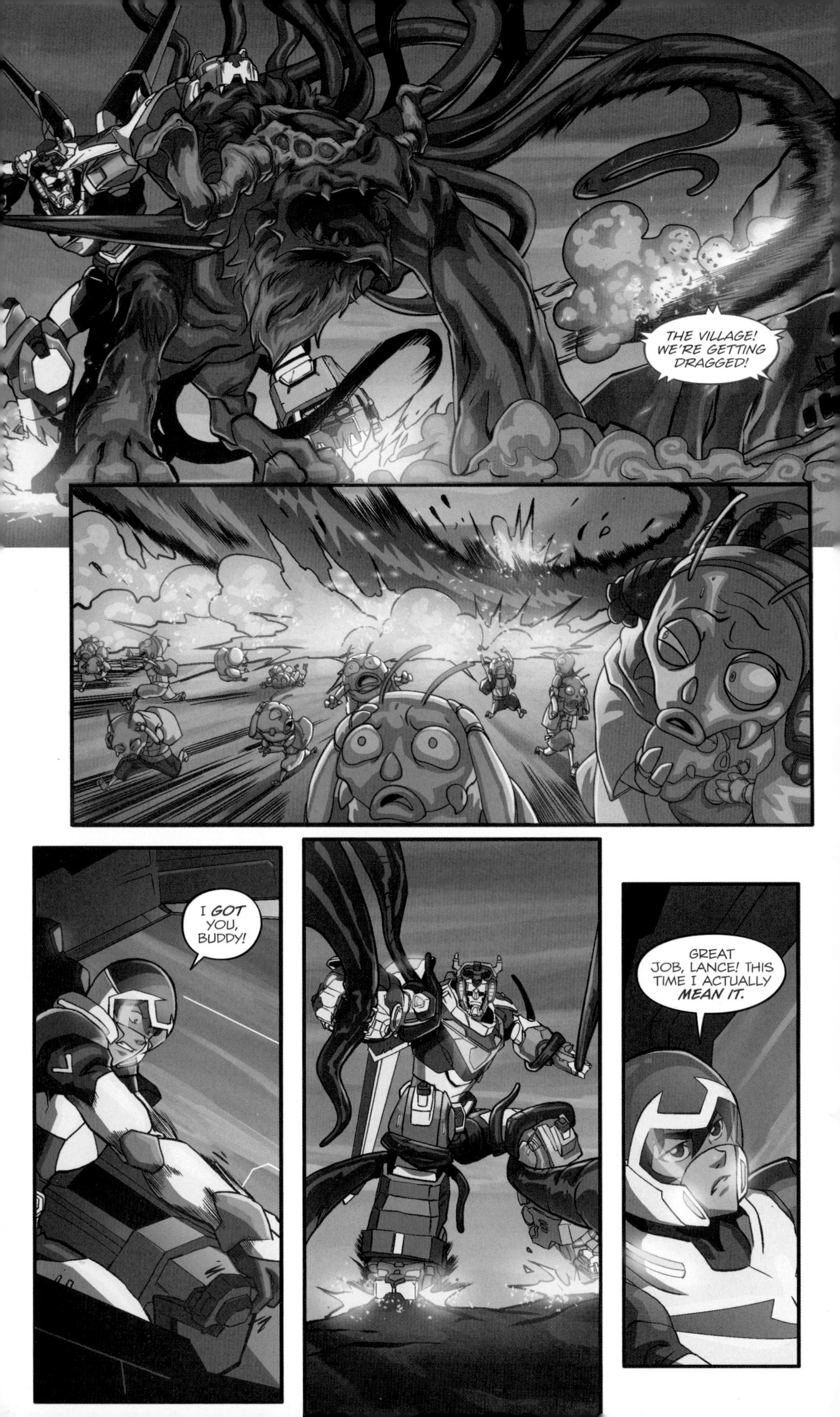
THE VILLAGE! WE'RE GETTING DRAGGED!
I GOT YOU, BUDDY!
GREAT JOB, LANCE! THIS TIME I ACTUALLY MEAN IT.

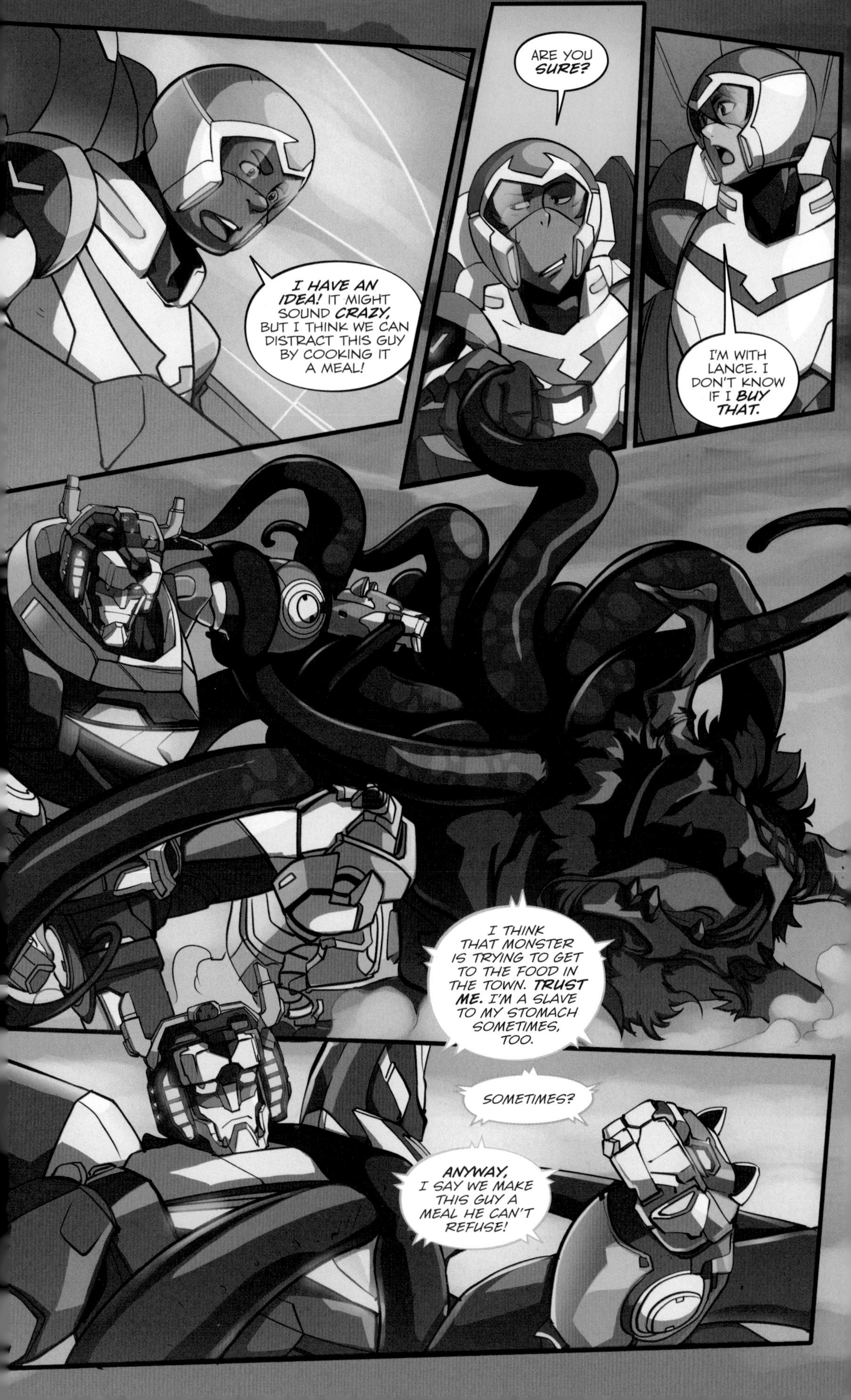
I HAVE AN IDEA! IT MIGHT SOUND CRAZY, BUT I THINK WE CAN DISTRACT THIS GUY BY COOKING IT A MEAL!
ARE YOU SURE?
I'M WITH LANCE. I DON'T KNOW IF I BUY THAT.
I THINK THAT MONSTER IS TRYING TO GET TO THE FOOD IN THE TOWN. TRUST ME. I'M A SLAVE TO MY STOMACH SOMETIMES, TOO.
SOMETIMES?
ANYWAY, I SAY WE MAKE THIS GUY A MEAL HE CAN'T REFUSE!

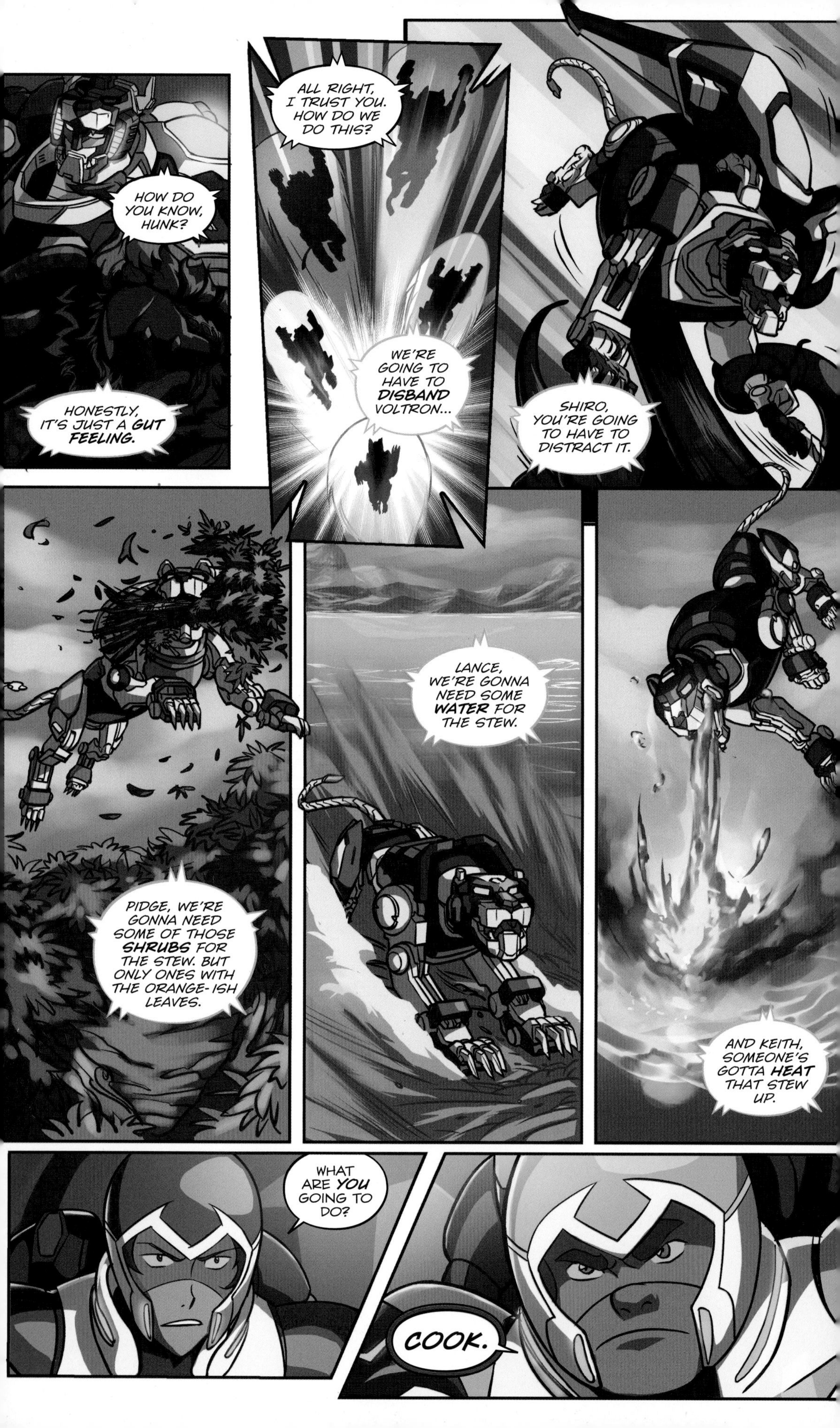
HOW DO YOU KNOW, HUNK?
HONESTLY, IT'S JUST A GUT FEELING.
ALL RIGHT, I TRUST YOU. HOW DO WE DO THIS?
WE'RE GOING TO HAVE TO DISBAND VOLTRON...
SHIRO, YOU'RE GOING TO HAVE TO DISTRACT IT.
PIDGE, WE'RE GONNA NEED SOME OF THOSE SHRUBS FOR THE STEW. BUT ONLY ONES WITH THE ORANGE-ISH LEAVES.
LANCE, WE'RE GONNA NEED SOME WATER FOR THE STEW.
AND KEITH, SOMEONE'S GOTTA HEAT THAT STEW UP.
WHAT ARE YOU GOING TO DO?
COOK.

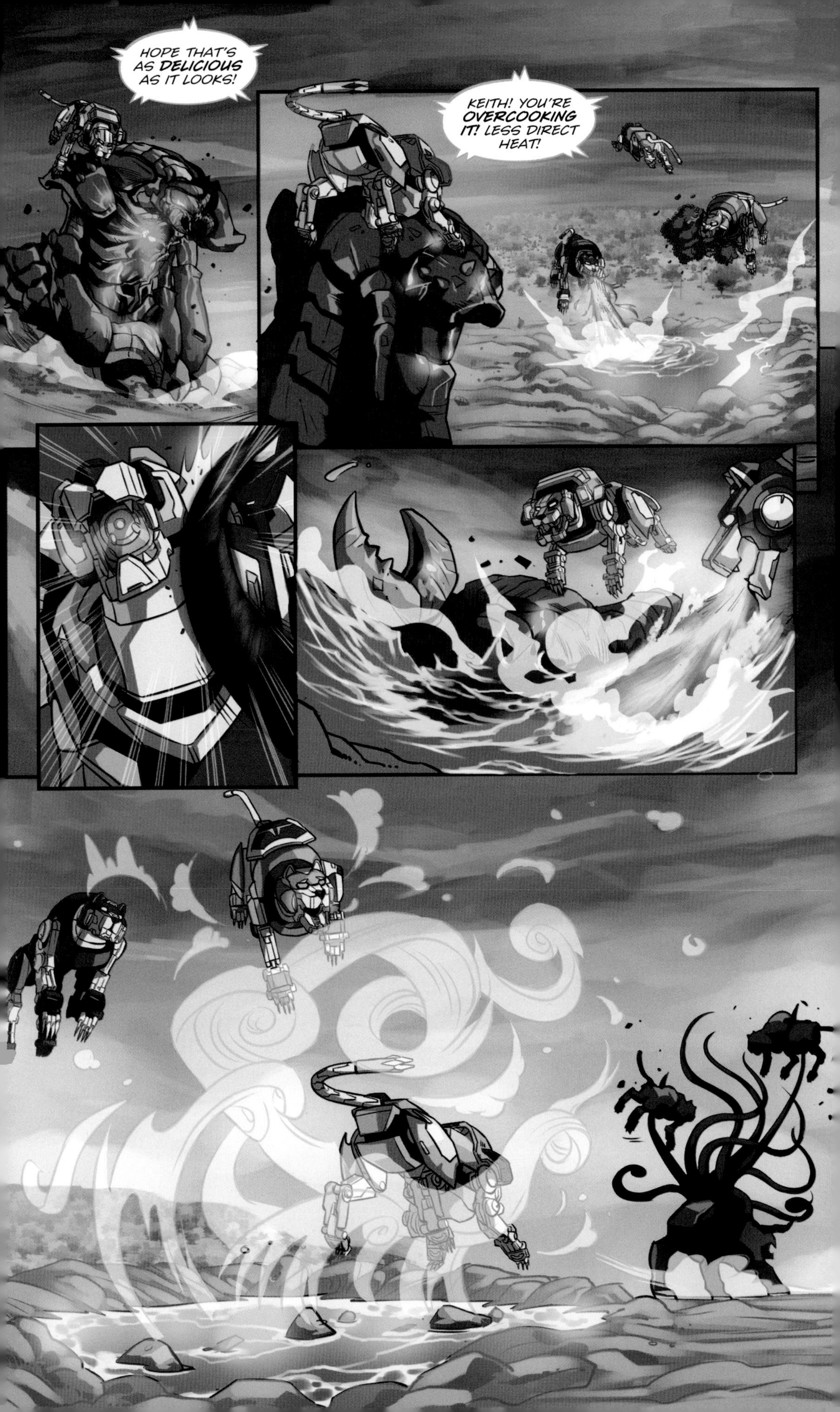
HOPE THAT'S AS **DELICIOUS** AS IT LOOKS!
KEITH! YOU'RE **OVERCOOKING IT!** LESS DIRECT HEAT!

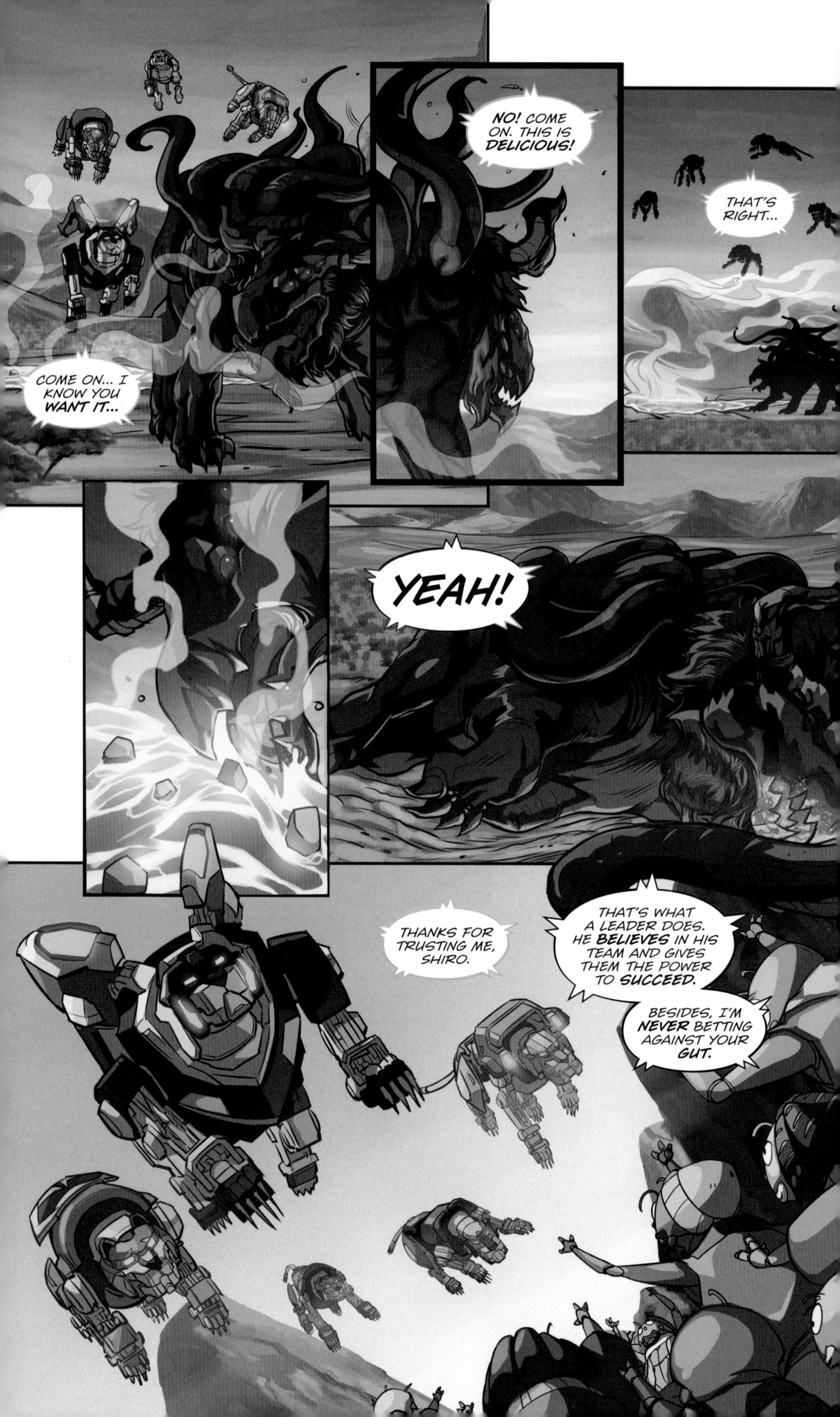
COME ON... I KNOW YOU WANT IT...
NO! COME ON. THIS IS DELICIOUS!
THAT'S RIGHT...
YEAH!
THANKS FOR TRUSTING ME, SHIRO.
THAT'S WHAT A LEADER DOES. HE BELIEVES IN HIS TEAM AND GIVES THEM THE POWER TO SUCCEED.
BESIDES, I'M NEVER BETTING AGAINST YOUR GUT.

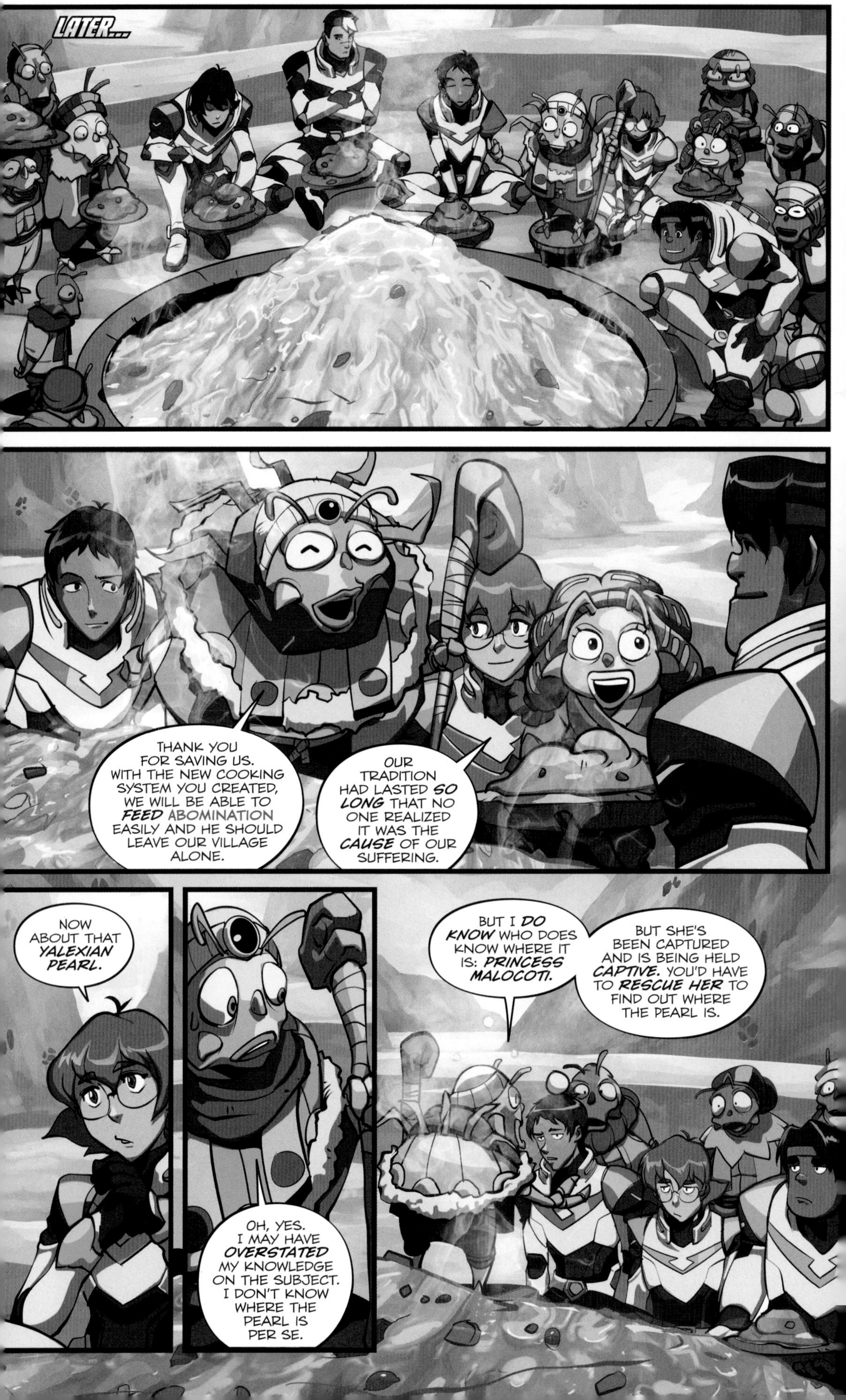
LATER...
THANK YOU FOR SAVING US. WITH THE NEW COOKING SYSTEM YOU CREATED, WE WILL BE ABLE TO FEED ABOMINATION EASILY AND HE SHOULD LEAVE OUR VILLAGE ALONE.
OUR TRADITION HAD LASTED SO LONG THAT NO ONE REALIZED IT WAS THE CAUSE OF OUR SUFFERING.
NOW ABOUT THAT YALEXIAN PEARL.
OH, YES. I MAY HAVE OVERSTATED MY KNOWLEDGE ON THE SUBJECT. I DON'T KNOW WHERE THE PEARL IS PER SE.
BUT I DO KNOW WHO DOES KNOW WHERE IT IS: PRINCESS MALOCOTI.
BUT SHE'S BEEN CAPTURED AND IS BEING HELD CAPTIVE. YOU'D HAVE TO RESCUE HER TO FIND OUT WHERE THE PEARL IS.

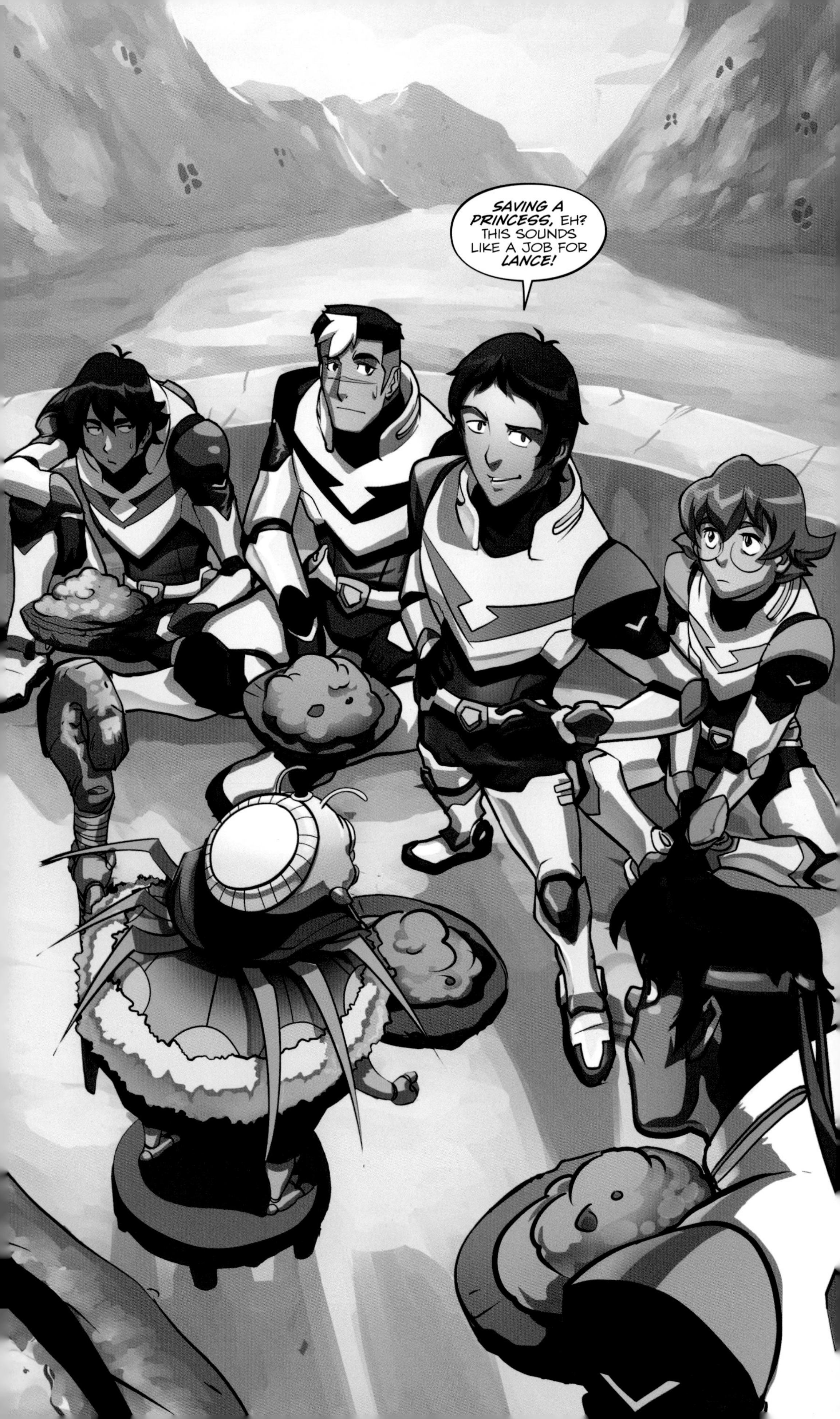
SAVING A PRINCESS, EH? THIS SOUNDS LIKE A JOB FOR LANCE!

CHAPTER THREE:
THE TALE OF LANCE AND THE DRAGON

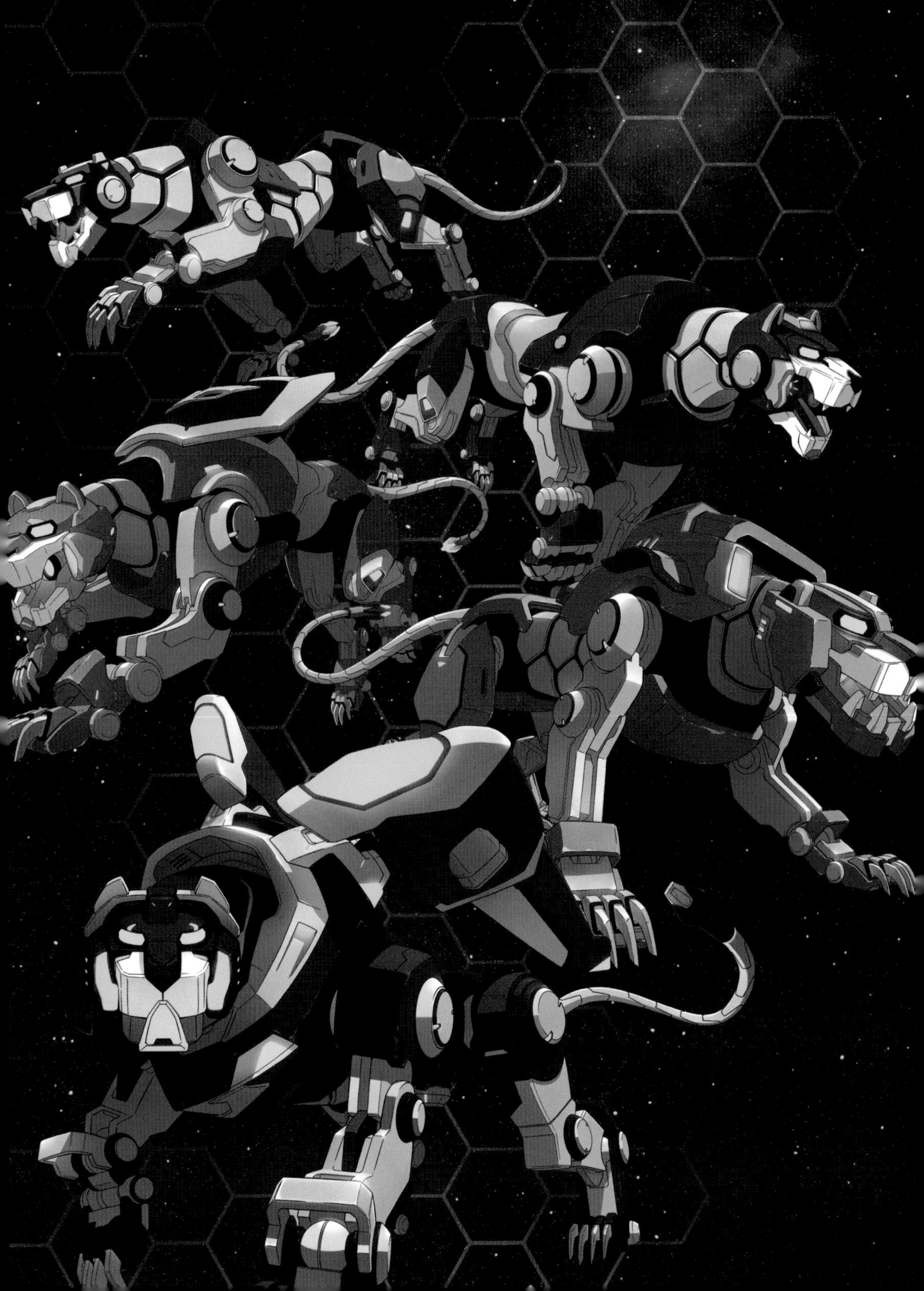

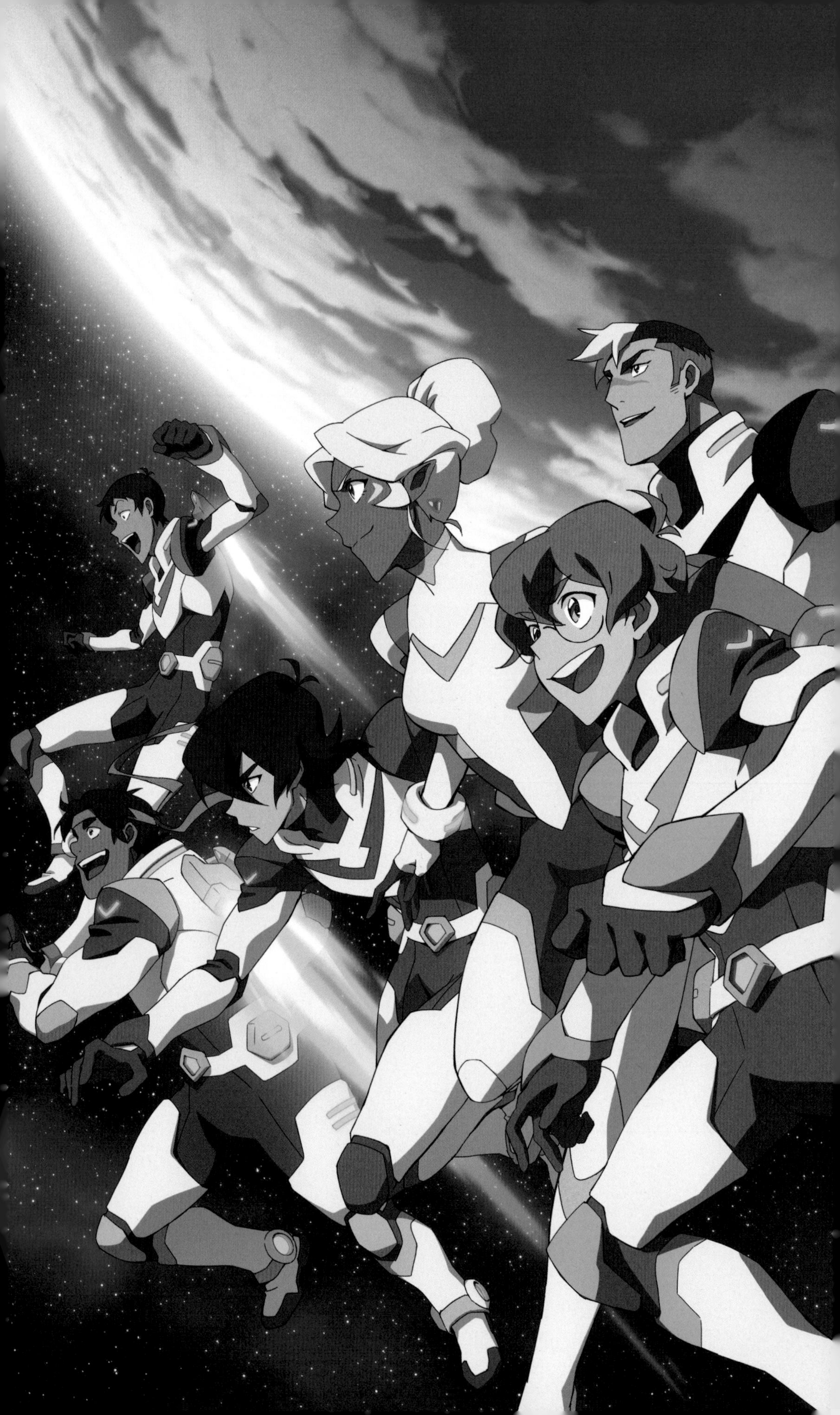

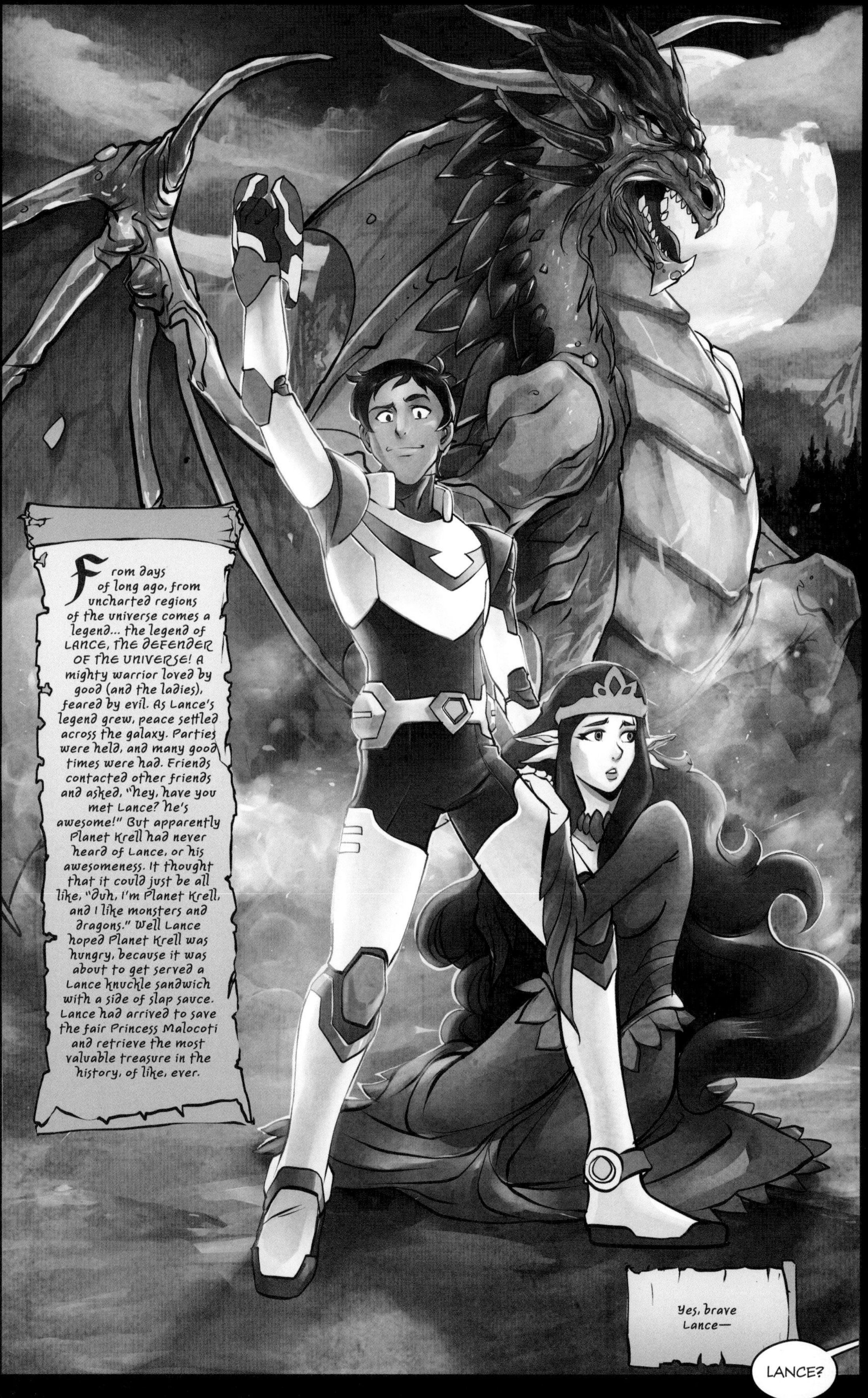
From days of long ago, from uncharted regions of the universe comes a legend... the legend of LANCE, THE DEFENDER OF THE UNIVERSE! A mighty warrior loved by good (and the ladies), feared by evil. As Lance's legend grew, peace settled across the galaxy. Parties were held, and many good times were had. Friends contacted other friends and asked, "Hey, have you met Lance? He's awesome!" But apparently Planet Krell had never heard of Lance, or his awesomeness. It thought that it could just be all like, "Duh, I'm Planet Krell, and I like monsters and dragons." Well Lance hoped Planet Krell was hungry, because it was about to get served a Lance knuckle sandwich with a side of slap sauce. Lance had arrived to save the fair Princess Malocoti and retrieve the most valuable treasure in the history, of like, ever.
Yes, brave Lance—
LANCE?

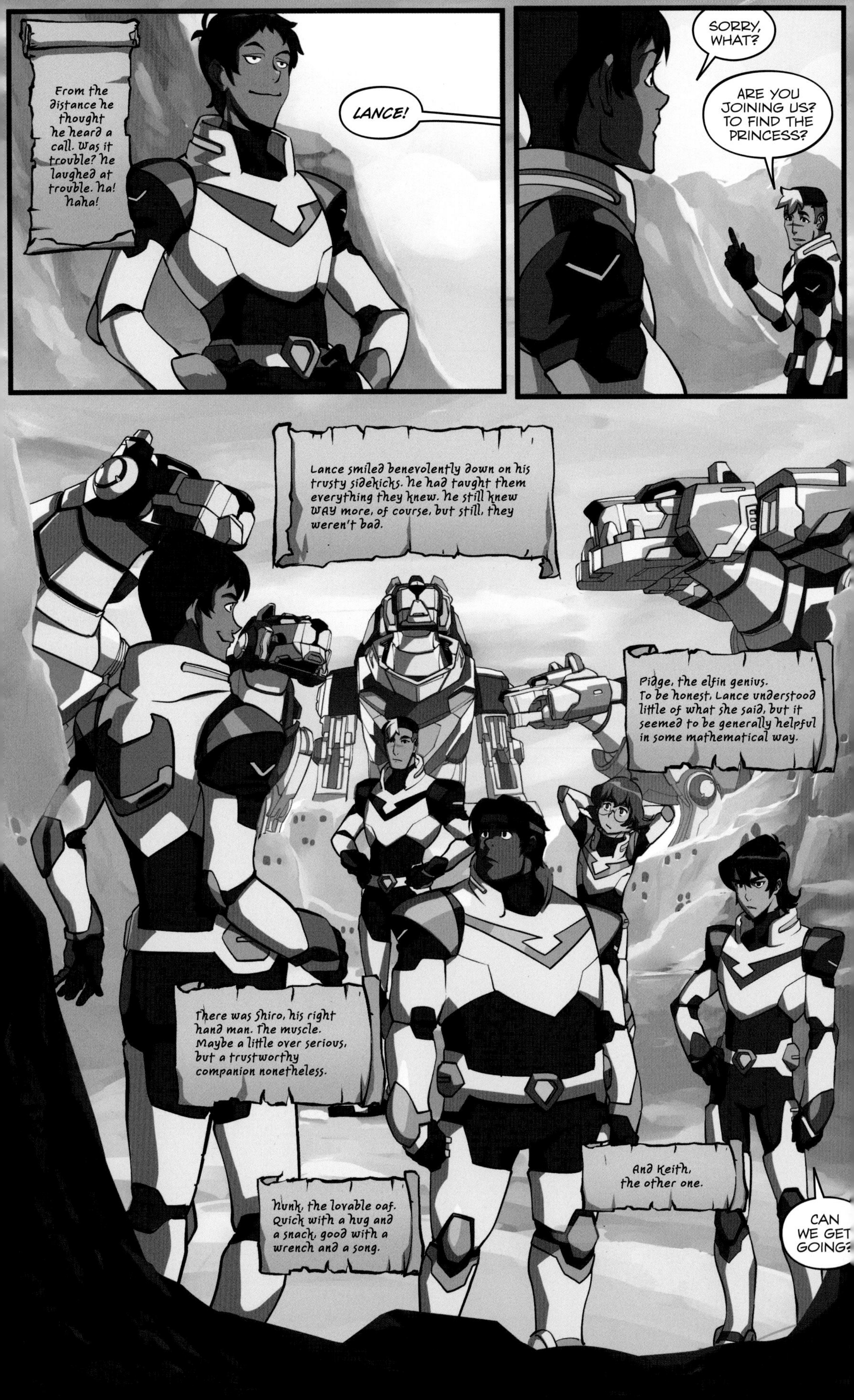

From the distance he thought he heard a call. Was it trouble? He laughed at trouble. Ha! Haha!
LANCE!
SORRY, WHAT?
ARE YOU JOINING US? TO FIND THE PRINCESS?
Lance smiled benevolently down on his trusty sidekicks. He had taught them everything they knew. He still knew WAY more, of course, but still, they weren't bad.
Pidge, the elfin genius. To be honest, Lance understood little of what she said, but it seemed to be generally helpful in some mathematical way.
There was Shiro, his right hand man. The muscle. Maybe a little over serious, but a trustworthy companion nonetheless.
Hunk, the lovable oaf. Quick with a hug and a snack, good with a wrench and a song.
And Keith, the other one.
CAN WE GET GOING?

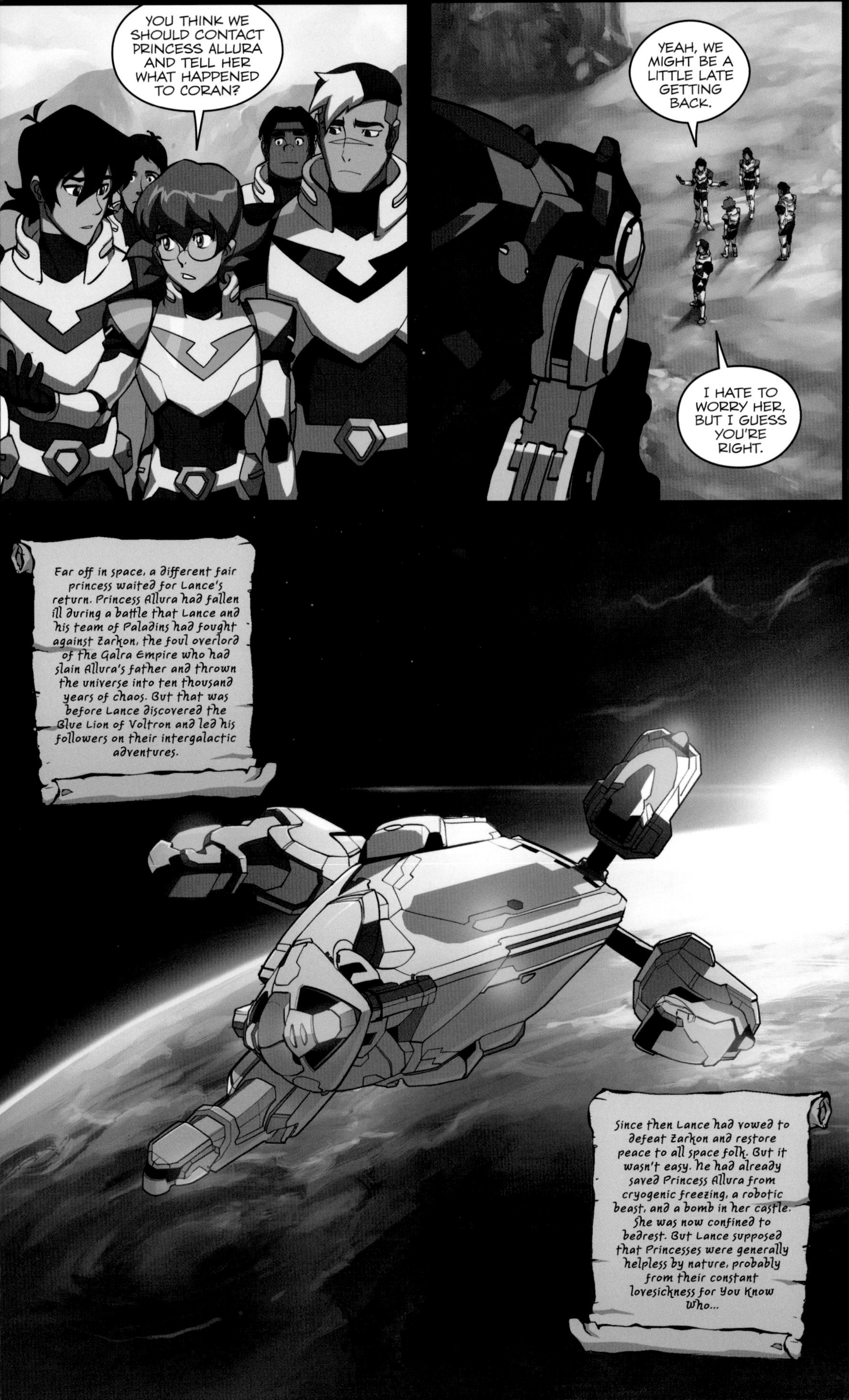
YOU THINK WE SHOULD CONTACT PRINCESS ALLURA AND TELL HER WHAT HAPPENED TO CORAN?
YEAH, WE MIGHT BE A LITTLE LATE GETTING BACK.
I HATE TO WORRY HER, BUT I GUESS YOU'RE RIGHT.
Far off in space, a different fair princess waited for Lance's return. Princess Allura had fallen ill during a battle that Lance and his team of Paladins had fought against Zarkon, the foul overlord of the Galra Empire who had slain Allura's father and thrown the universe into ten thousand years of chaos. But that was before Lance discovered the Blue Lion of Voltron and led his followers on their intergalactic adventures.
Since then Lance had vowed to defeat Zarkon and restore peace to all space folk. But it wasn't easy. He had already saved Princess Allura from cryogenic freezing, a robotic beast, and a bomb in her castle. She was now confined to bedrest. But Lance supposed that Princesses were generally helpless by nature, probably from their constant lovesickness for You Know Who...

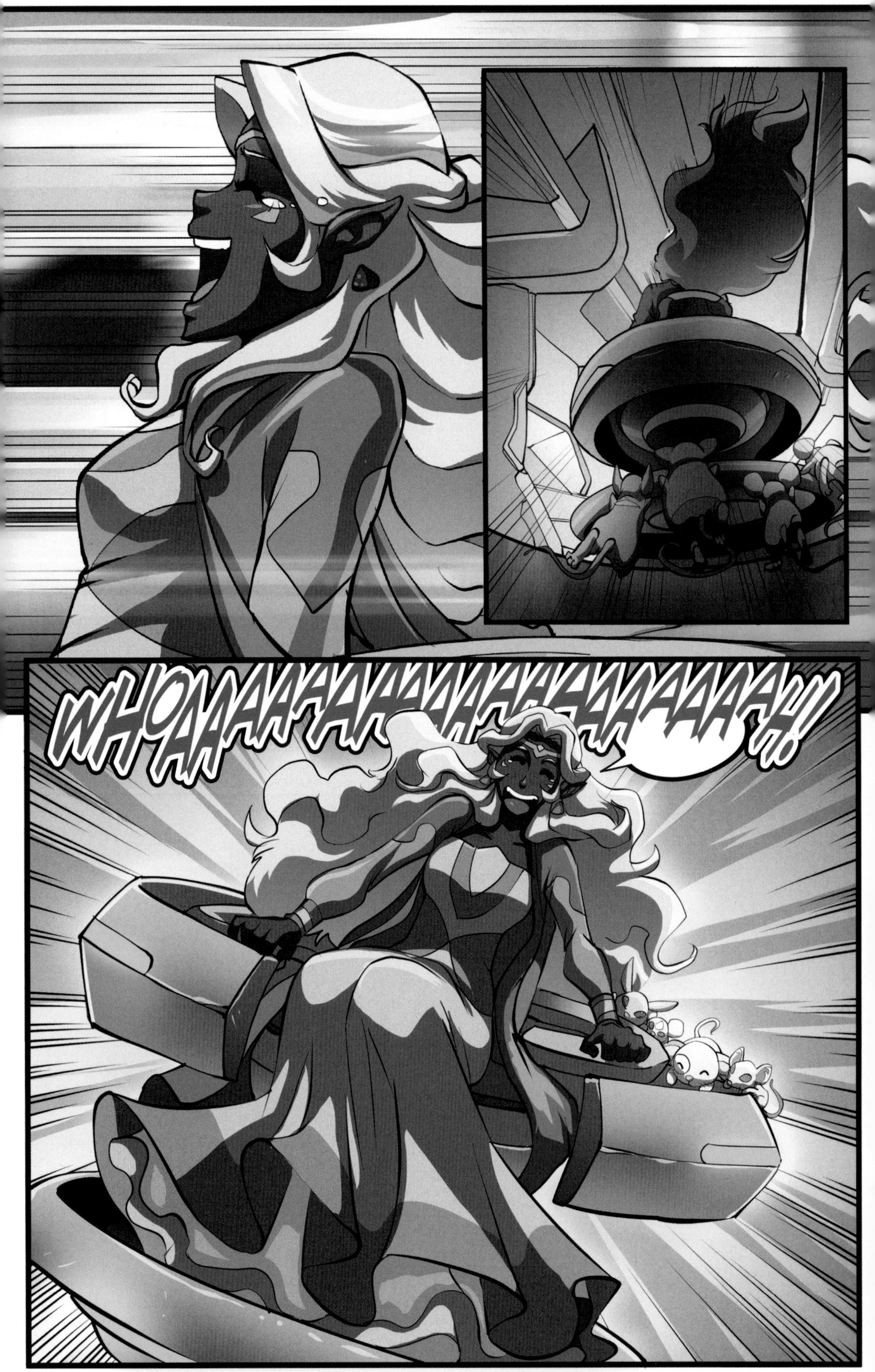
WHOAAAAAAAAAAAAAAAAAAAH!!

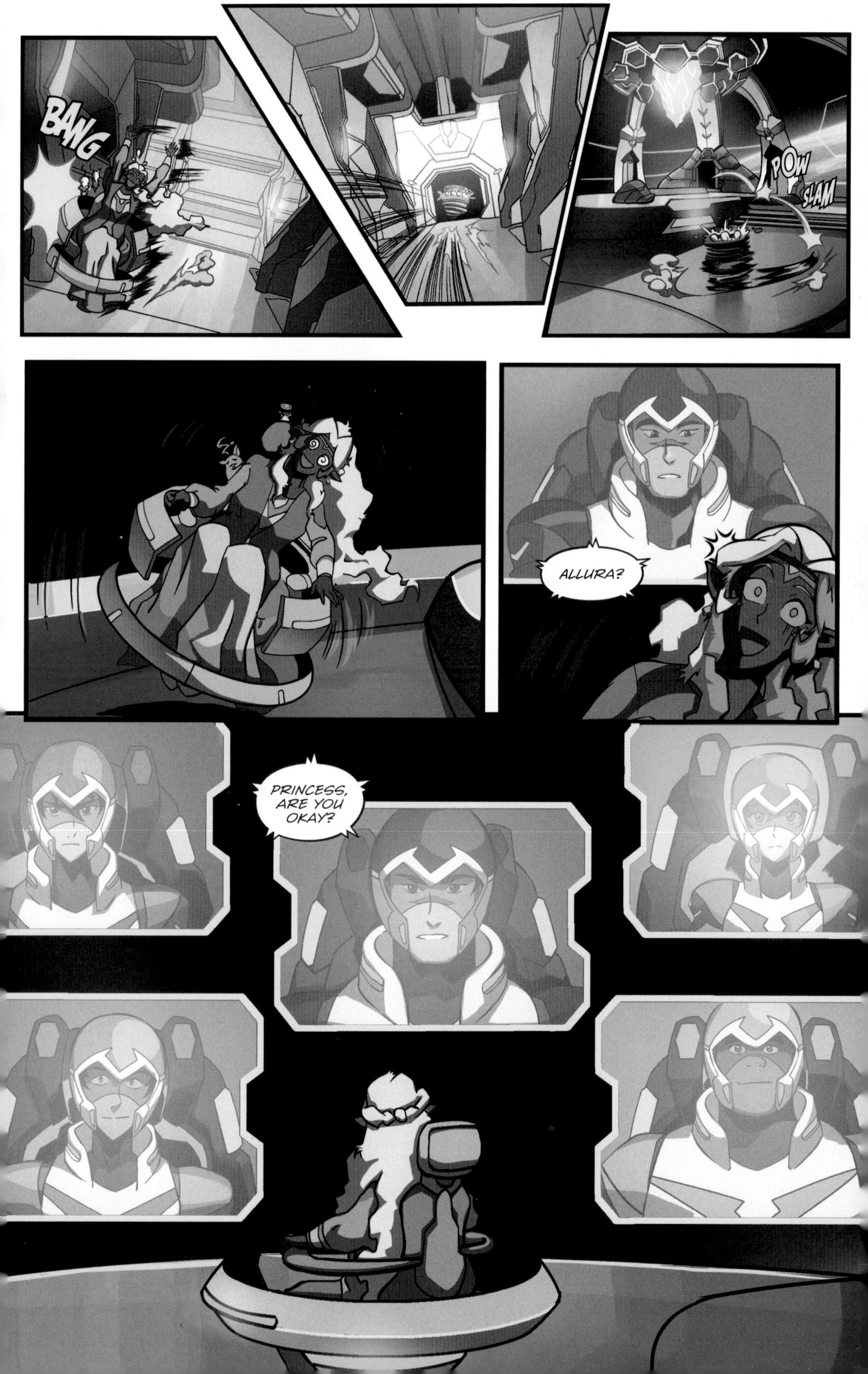
BANG
POW
SLAM
ALLURA?
PRINCESS, ARE YOU OKAY?

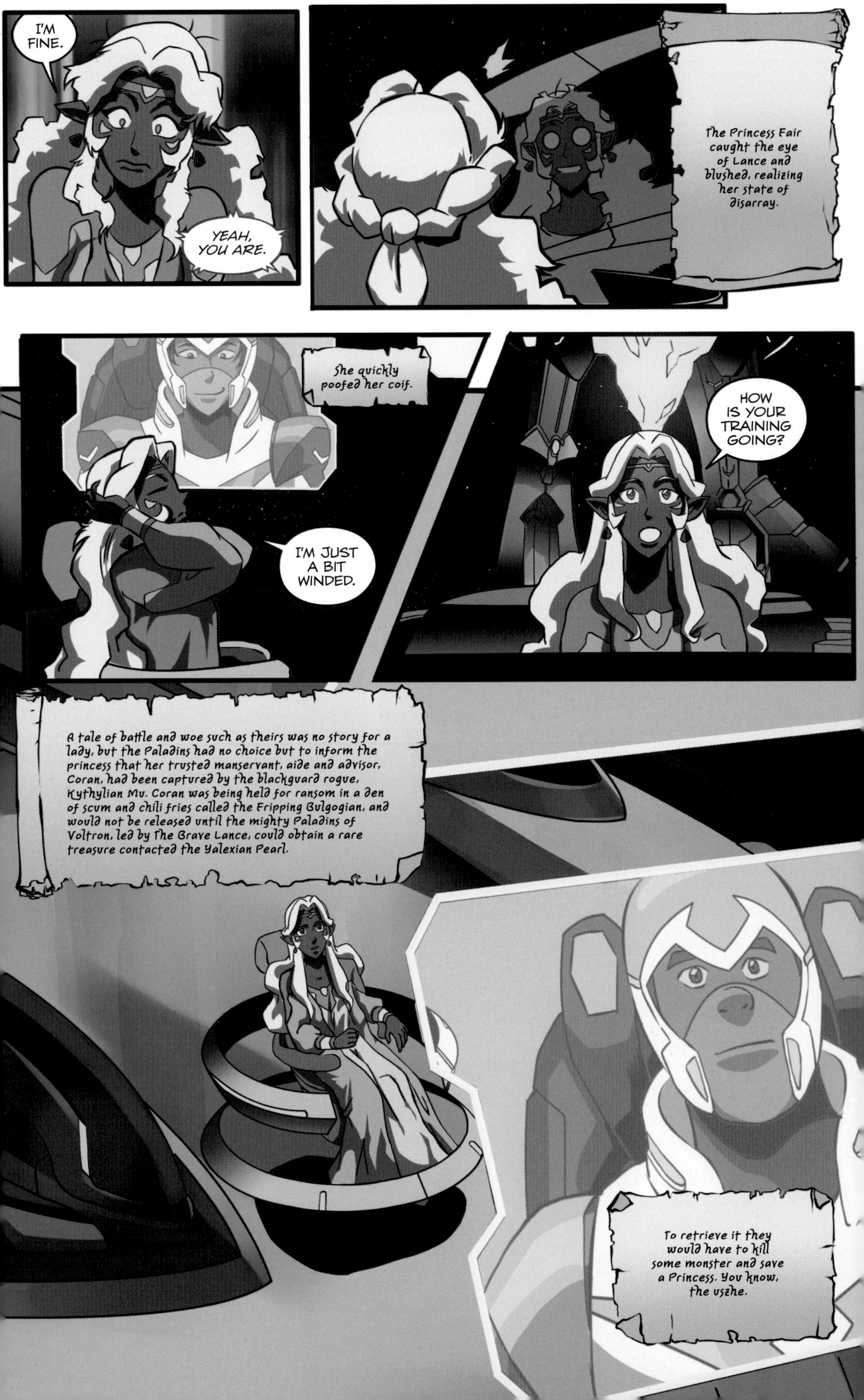
I'M FINE.
YEAH, YOU ARE.
The Princess Fair caught the eye of Lance and blushed, realizing her state of disarray.
She quickly poofed her coif.
I'M JUST A BIT WINDED.
HOW IS YOUR TRAINING GOING?
A tale of battle and woe such as theirs was no story for a lady, but the Paladins had no choice but to inform the princess that her trusted manservant, aide and advisor, Coran, had been captured by the blackguard rogue, Kythylian Mu. Coran was being held for ransom in a den of scum and chili fries called the Fripping Bulgogian, and would not be released until the mighty Paladins of Voltron, led by the Brave Lance, could obtain a rare treasure contacted the Yalexian Pearl.
To retrieve it they would have to kill some monster and save a Princess. You know, the uszhe.

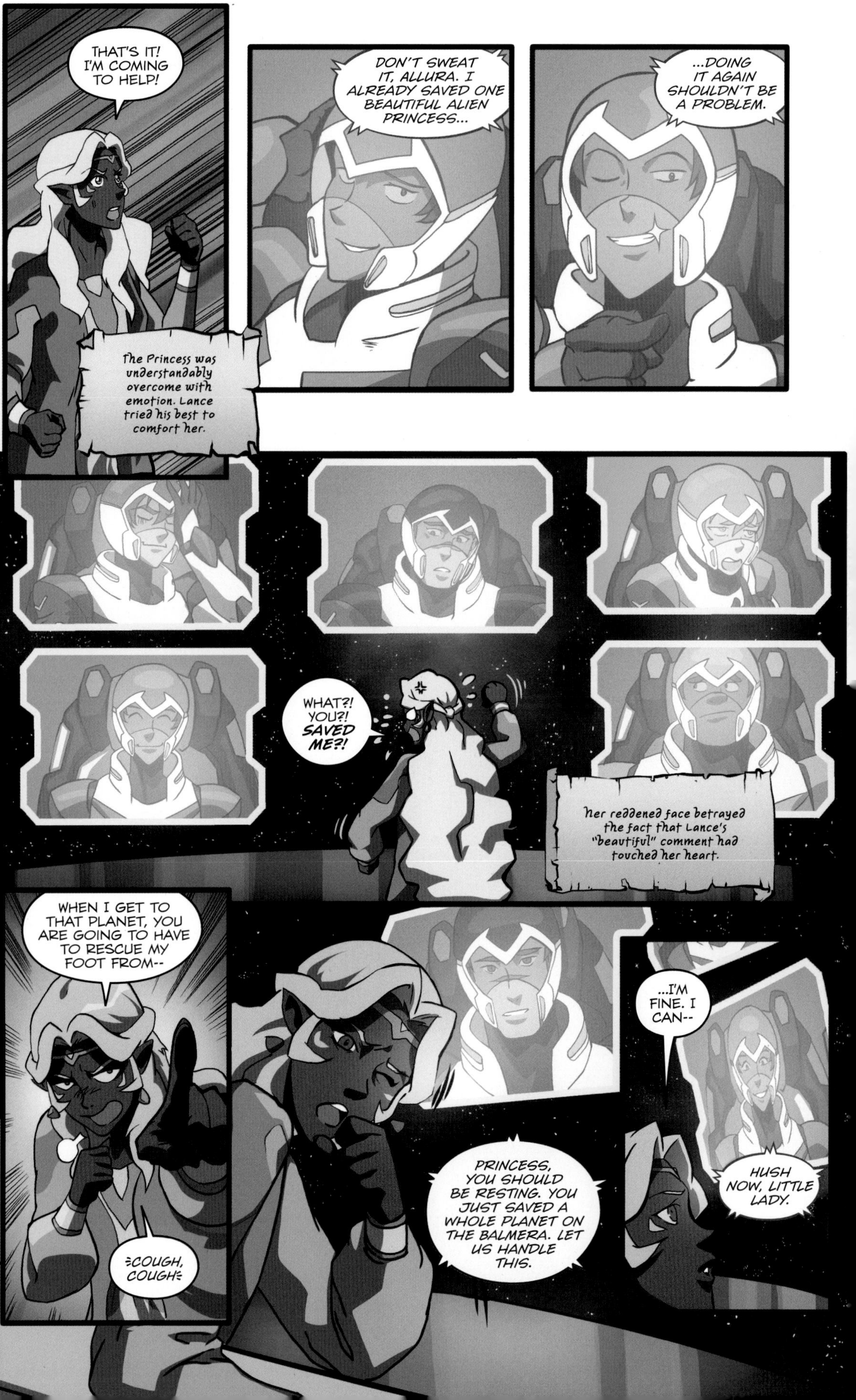
THAT'S IT! I'M COMING TO HELP!
The Princess was understandably overcome with emotion. Lance tried his best to comfort her.
DON'T SWEAT IT, ALLURA. I ALREADY SAVED ONE BEAUTIFUL ALIEN PRINCESS...
...DOING IT AGAIN SHOULDN'T BE A PROBLEM.
WHAT?! YOU?! SAVED ME?!
Her reddened face betrayed the fact that Lance's "beautiful" comment had touched her heart.
WHEN I GET TO THAT PLANET, YOU ARE GOING TO HAVE TO RESCUE MY FOOT FROM--
≈COUGH, COUGH≈
PRINCESS, YOU SHOULD BE RESTING. YOU JUST SAVED A WHOLE PLANET ON THE BALMERA. LET US HANDLE THIS.
...I'M FINE. I CAN--
HUSH NOW, LITTLE LADY.

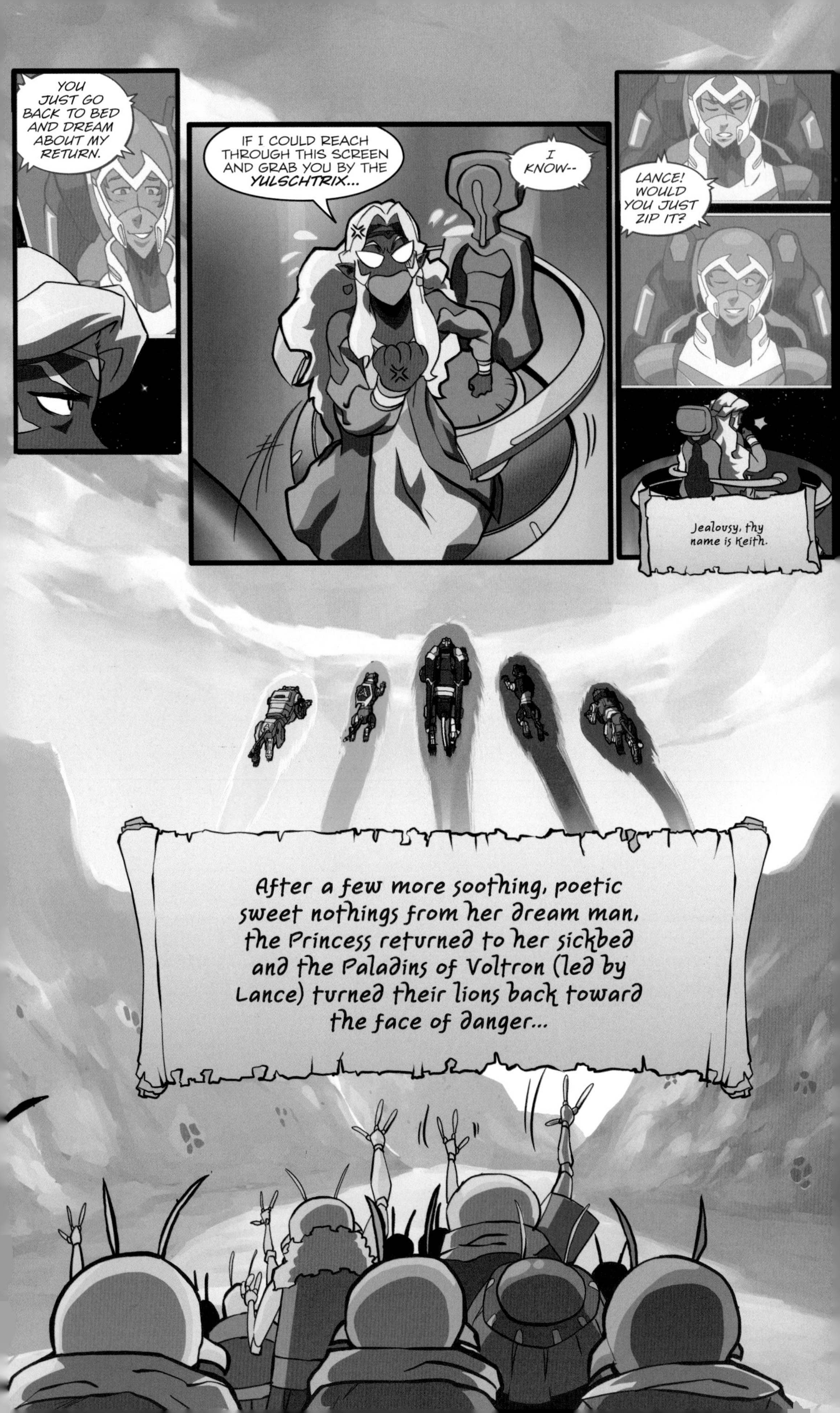
YOU JUST GO BACK TO BED AND DREAM ABOUT MY RETURN.
IF I COULD REACH THROUGH THIS SCREEN AND GRAB YOU BY THE YULSCHTRIX...
I KNOW--
LANCE! WOULD YOU JUST ZIP IT?
Jealousy, thy name is Keith.
After a few more soothing, poetic sweet nothings from her dream man, the Princess returned to her sickbed and the Paladins of Voltron (led by Lance) turned their lions back toward the face of danger...

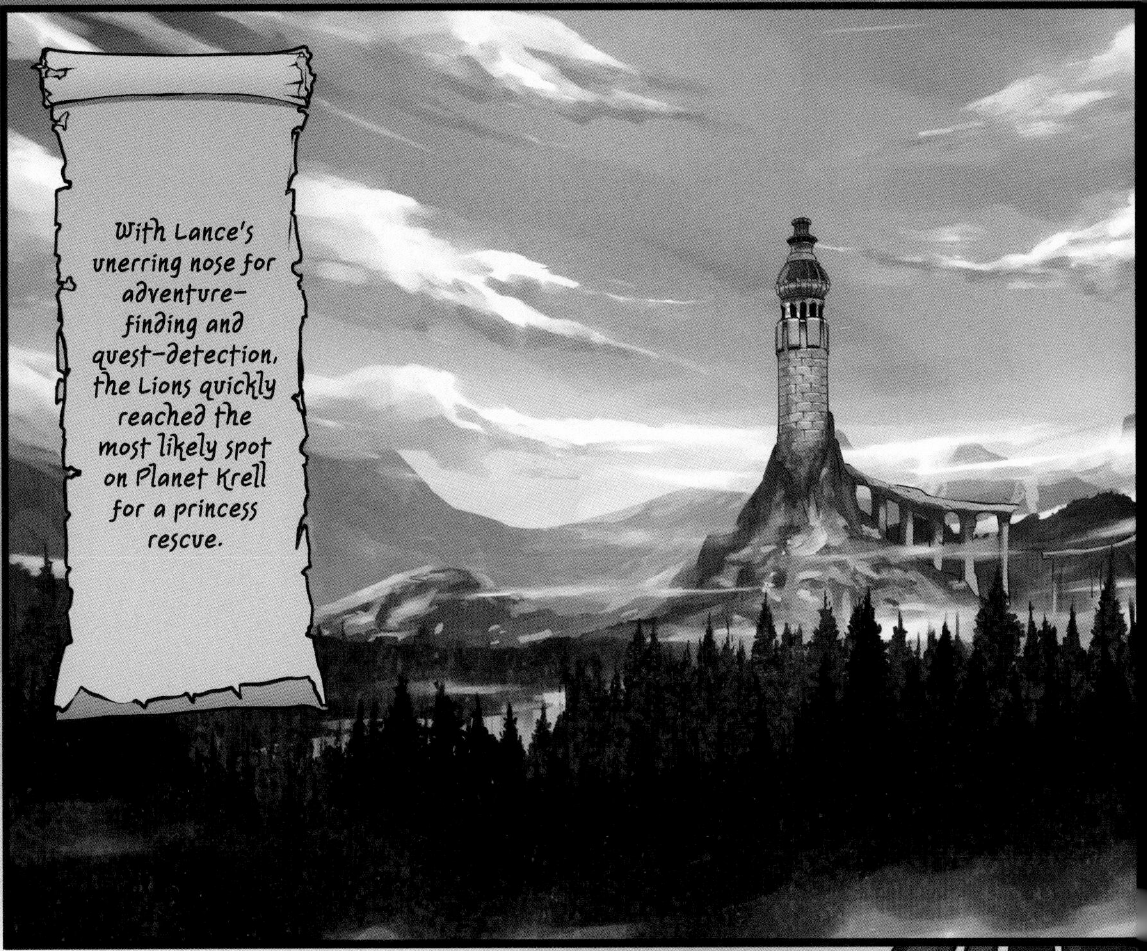
With Lance's unerring nose for adventure-finding and quest-detection, the Lions quickly reached the most likely spot on Planet Krell for a princess rescue.

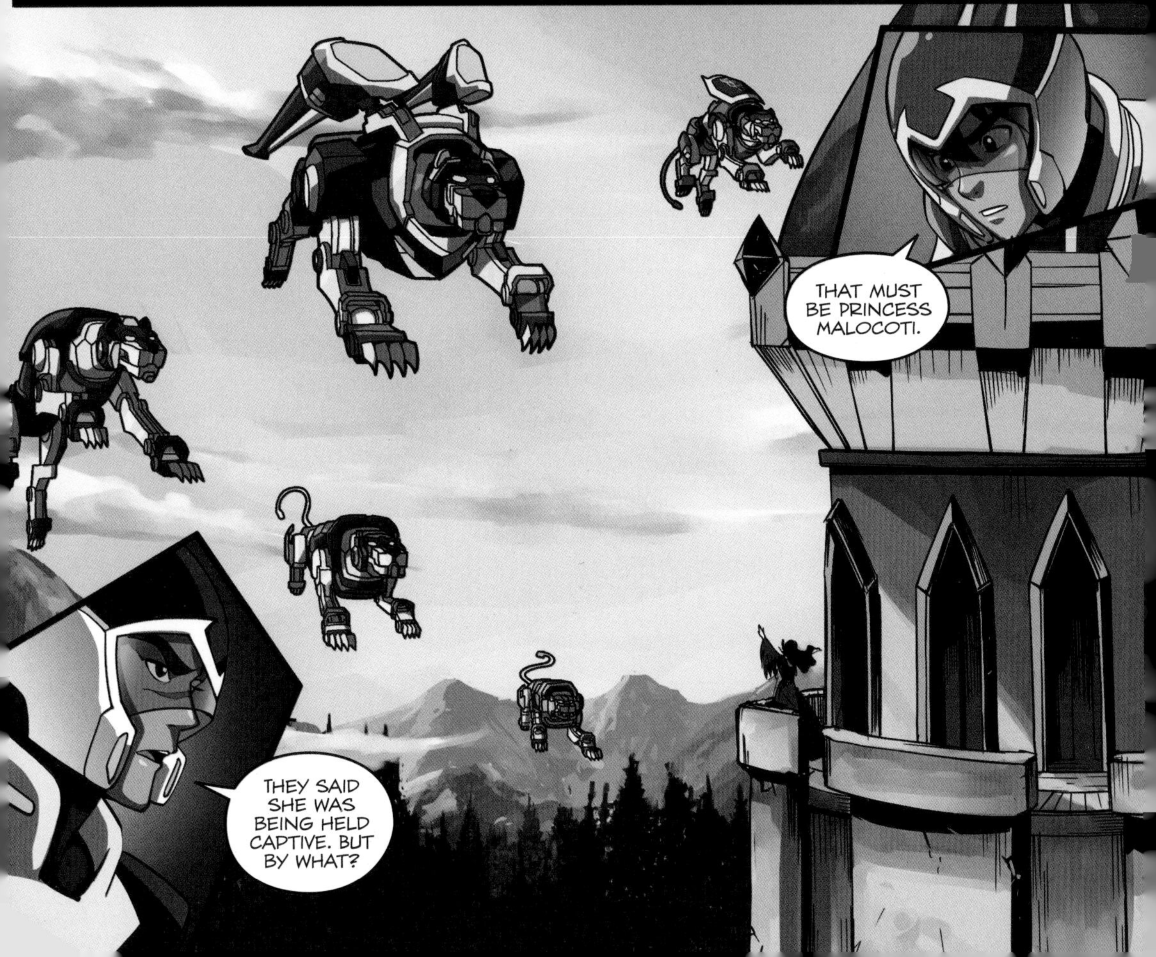
THAT MUST BE PRINCESS MALOCOTI.
THEY SAID SHE WAS BEING HELD CAPTIVE. BUT BY WHAT?

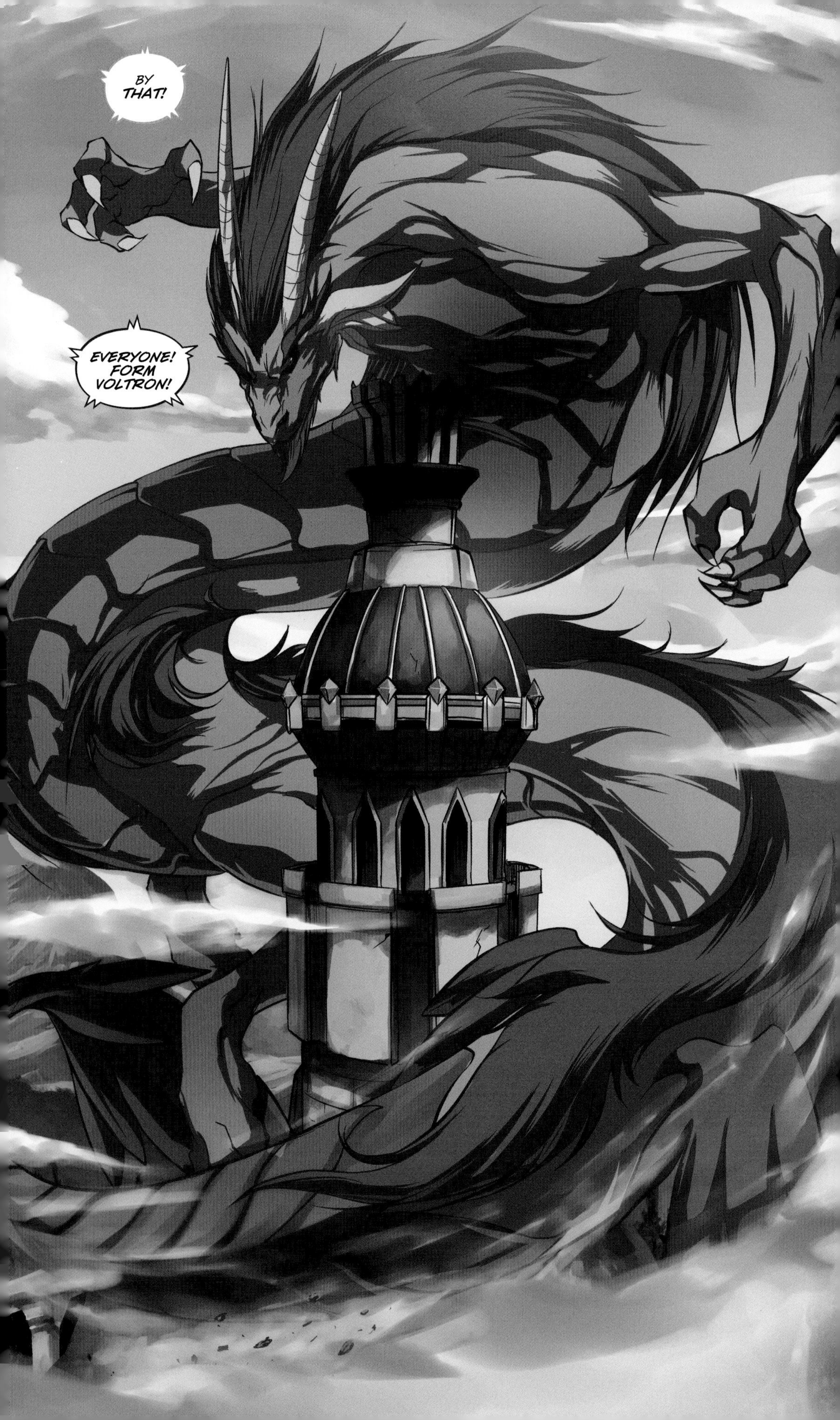
BY THAT!
EVERYONE! FORM VOLTRON!

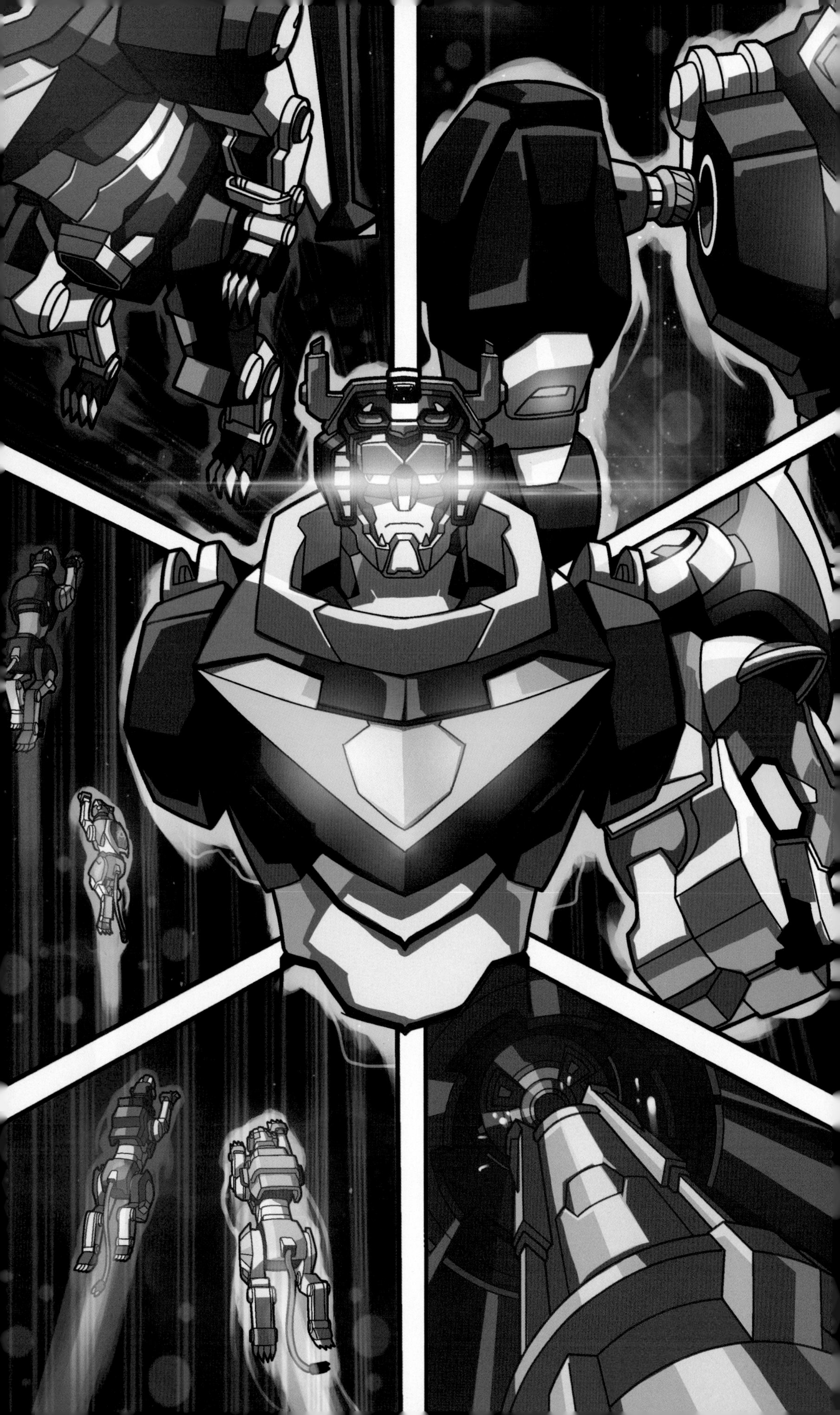

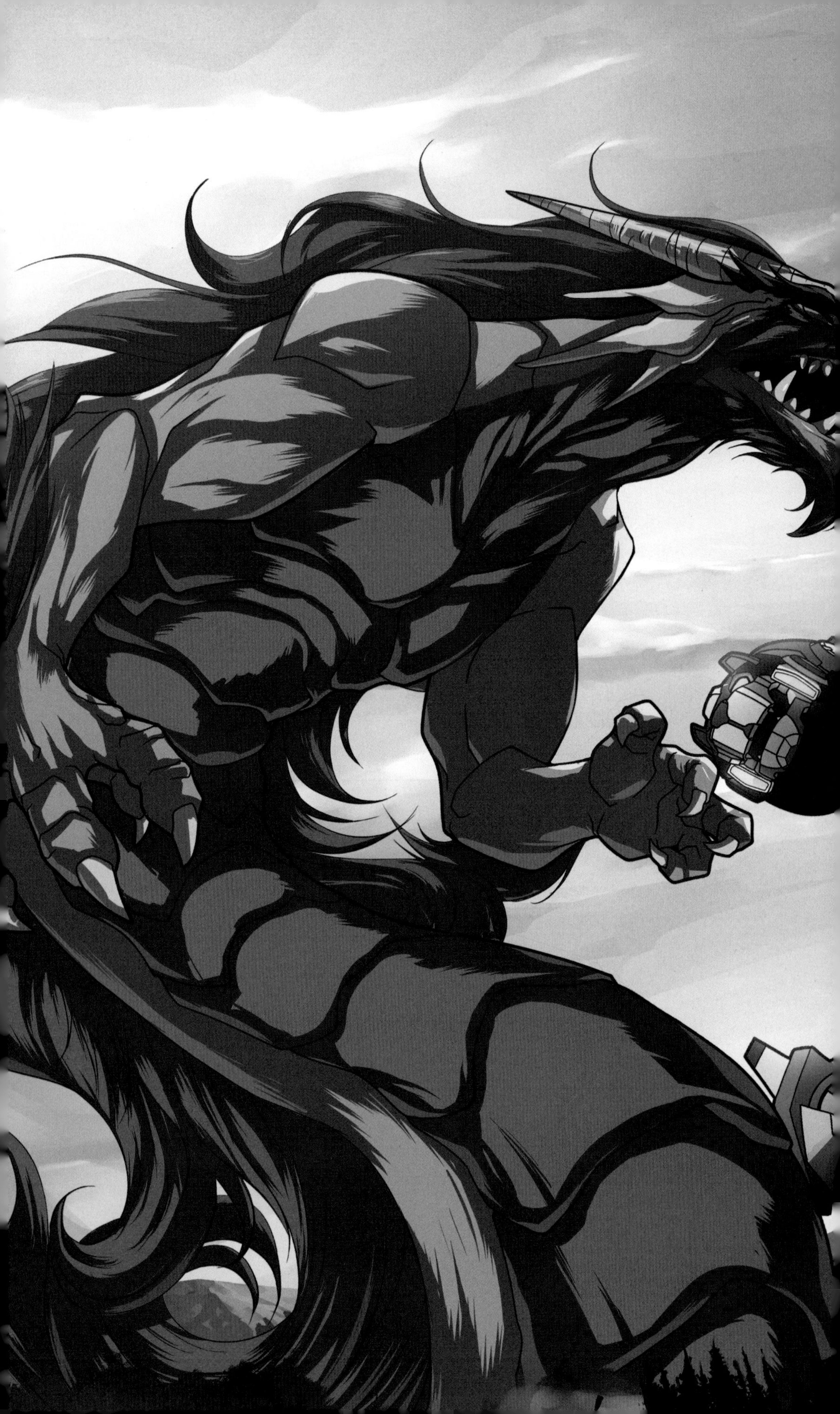

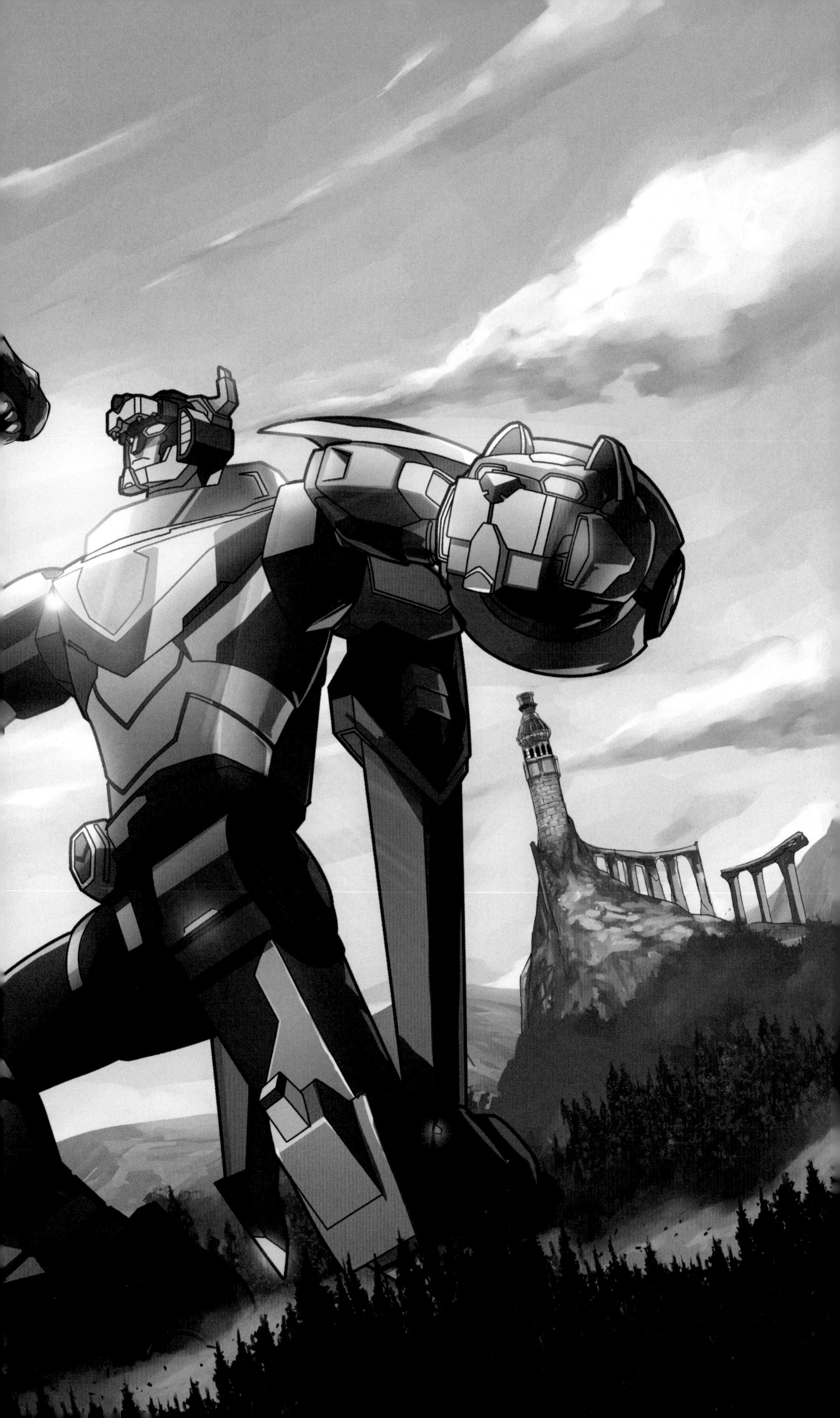

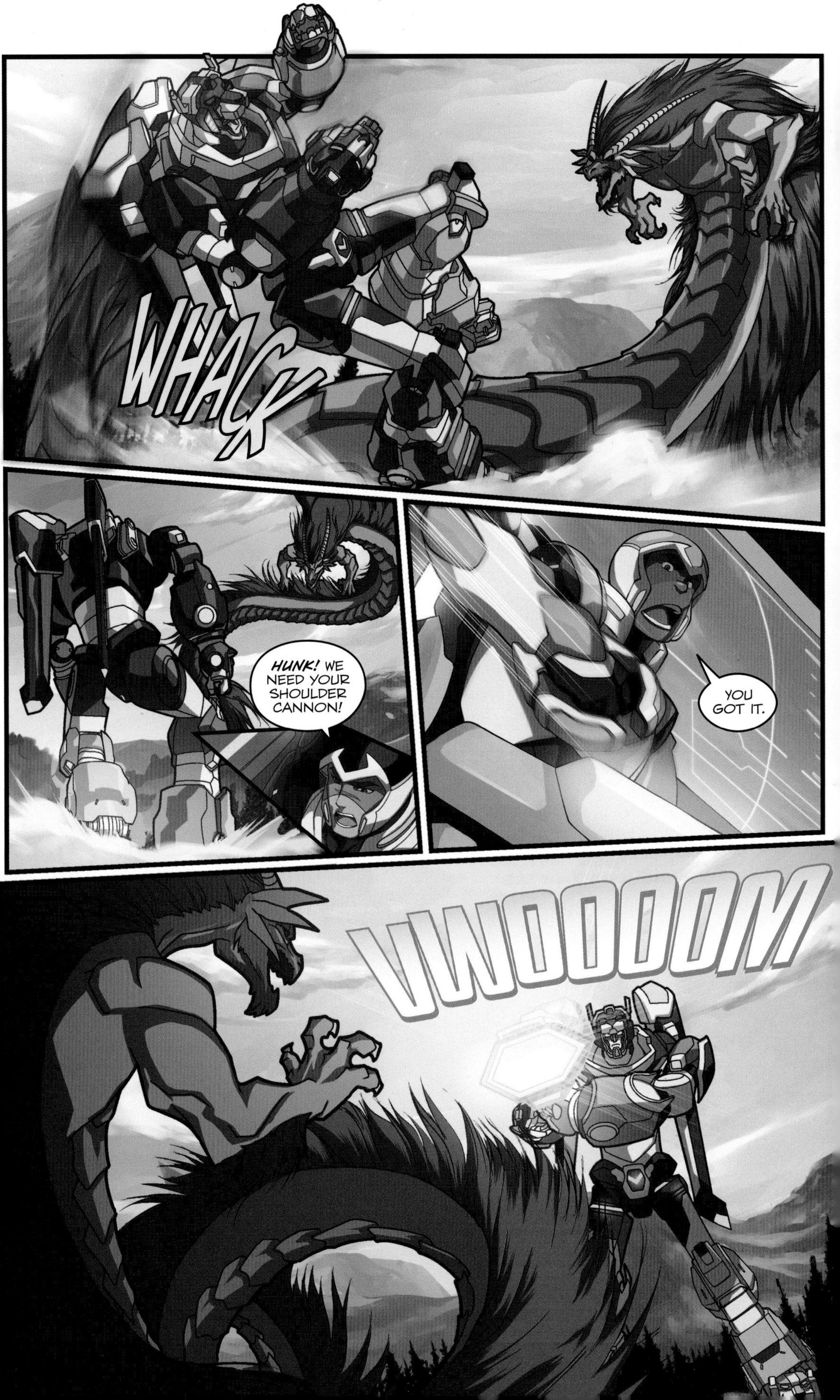
WHACK
HUNK! WE NEED YOUR SHOULDER CANNON!
YOU GOT IT.
VWOOOOM

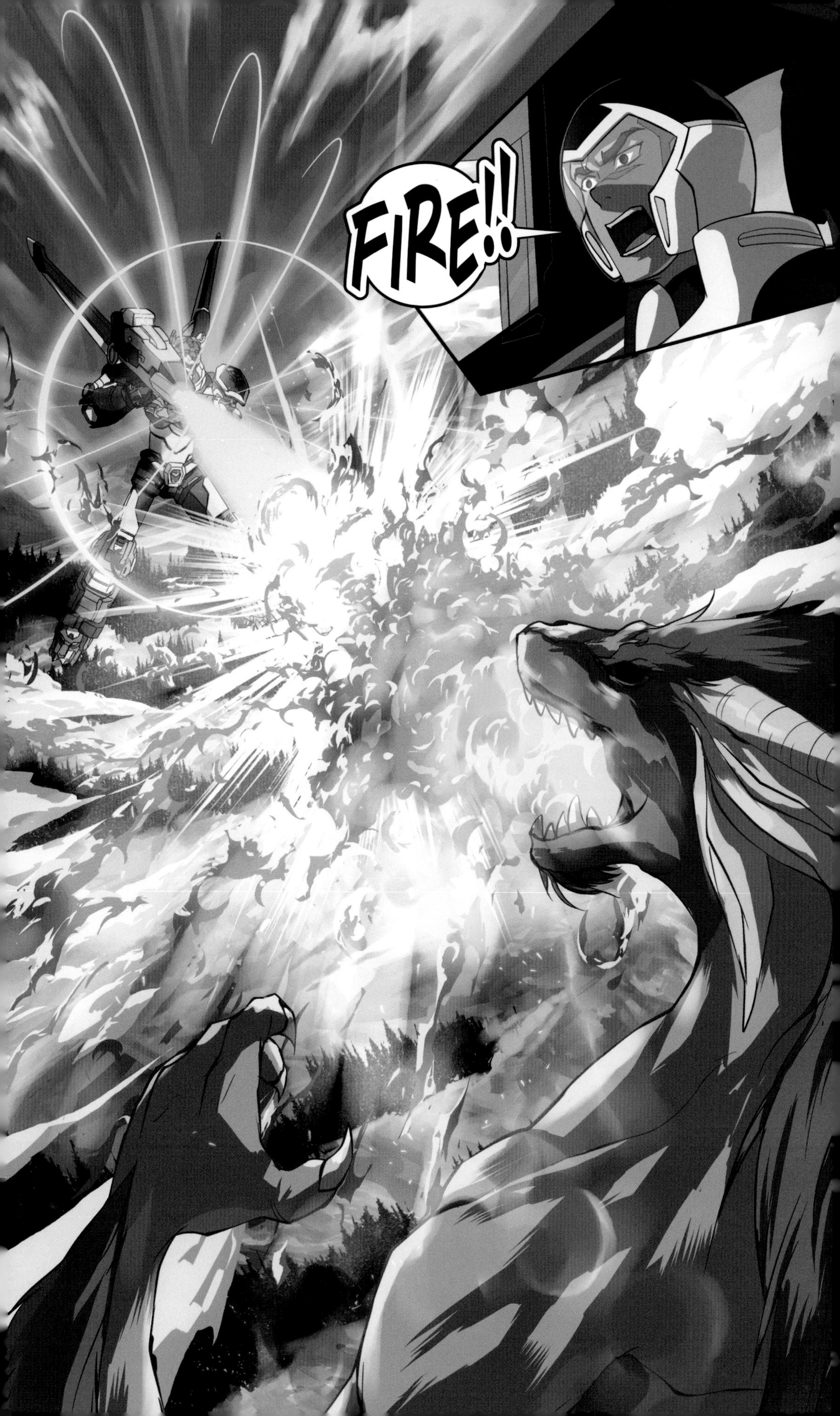
FIRE!!

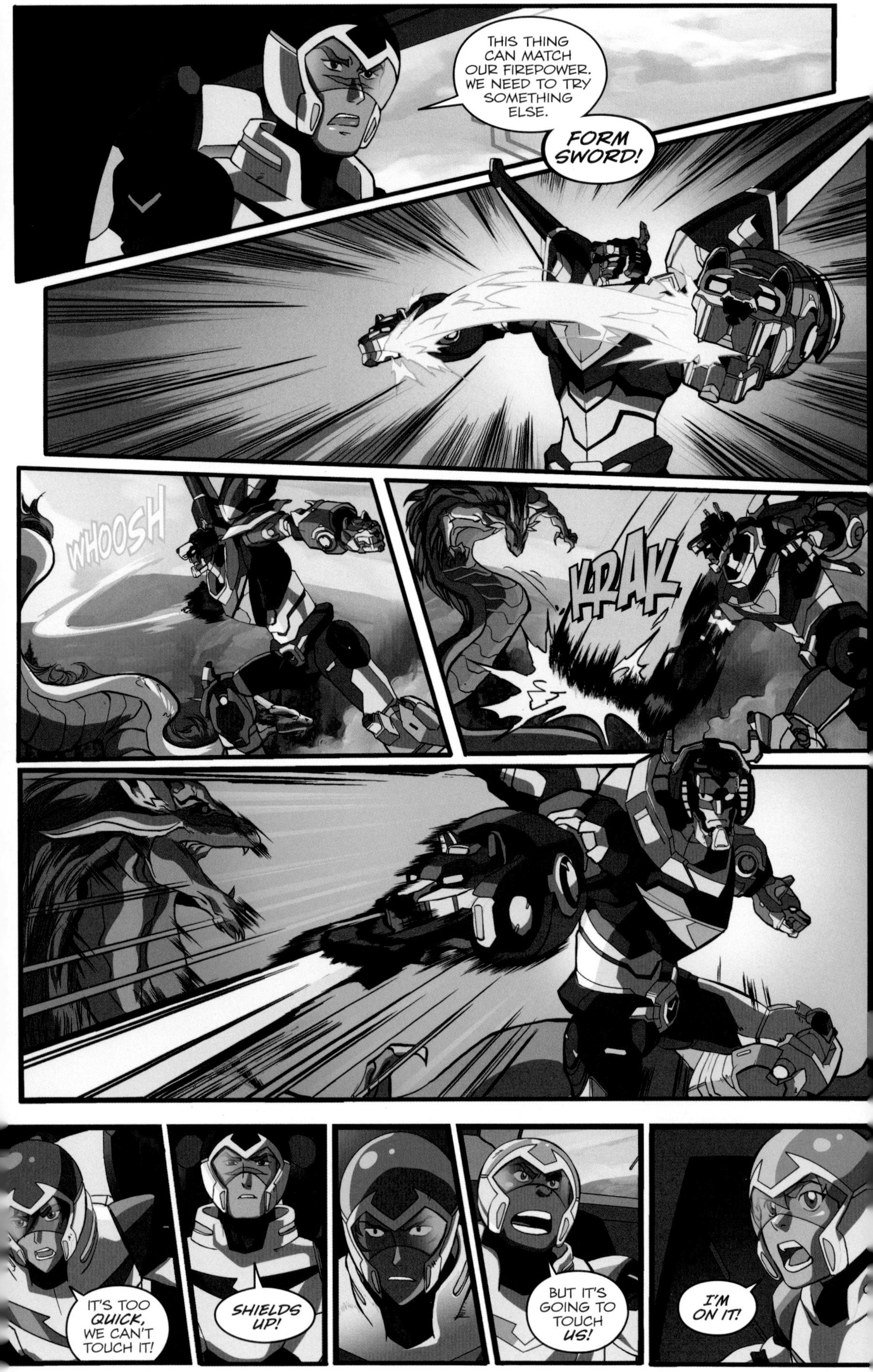
THIS THING CAN MATCH OUR FIREPOWER. WE NEED TO TRY SOMETHING ELSE.
FORM SWORD!
WHOOSH
KRAK
IT'S TOO QUICK, WE CAN'T TOUCH IT!
SHIELDS UP!
BUT IT'S GOING TO TOUCH US!
I'M ON IT!

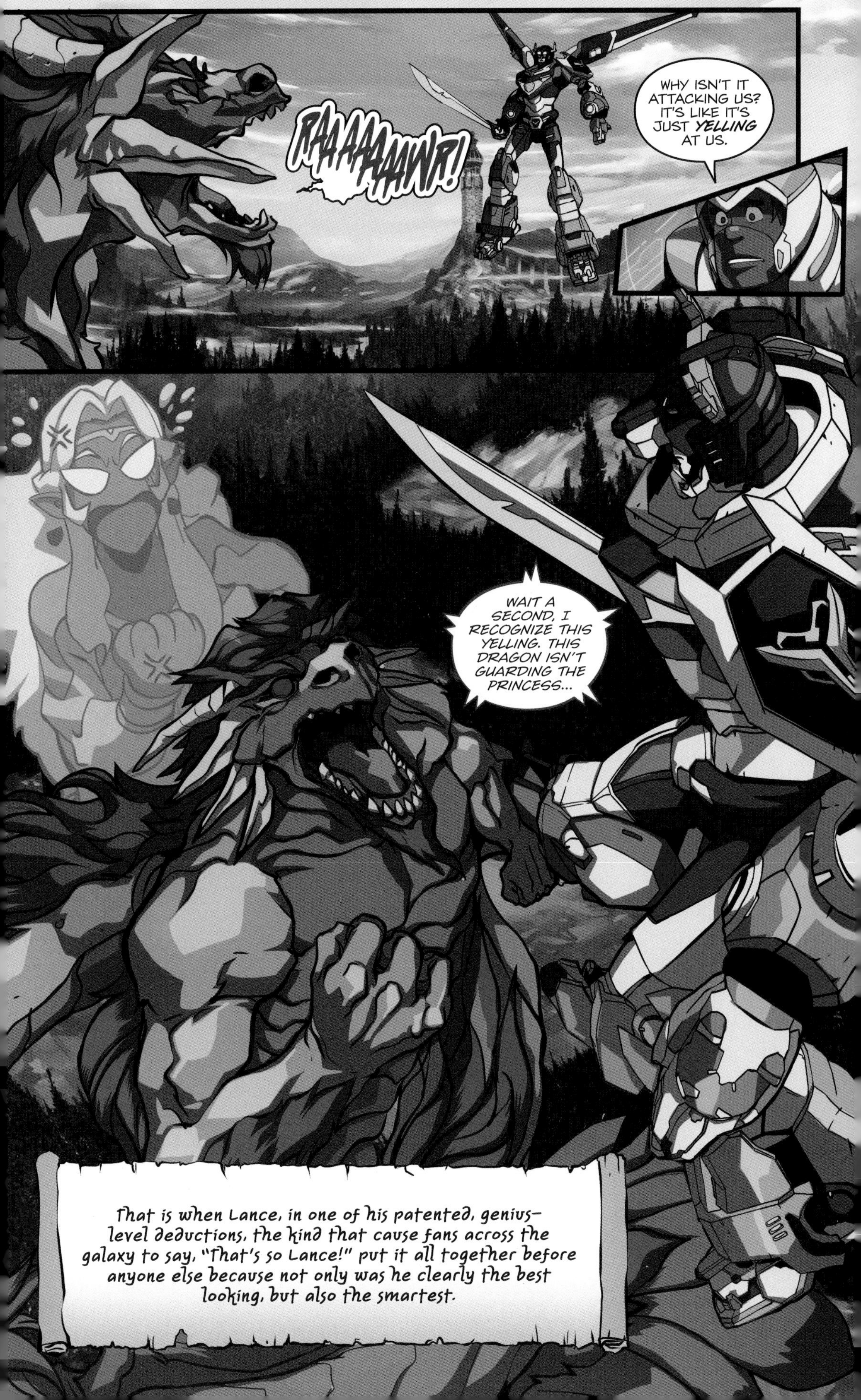
RAAAAAAAAWR!
WHY ISN'T IT ATTACKING US? IT'S LIKE IT'S JUST YELLING AT US.
WAIT A SECOND, I RECOGNIZE THIS YELLING. THIS DRAGON ISN'T GUARDING THE PRINCESS...
That is when Lance, in one of his patented, genius-level deductions, the kind that cause fans across the galaxy to say, "That's so Lance!" put it all together before anyone else because not only was he clearly the best looking, but also the smartest.

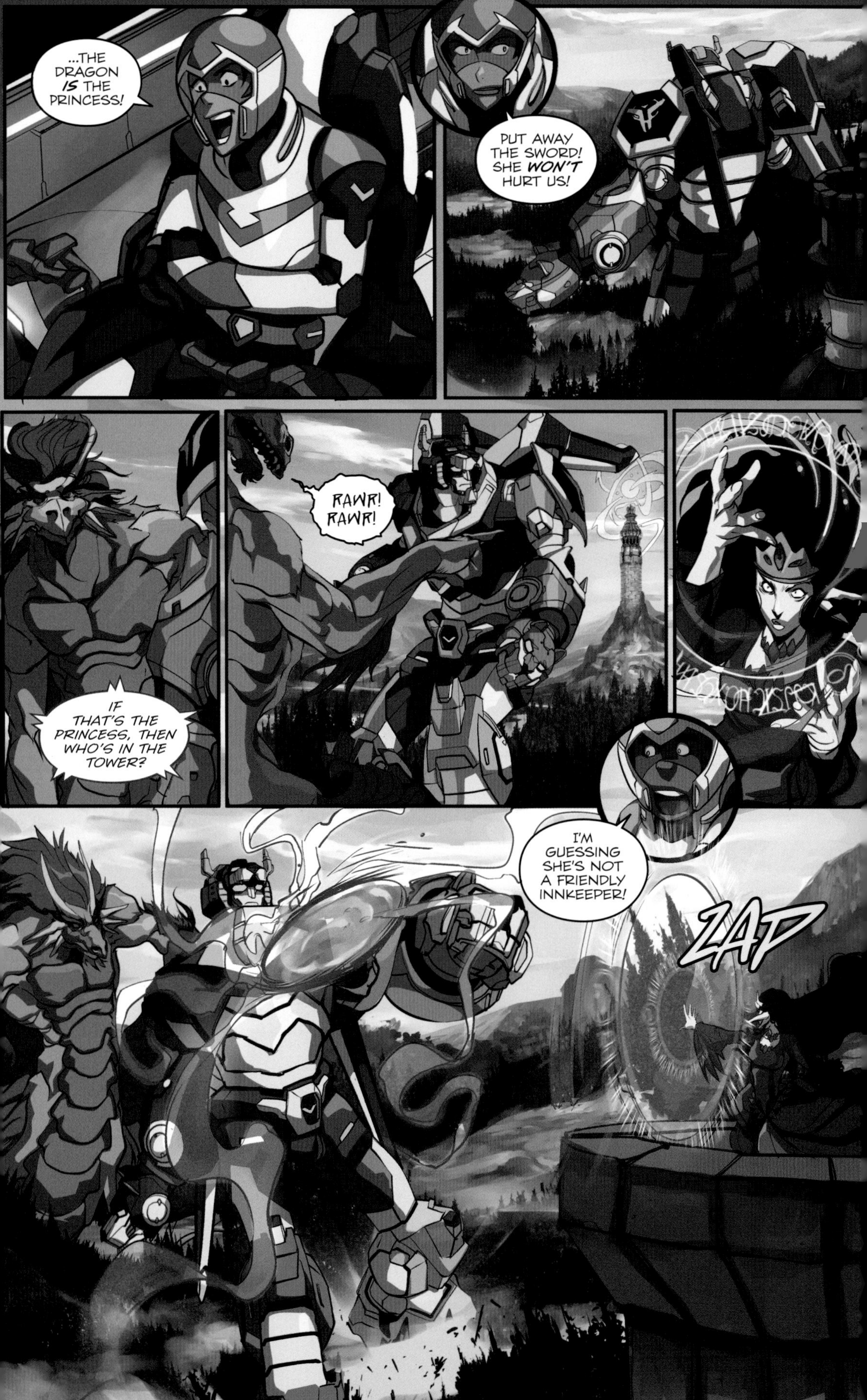
...THE DRAGON *IS* THE PRINCESS!
PUT AWAY THE SWORD! SHE *WON'T* HURT US!
RAWR! RAWR!
IF THAT'S THE PRINCESS, THEN WHO'S IN THE TOWER?
I'M GUESSING SHE'S NOT A FRIENDLY INNKEEPER!
ZAP

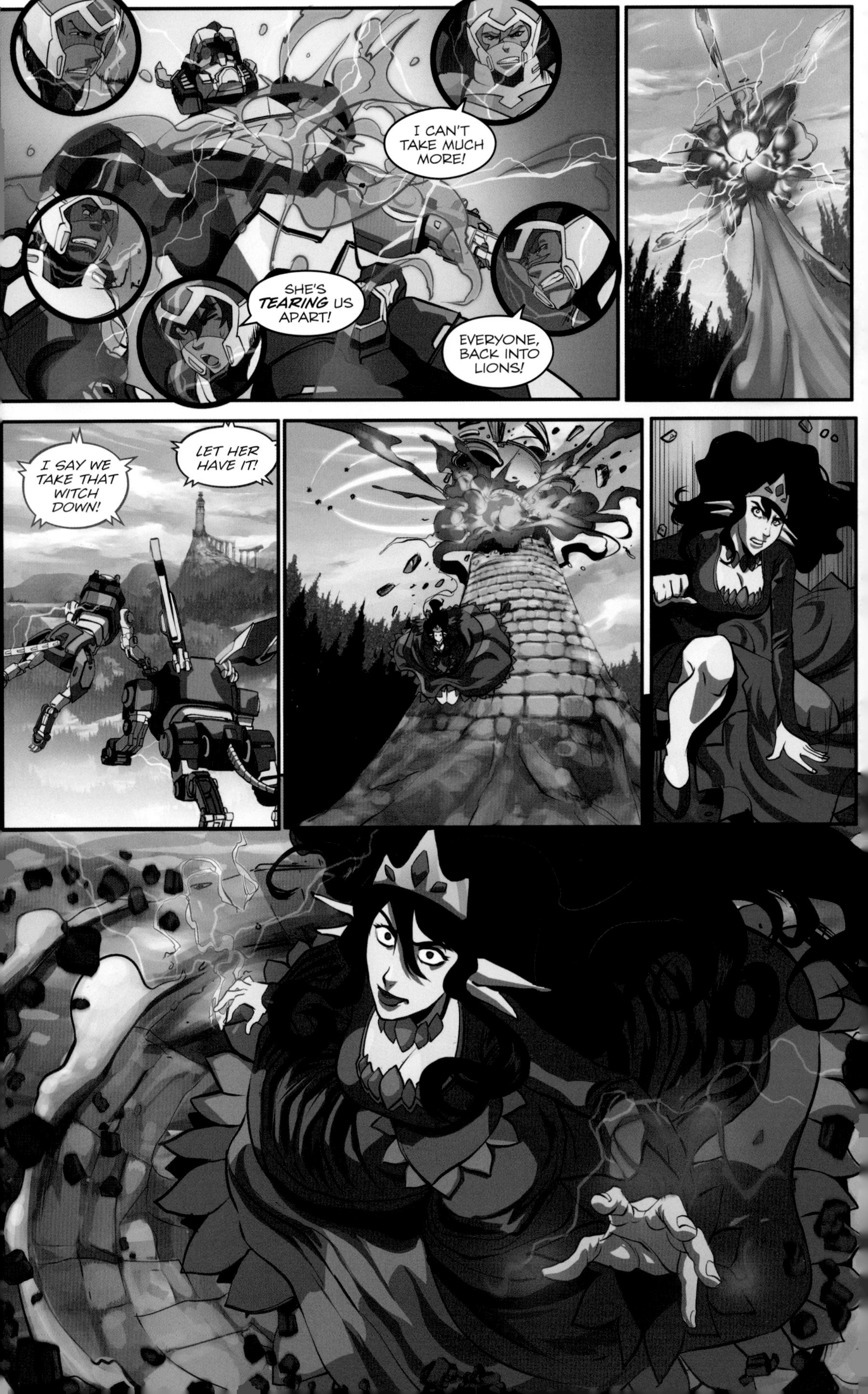
I CAN'T TAKE MUCH MORE!
SHE'S TEARING US APART!
EVERYONE, BACK INTO LIONS!
I SAY WE TAKE THAT WITCH DOWN!
LET HER HAVE IT!

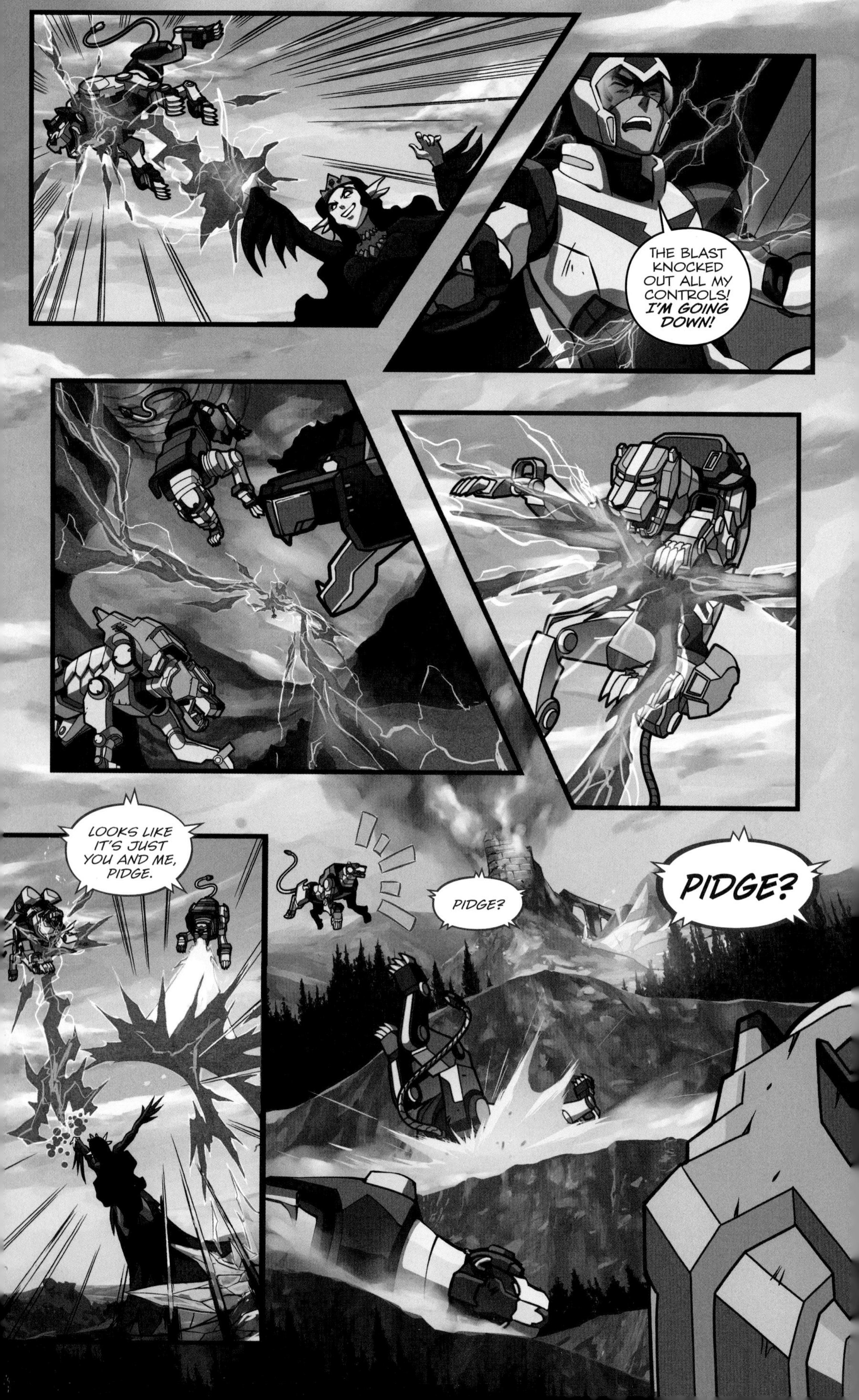
THE BLAST KNOCKED OUT ALL MY CONTROLS! I'M GOING DOWN!
LOOKS LIKE IT'S JUST YOU AND ME, PIDGE.
PIDGE?
PIDGE?

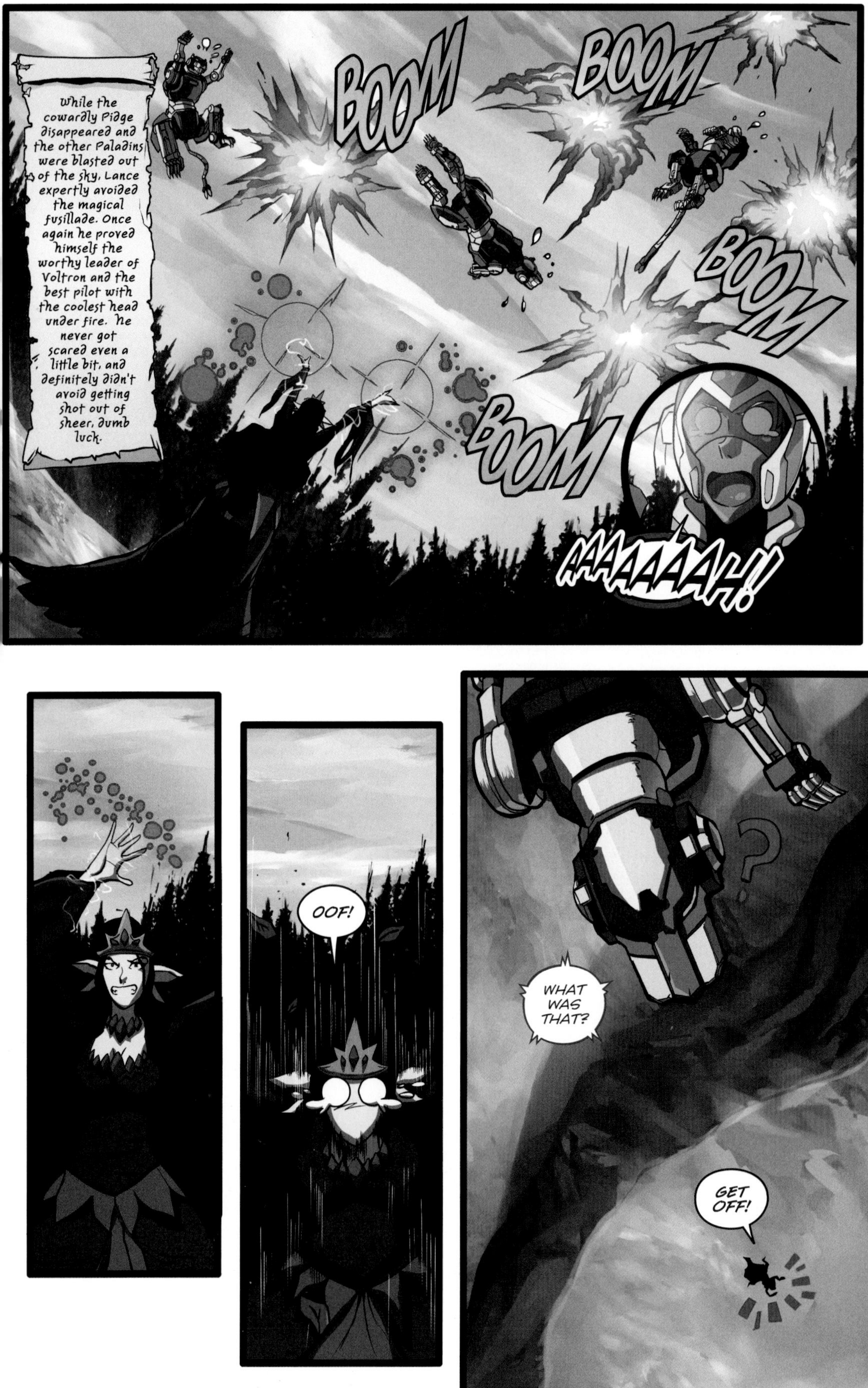
While the cowardly Pidge disappeared and the other Paladins were blasted out of the sky, Lance expertly avoided the magical fusillade. Once again he proved himself the worthy leader of Voltron and the best pilot with the coolest head under fire. He never got scared even a little bit, and definitely didn't avoid getting shot out of sheer, dumb luck.
BOOM
BOOM
BOOM
BOOM
AAAAAAAH!!
OOF!
?
WHAT WAS THAT?
GET OFF!

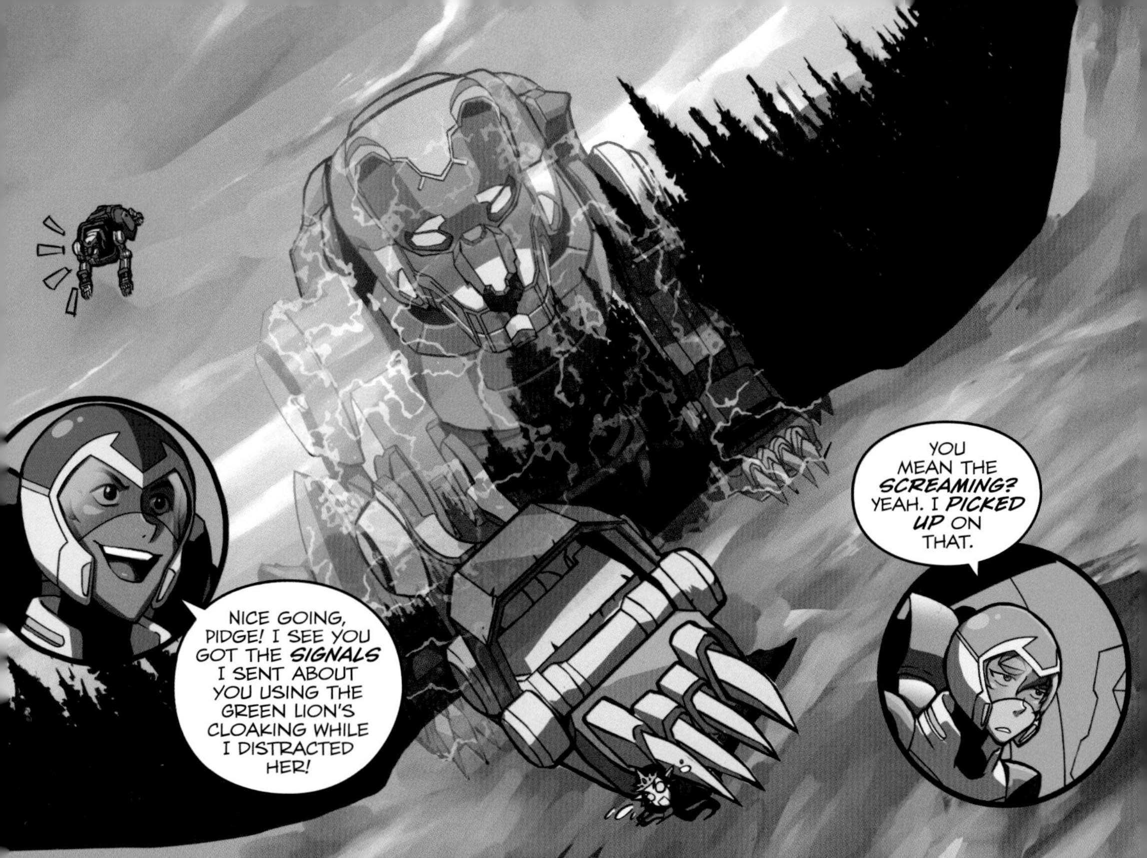
NICE GOING, PIDGE! I SEE YOU GOT THE SIGNALS I SENT ABOUT YOU USING THE GREEN LION'S CLOAKING WHILE I DISTRACTED HER!
YOU MEAN THE SCREAMING? YEAH. I PICKED UP ON THAT.

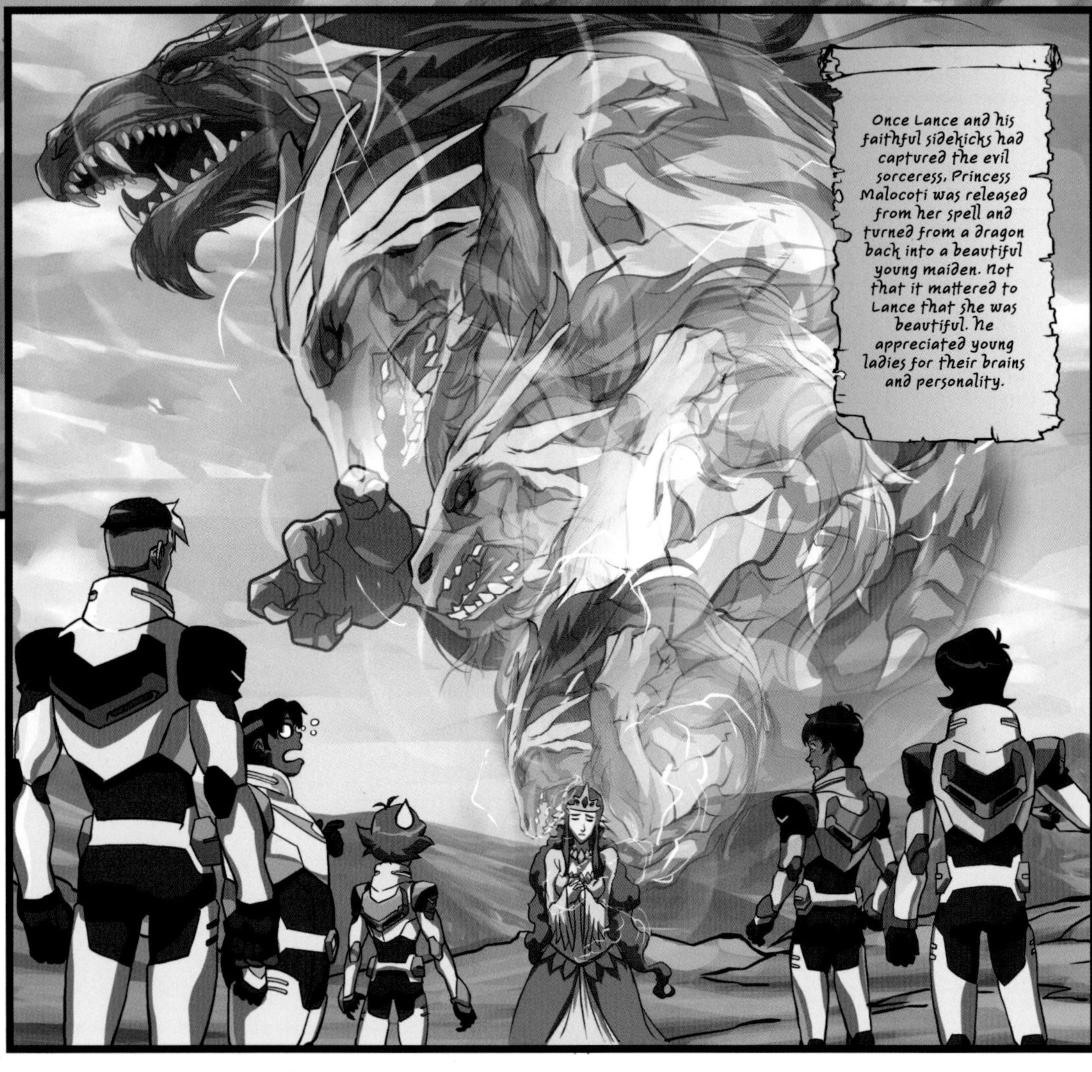
Once Lance and his faithful sidekicks had captured the evil sorceress, Princess Malocoti was released from her spell and turned from a dragon back into a beautiful young maiden. Not that it mattered to Lance that she was beautiful. He appreciated young ladies for their brains and personality.

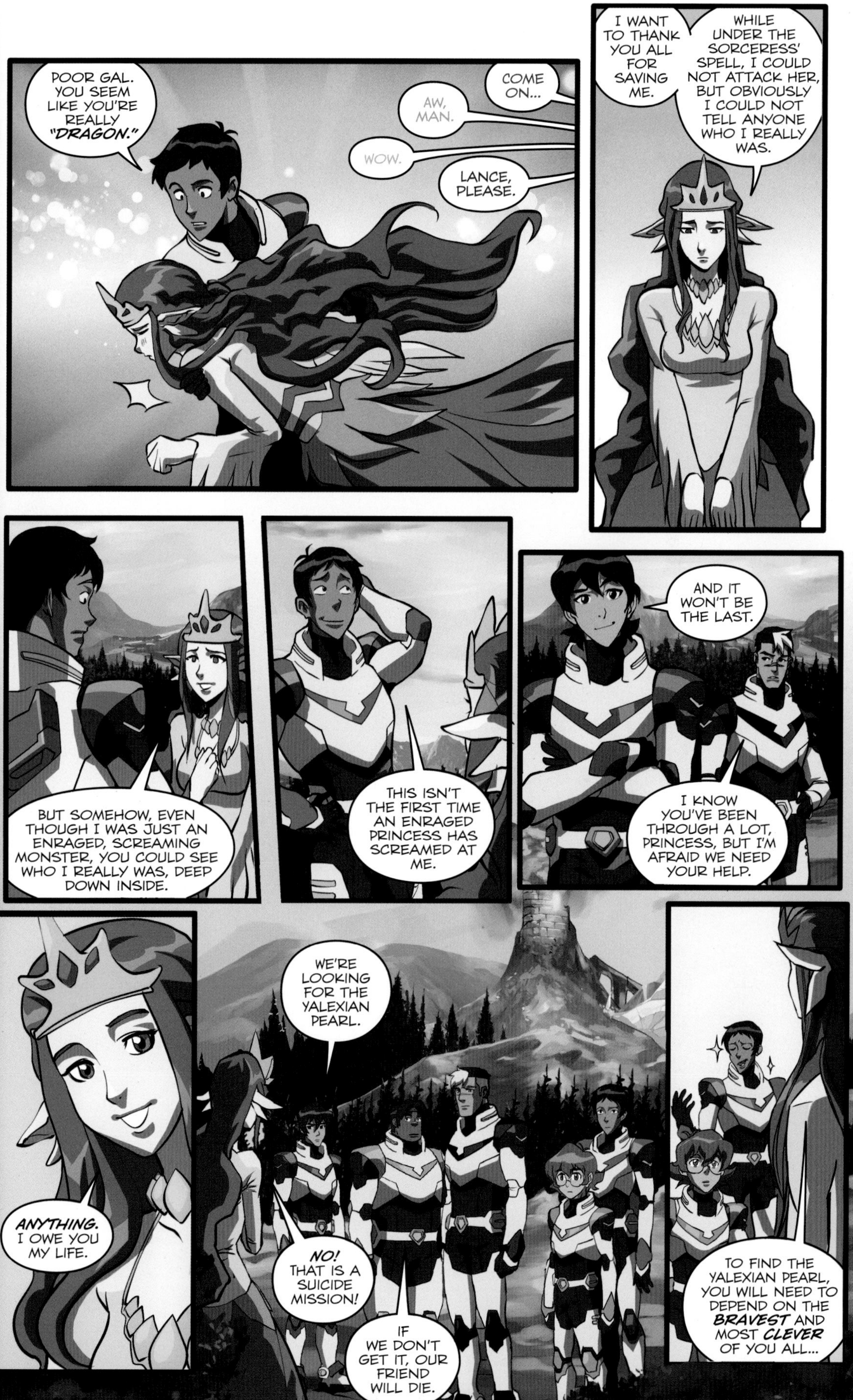
POOR GAL. YOU SEEM LIKE YOU'RE REALLY "DRAGON."
COME ON...
AW, MAN.
WOW.
LANCE, PLEASE.
I WANT TO THANK YOU ALL FOR SAVING ME.
WHILE UNDER THE SORCERESS' SPELL, I COULD NOT ATTACK HER, BUT OBVIOUSLY I COULD NOT TELL ANYONE WHO I REALLY WAS.
BUT SOMEHOW, EVEN THOUGH I WAS JUST AN ENRAGED, SCREAMING MONSTER, YOU COULD SEE WHO I REALLY WAS, DEEP DOWN INSIDE.
THIS ISN'T THE FIRST TIME AN ENRAGED PRINCESS HAS SCREAMED AT ME.
AND IT WON'T BE THE LAST.
I KNOW YOU'VE BEEN THROUGH A LOT, PRINCESS, BUT I'M AFRAID WE NEED YOUR HELP.
ANYTHING. I OWE YOU MY LIFE.
WE'RE LOOKING FOR THE YALEXIAN PEARL.
NO! THAT IS A SUICIDE MISSION!
IF WE DON'T GET IT, OUR FRIEND WILL DIE.
TO FIND THE YALEXIAN PEARL, YOU WILL NEED TO DEPEND ON THE BRAVEST AND MOST CLEVER OF YOU ALL...

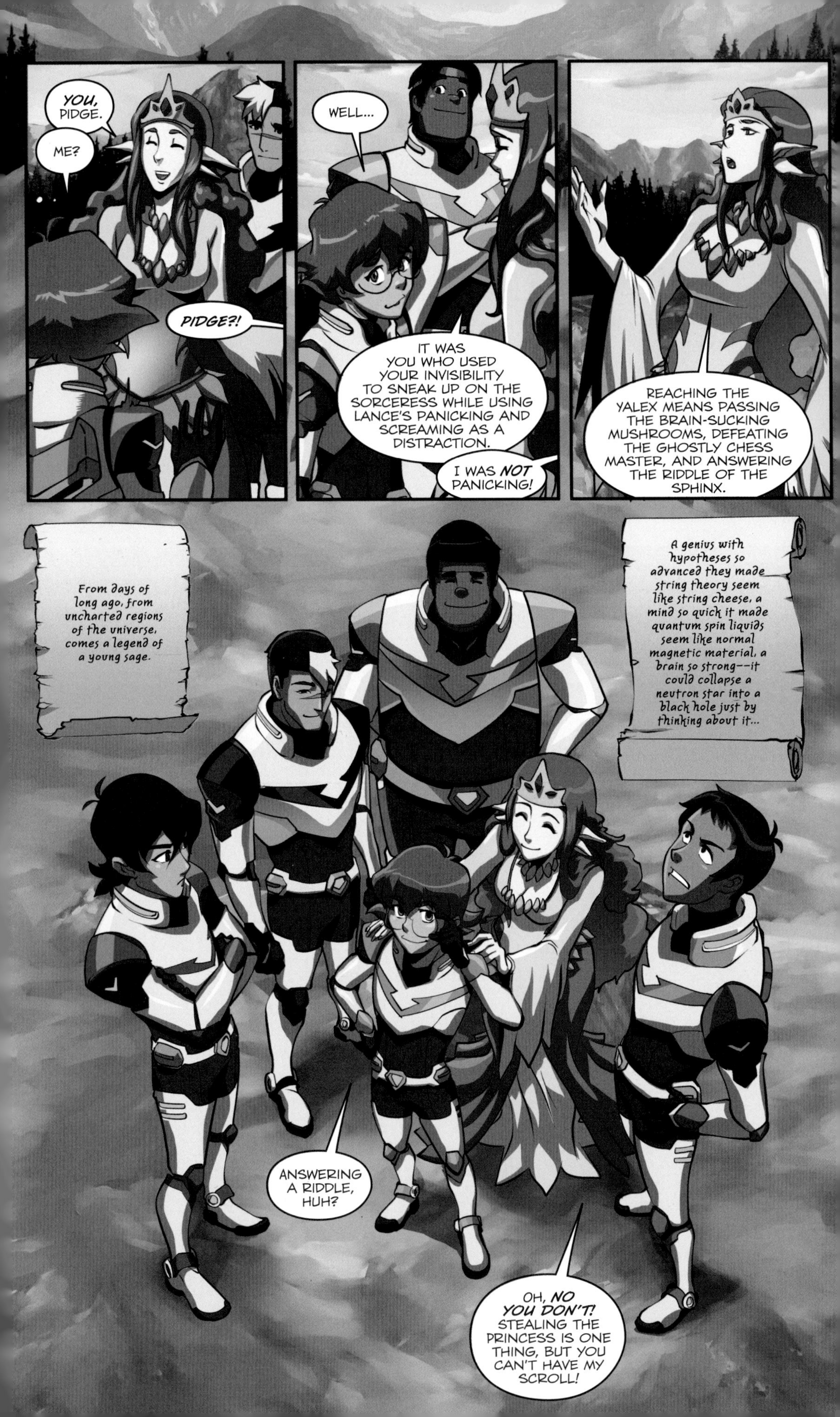
YOU, PIDGE.
ME?
PIDGE?!
WELL...
IT WAS YOU WHO USED YOUR INVISIBILITY TO SNEAK UP ON THE SORCERESS WHILE USING LANCE'S PANICKING AND SCREAMING AS A DISTRACTION.
I WAS NOT PANICKING!
REACHING THE YALEX MEANS PASSING THE BRAIN-SUCKING MUSHROOMS, DEFEATING THE GHOSTLY CHESS MASTER, AND ANSWERING THE RIDDLE OF THE SPHINX.
From days of long ago, from uncharted regions of the universe, comes a legend of a young sage.
A genius with hypotheses so advanced they made string theory seem like string cheese, a mind so quick it made quantum spin liquids seem like normal magnetic material, a brain so strong--it could collapse a neutron star into a black hole just by thinking about it...
ANSWERING A RIDDLE, HUH?
OH, NO YOU DON'T! STEALING THE PRINCESS IS ONE THING, BUT YOU CAN'T HAVE MY SCROLL!

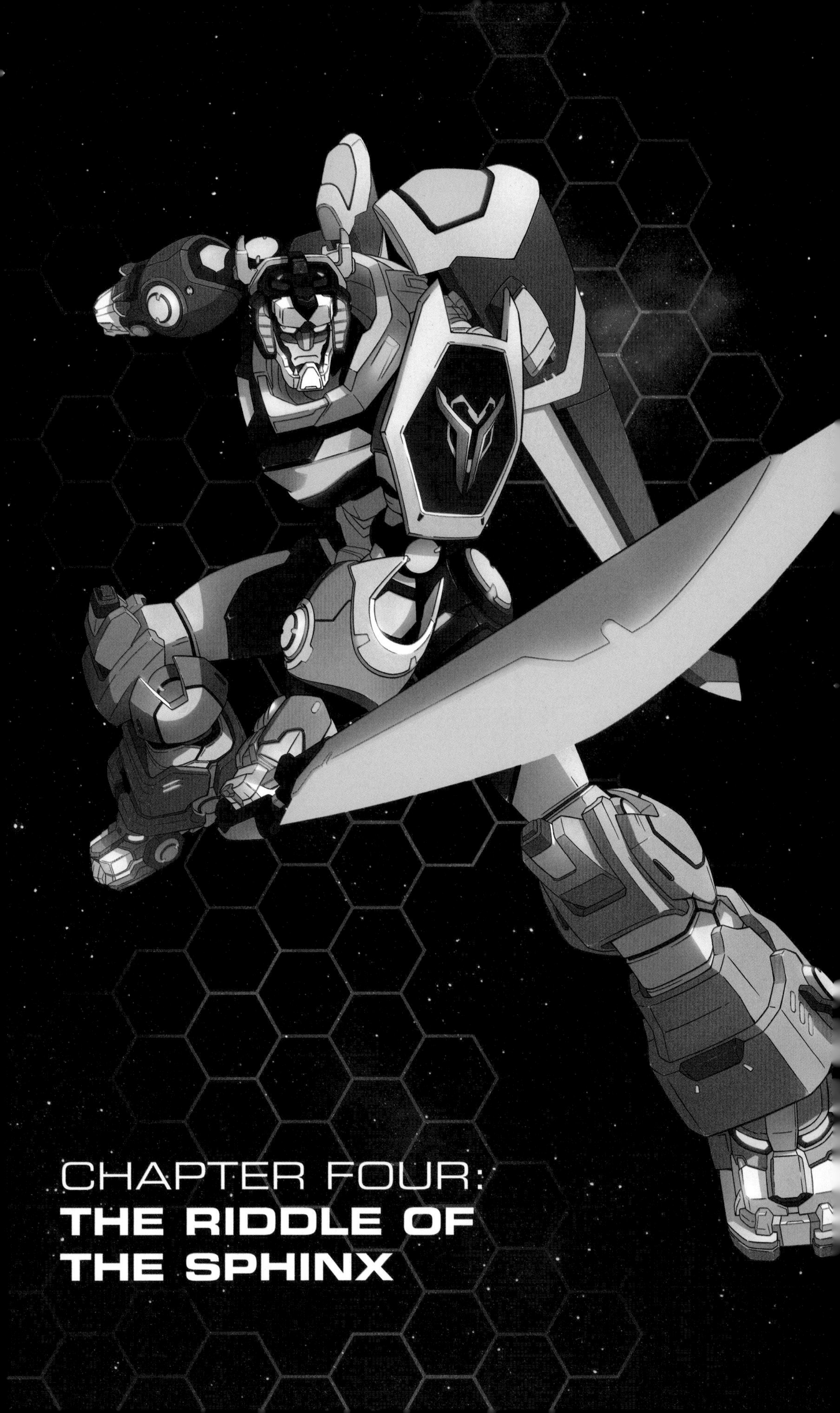

CHAPTER FOUR:
THE RIDDLE OF THE SPHINX

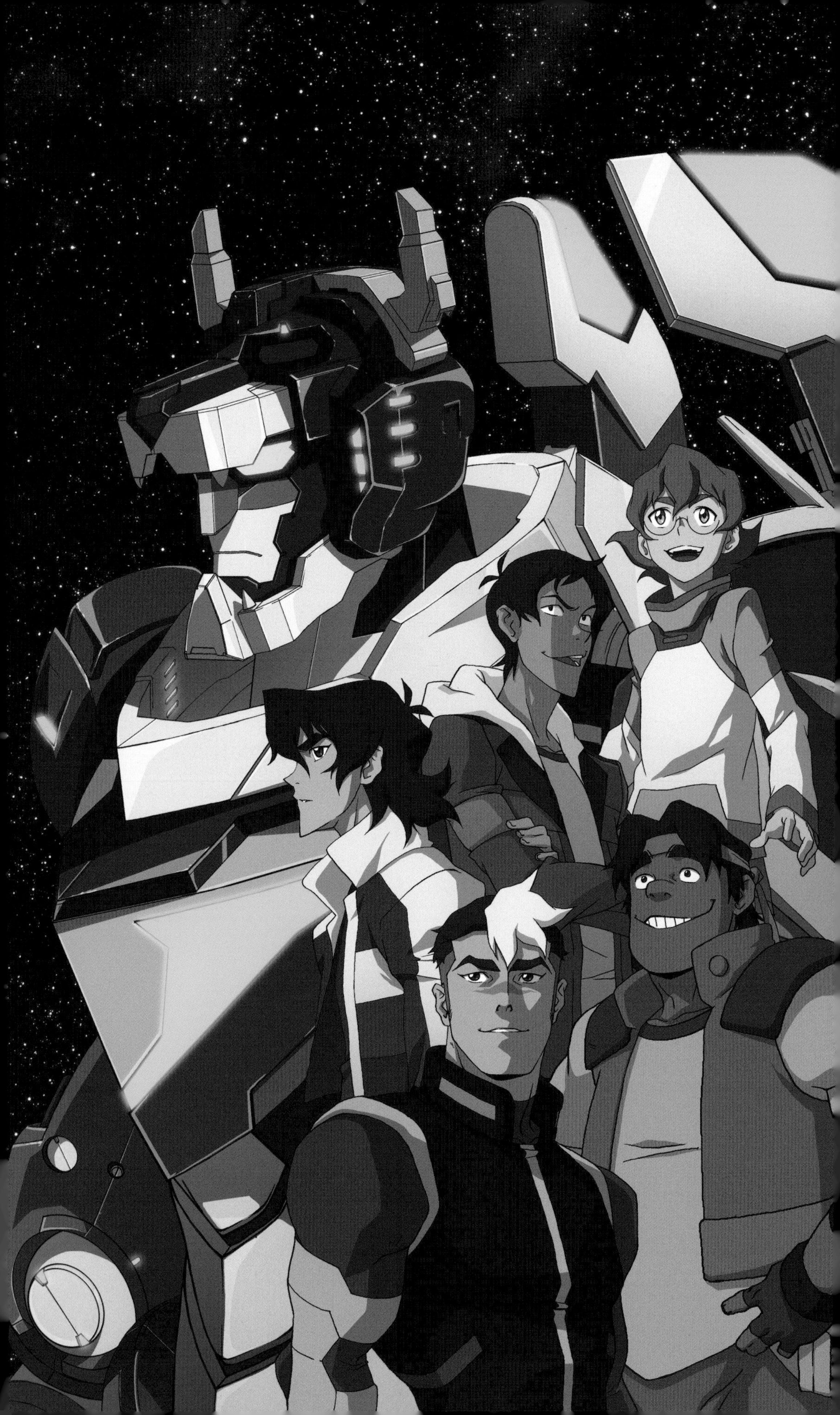

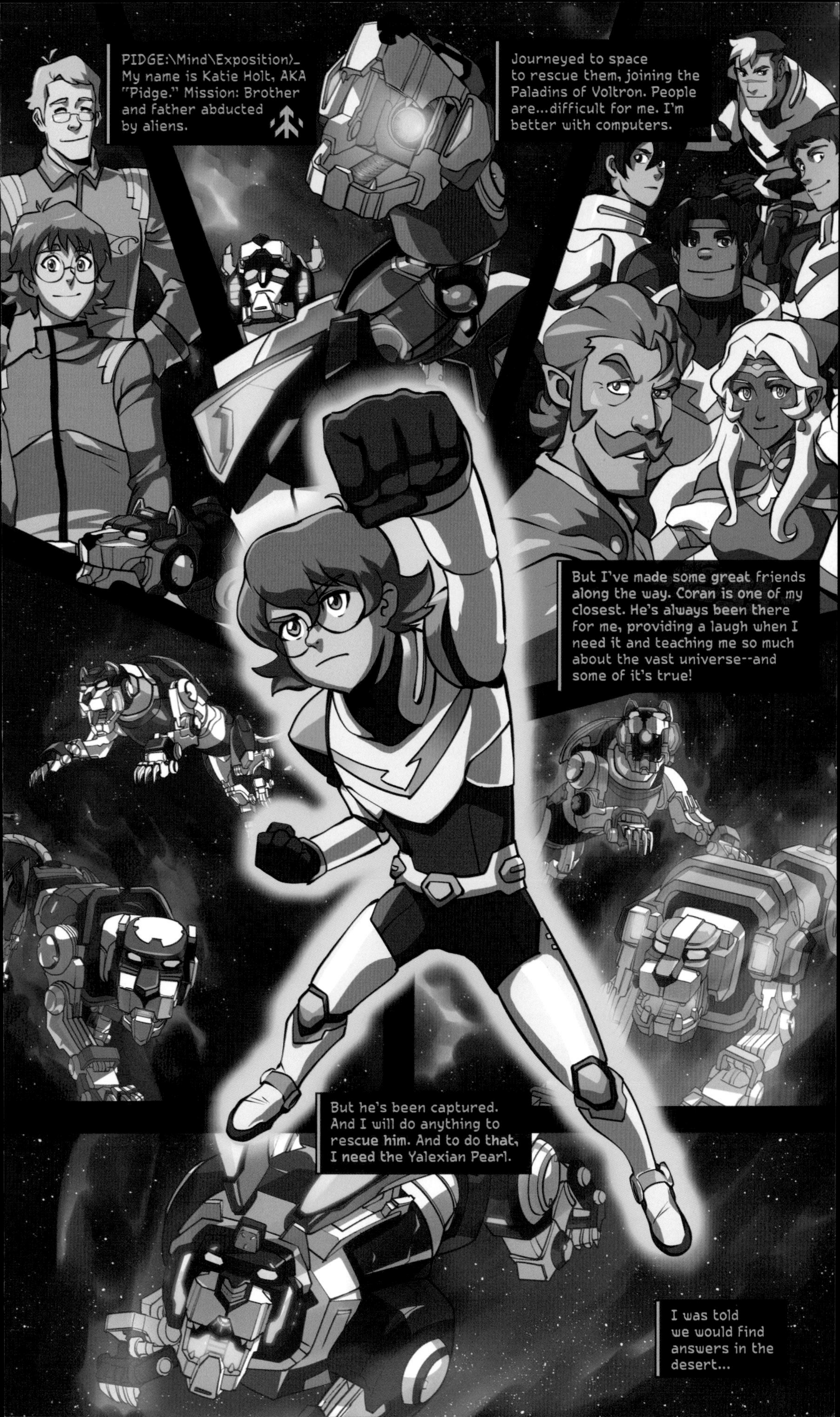

PIDGE:\Mind\Exposition)_ My name is Katie Holt, AKA "Pidge." Mission: Brother and father abducted by aliens.
Journeyed to space to rescue them, joining the Paladins of Voltron. People are...difficult for me. I'm better with computers.
But I've made some great friends along the way. Coran is one of my closest. He's always been there for me, providing a laugh when I need it and teaching me so much about the vast universe--and some of it's true!
But he's been captured. And I will do anything to rescue him. And to do that, I need the Yalexian Pearl.
I was told we would find answers in the desert...

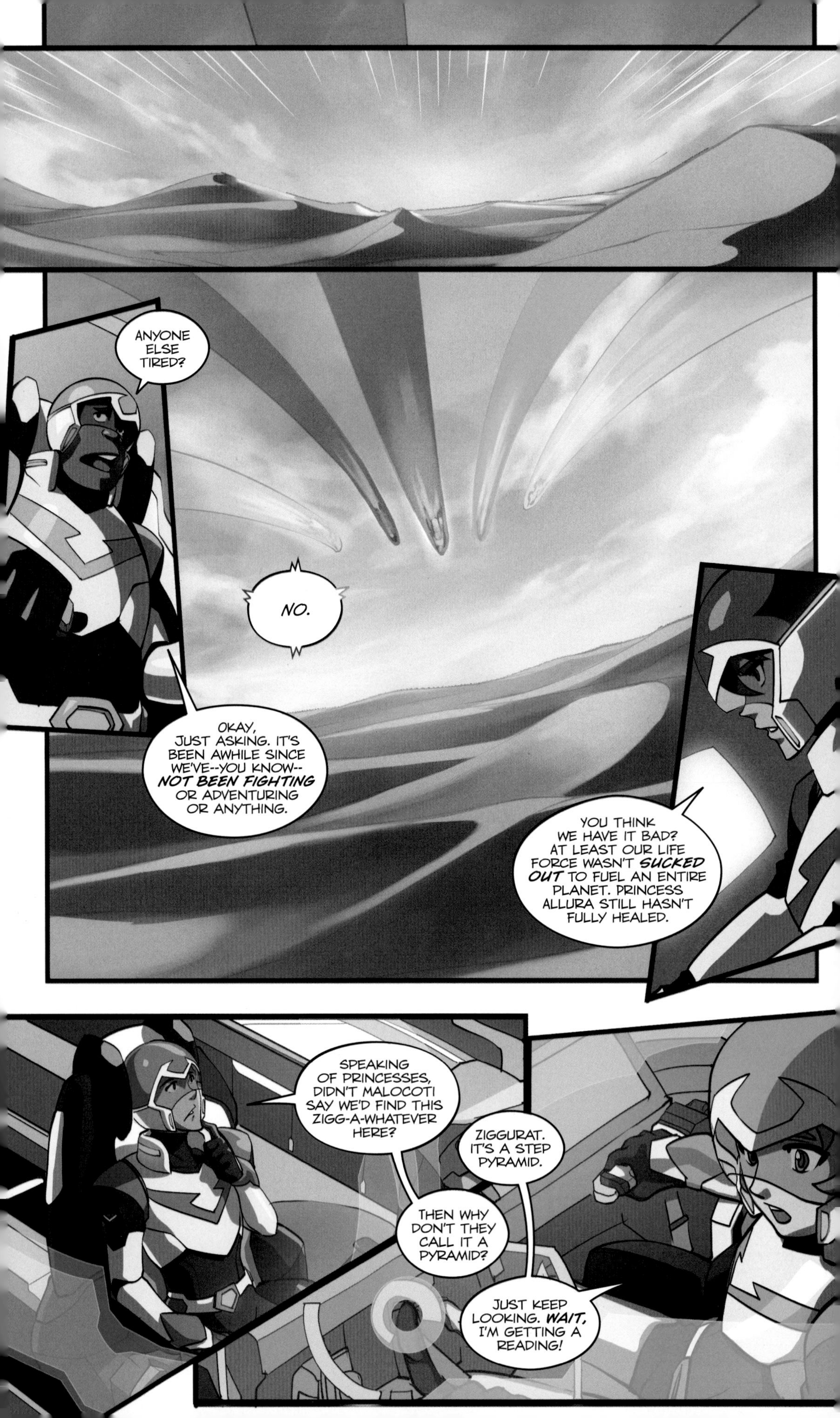
ANYONE ELSE TIRED?
NO.
OKAY, JUST ASKING. IT'S BEEN AWHILE SINCE WE'VE--YOU KNOW-- ***NOT BEEN FIGHTING*** OR ADVENTURING OR ANYTHING.
YOU THINK WE HAVE IT BAD? AT LEAST OUR LIFE FORCE WASN'T ***SUCKED OUT*** TO FUEL AN ENTIRE PLANET. PRINCESS ALLURA STILL HASN'T FULLY HEALED.
SPEAKING OF PRINCESSES, DIDN'T MALOCOTI SAY WE'D FIND THIS ZIGG-A-WHATEVER HERE?
ZIGGURAT. IT'S A STEP PYRAMID.
THEN WHY DON'T THEY CALL IT A PYRAMID?
JUST KEEP LOOKING. ***WAIT,*** I'M GETTING A READING!

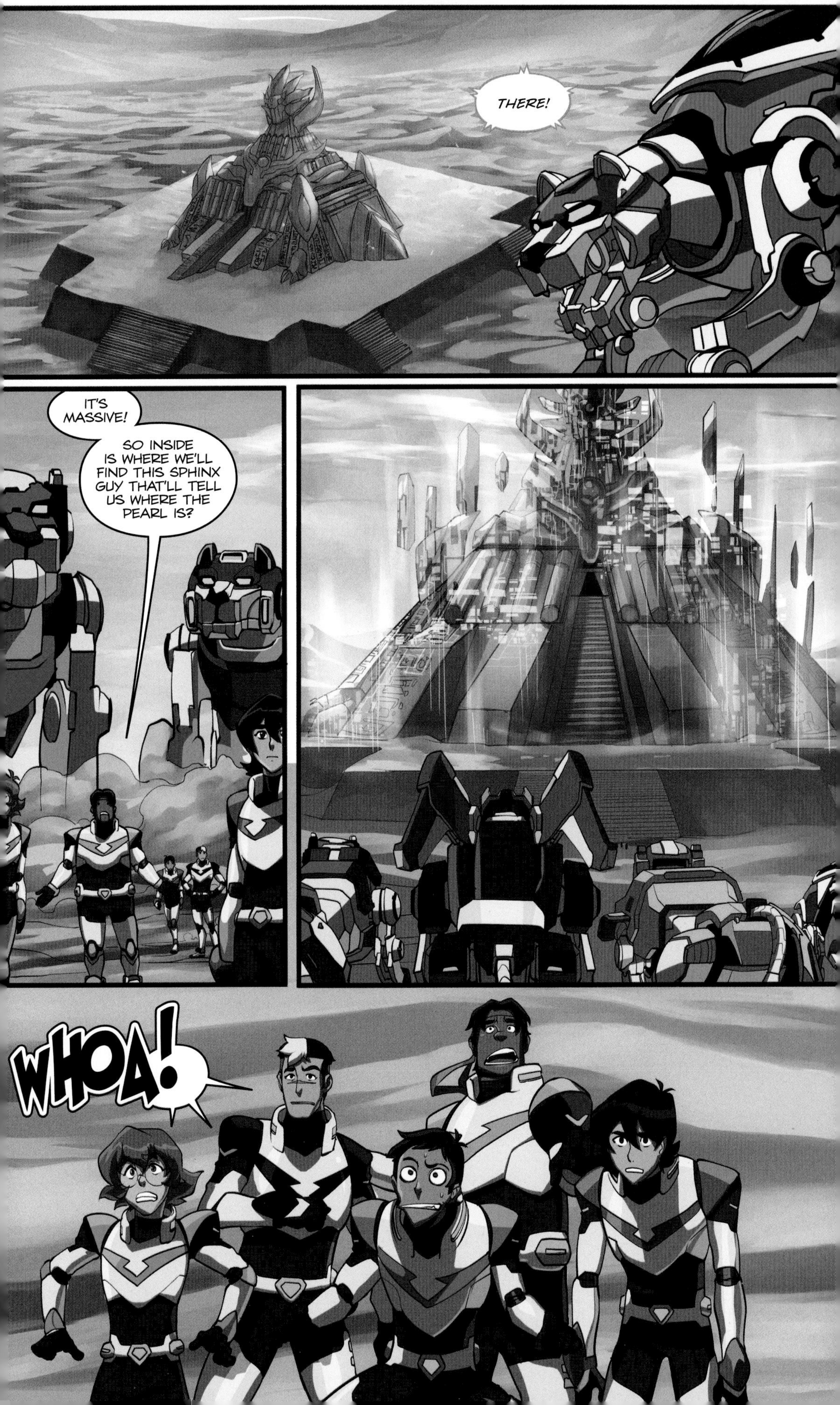
THERE!
IT'S MASSIVE!
SO INSIDE IS WHERE WE'LL FIND THIS SPHINX GUY THAT'LL TELL US WHERE THE PEARL IS?
WHOA!

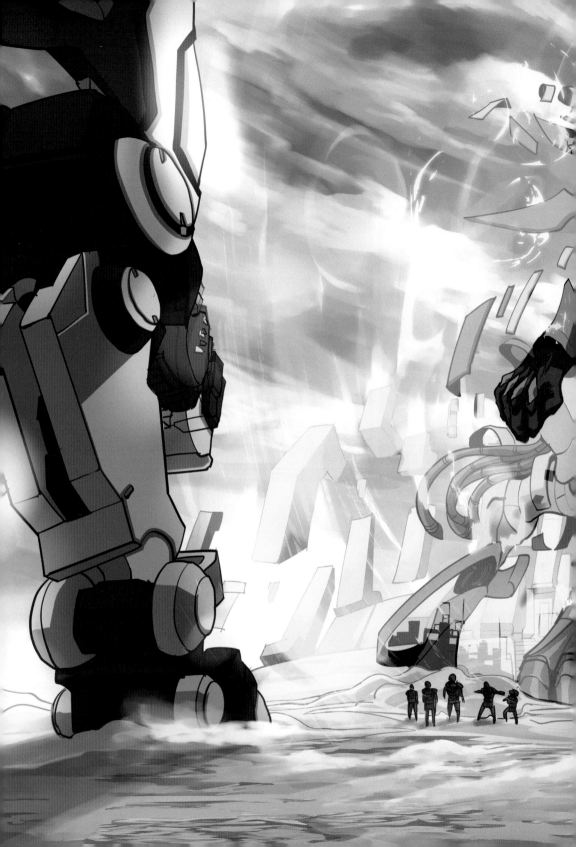

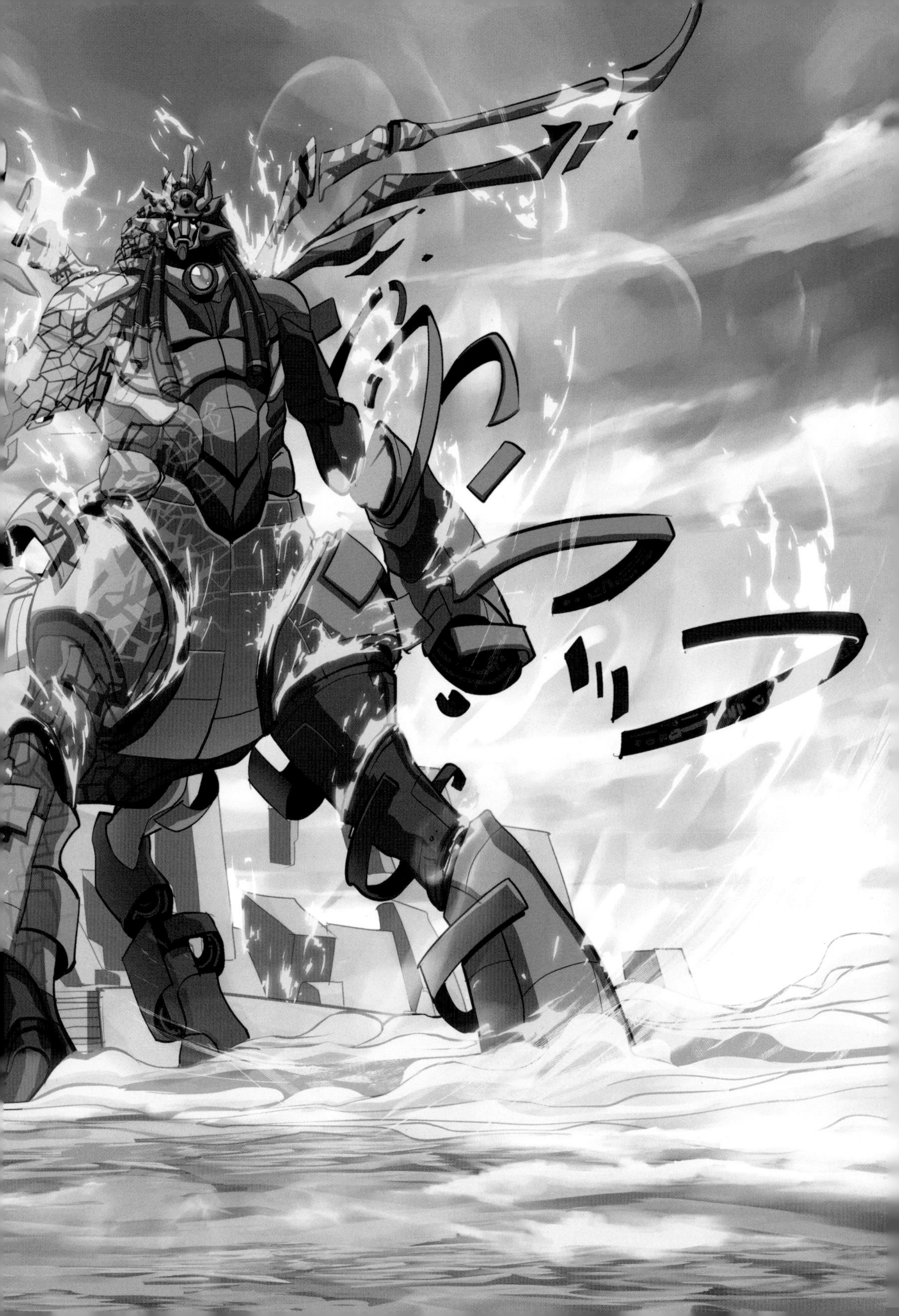

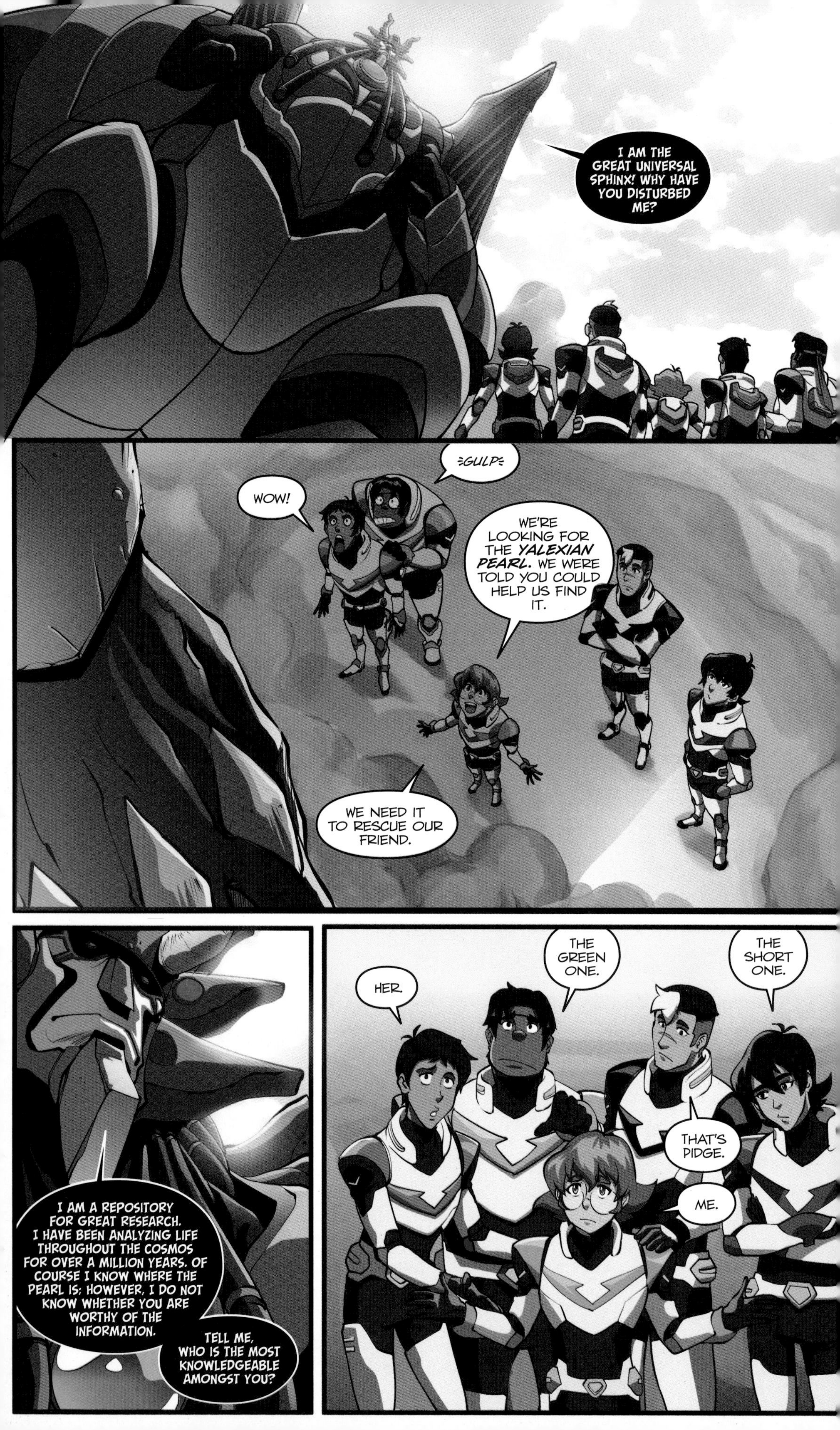
I AM THE GREAT UNIVERSAL SPHINX! WHY HAVE YOU DISTURBED ME?
GULP
WOW!
WE'RE LOOKING FOR THE YALEXIAN PEARL. WE WERE TOLD YOU COULD HELP US FIND IT.
WE NEED IT TO RESCUE OUR FRIEND.
I AM A REPOSITORY FOR GREAT RESEARCH. I HAVE BEEN ANALYZING LIFE THROUGHOUT THE COSMOS FOR OVER A MILLION YEARS. OF COURSE I KNOW WHERE THE PEARL IS; HOWEVER, I DO NOT KNOW WHETHER YOU ARE WORTHY OF THE INFORMATION.
TELL ME, WHO IS THE MOST KNOWLEDGEABLE AMONGST YOU?
HER.
THE GREEN ONE.
THE SHORT ONE.
THAT'S PIDGE.
ME.

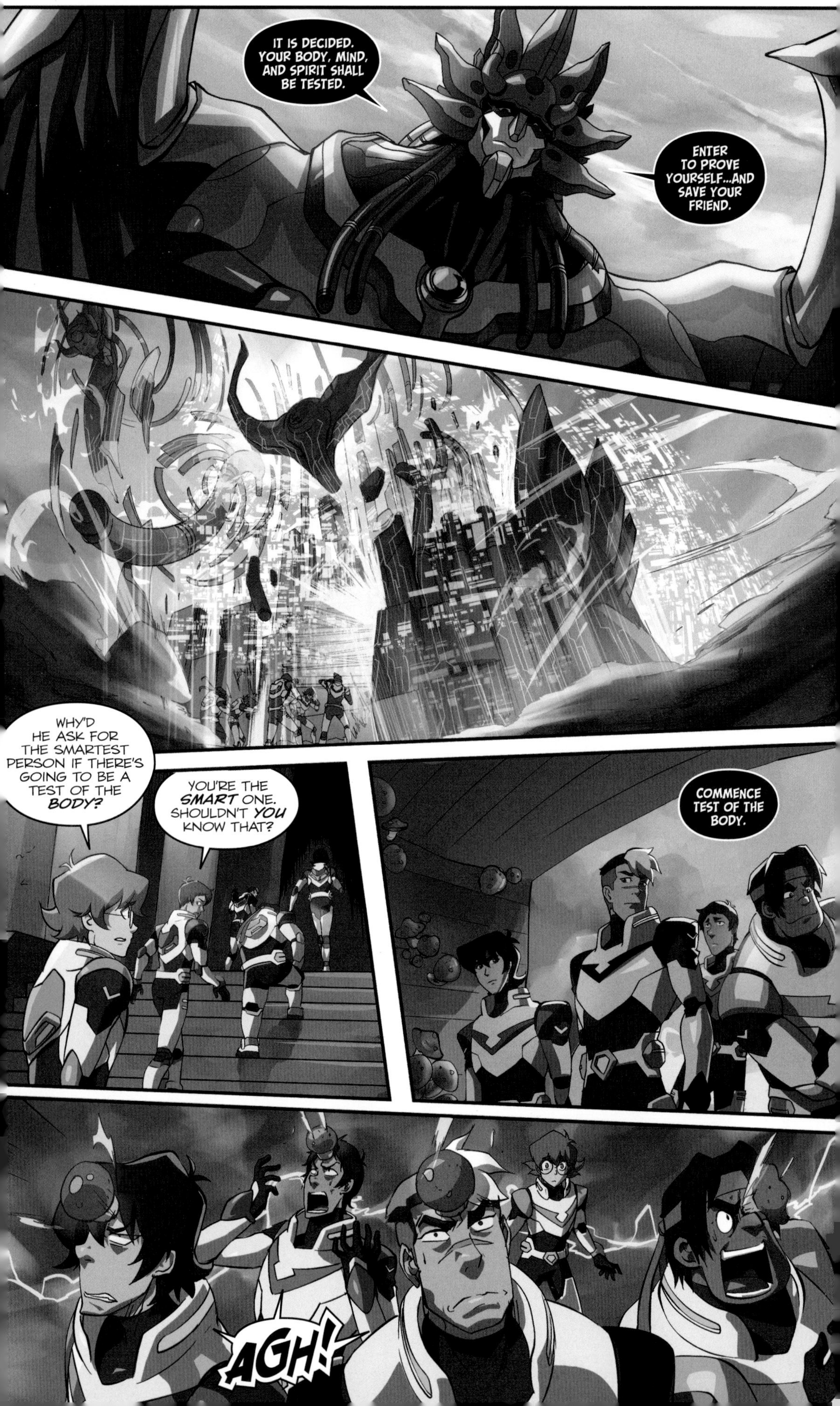
IT IS DECIDED. YOUR BODY, MIND, AND SPIRIT SHALL BE TESTED.
ENTER TO PROVE YOURSELF...AND SAVE YOUR FRIEND.
WHY'D HE ASK FOR THE SMARTEST PERSON IF THERE'S GOING TO BE A TEST OF THE *BODY?*
YOU'RE THE *SMART* ONE. SHOULDN'T *YOU* KNOW THAT?
COMMENCE TEST OF THE BODY.
AGH!

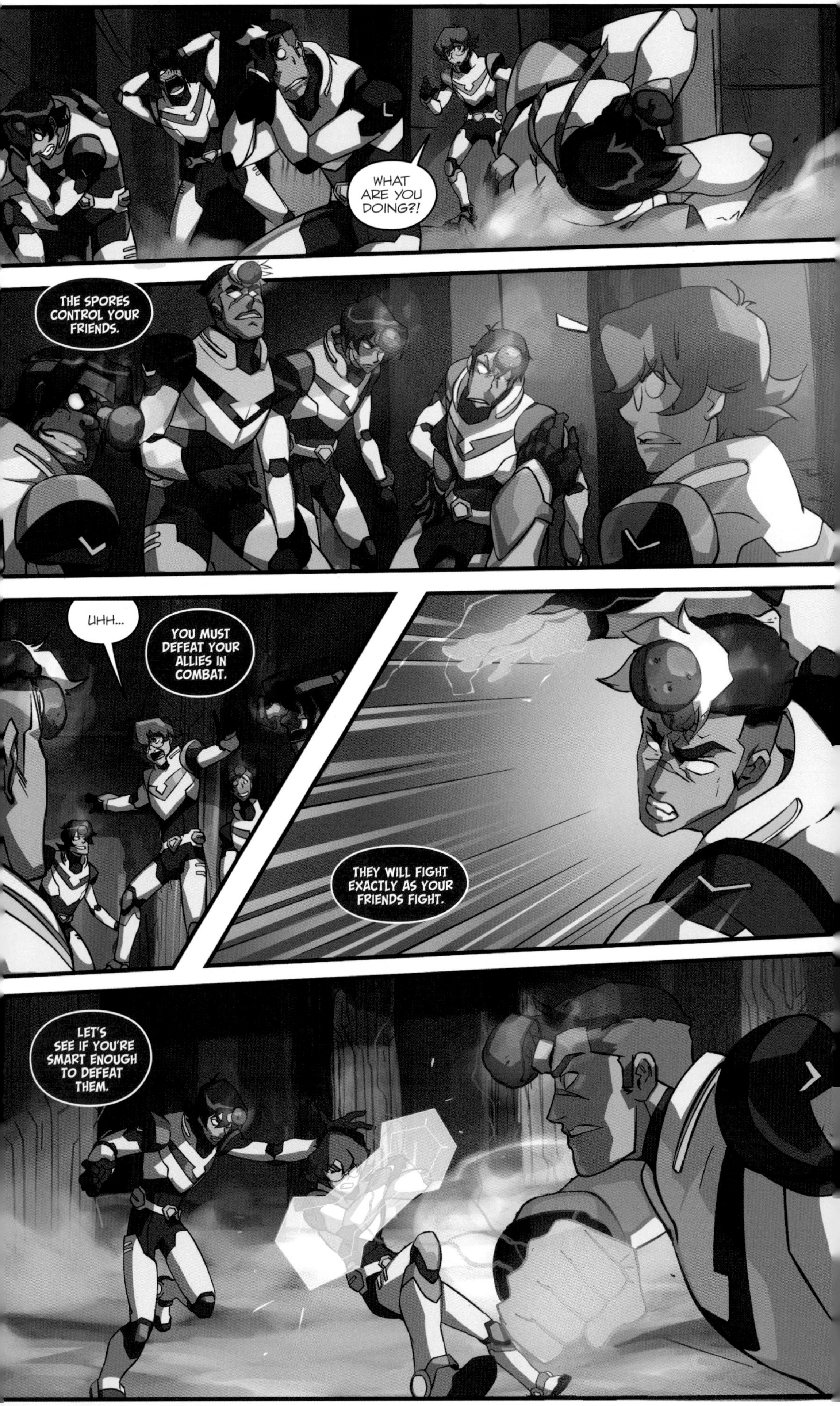
WHAT ARE YOU DOING?!
THE SPORES CONTROL YOUR FRIENDS.
UHH...
YOU MUST DEFEAT YOUR ALLIES IN COMBAT.
THEY WILL FIGHT EXACTLY AS YOUR FRIENDS FIGHT.
LET'S SEE IF YOU'RE SMART ENOUGH TO DEFEAT THEM.

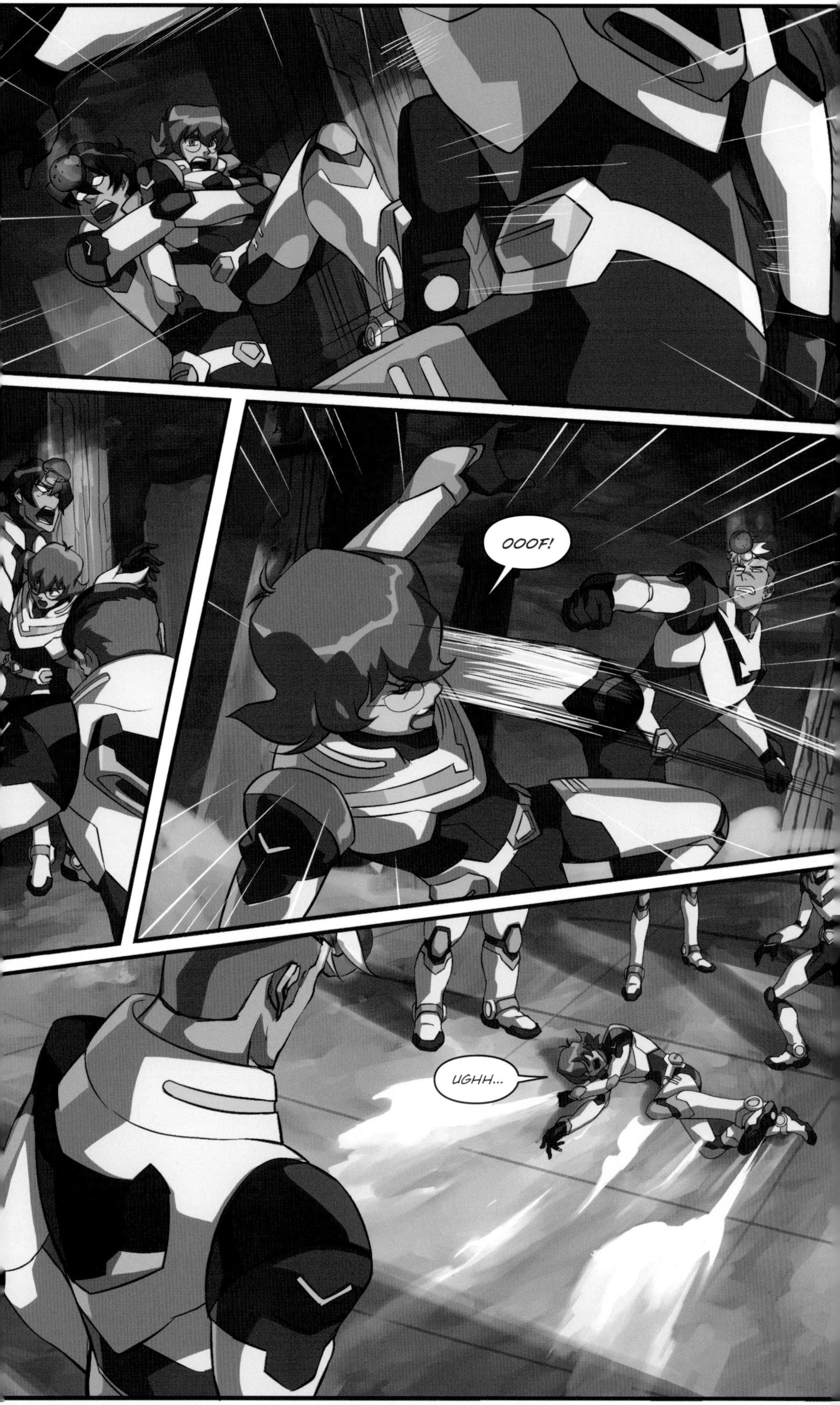
OOOF!
UGHH...

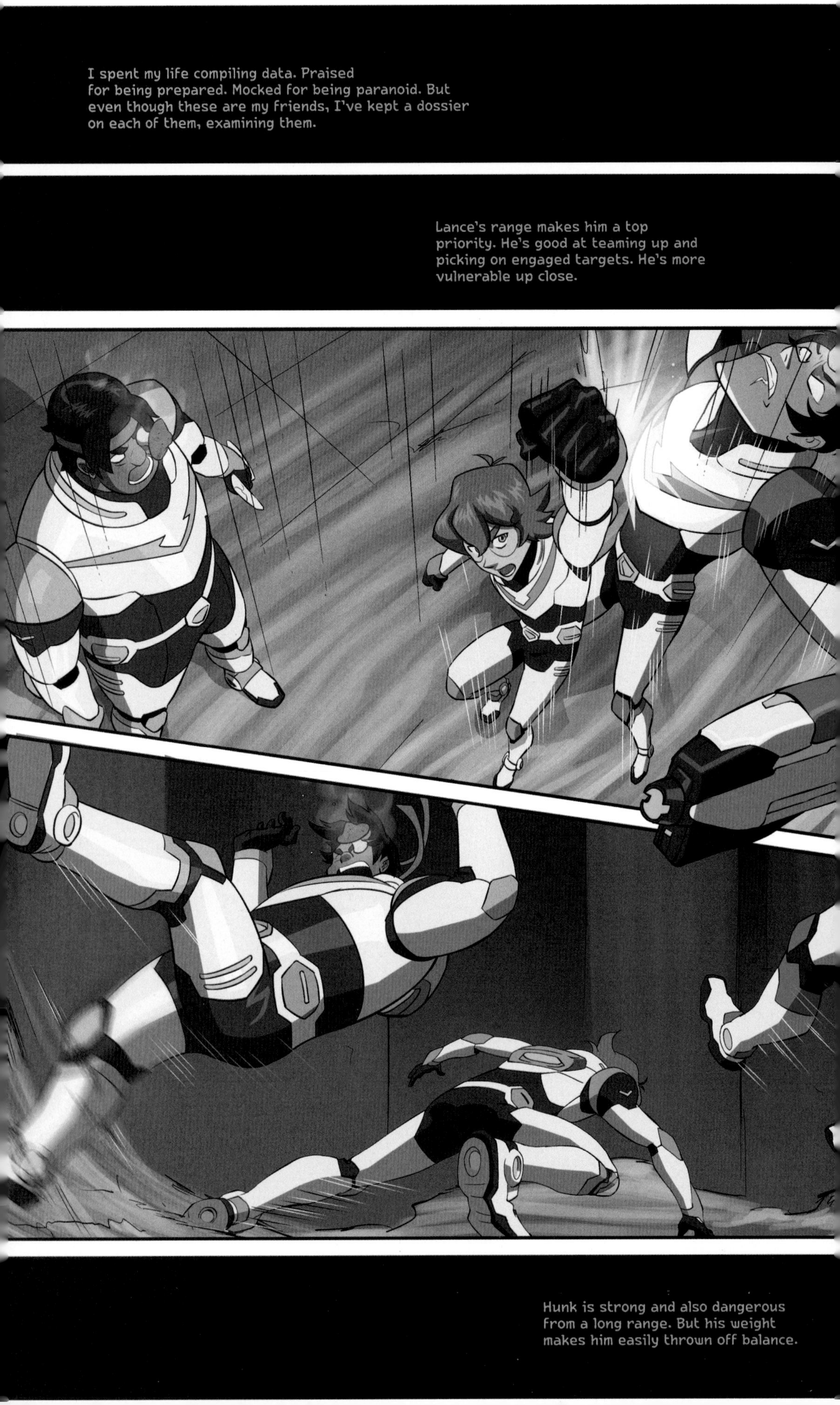
I spent my life compiling data. Praised for being prepared. Mocked for being paranoid. But even though these are my friends, I've kept a dossier on each of them, examining them.
Lance's range makes him a top priority. He's good at teaming up and picking on engaged targets. He's more vulnerable up close.
Hunk is strong and also dangerous from a long range. But his weight makes him easily thrown off balance.

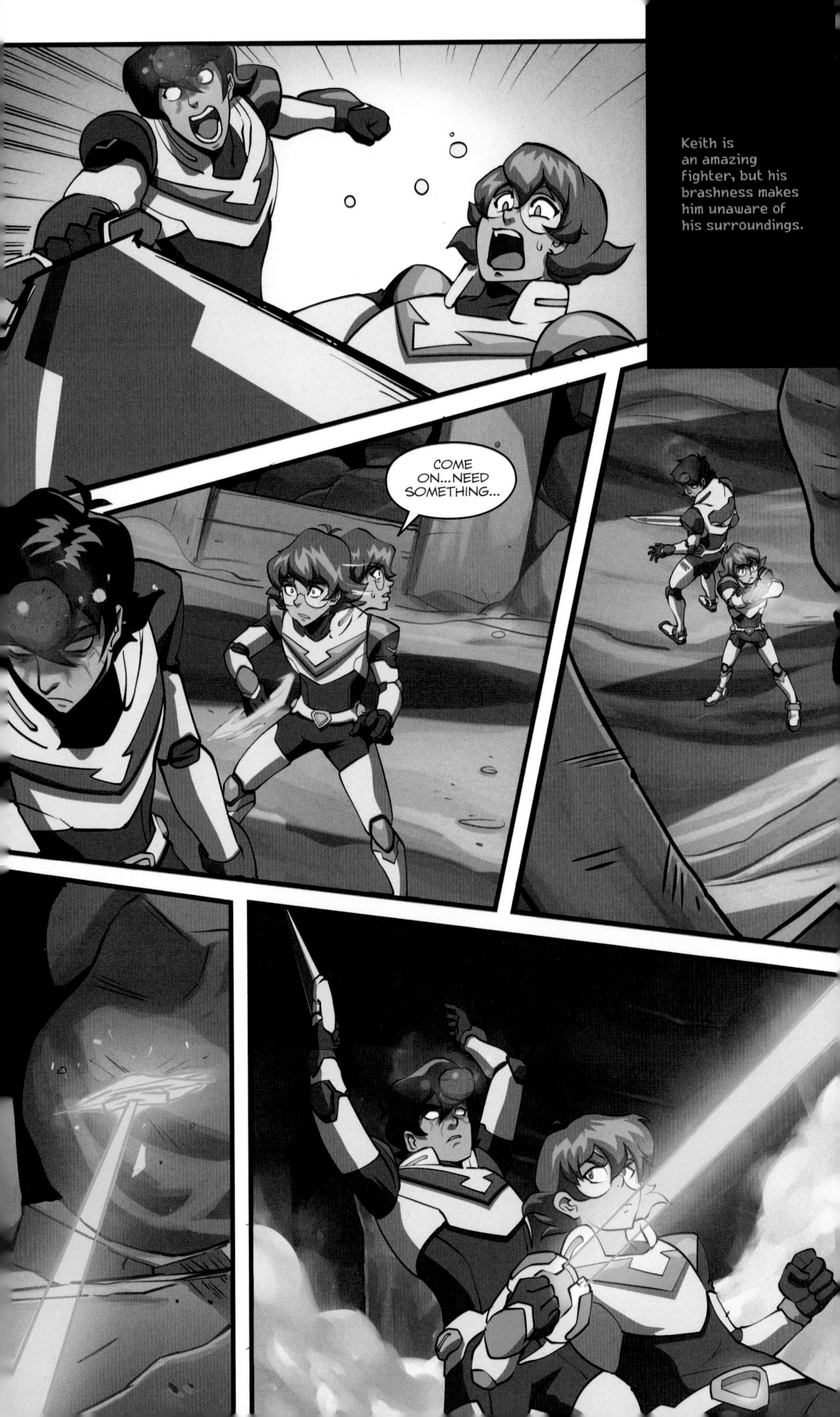
Keith is an amazing fighter, but his brashness makes him unaware of his surroundings.
COME ON...NEED SOMETHING...

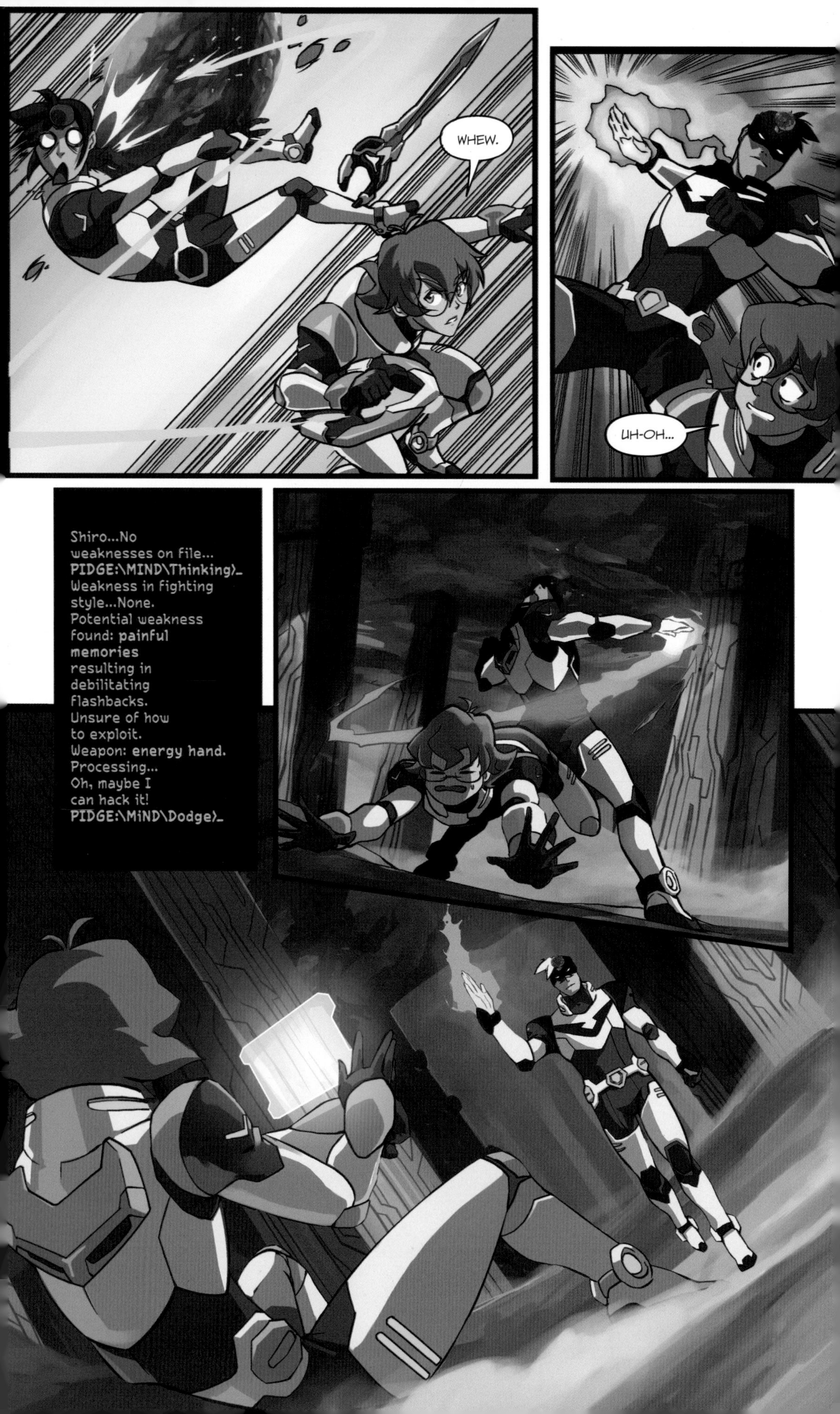
WHEW.
UH-OH...
Shiro...No weaknesses on file...
PIDGE:\MIND\Thinking>_
Weakness in fighting style...None.
Potential weakness found: painful memories resulting in debilitating flashbacks.
Unsure of how to exploit.
Weapon: energy hand.
Processing...
Oh, maybe I can hack it!
PIDGE:\MiND\Dodge>_

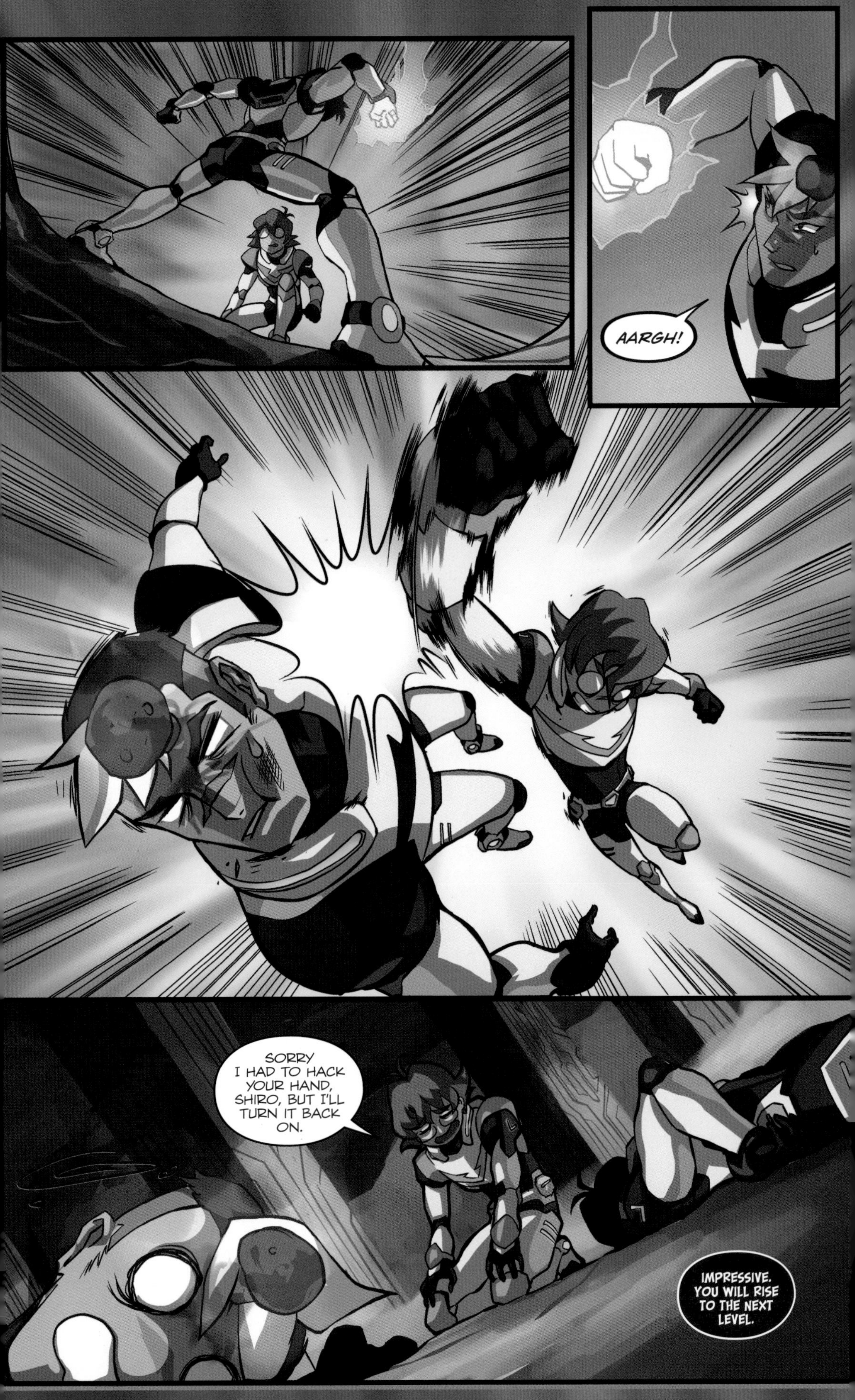
AARGH!
SORRY I HAD TO HACK YOUR HAND, SHIRO, BUT I'LL TURN IT BACK ON.
IMPRESSIVE. YOU WILL RISE TO THE NEXT LEVEL.

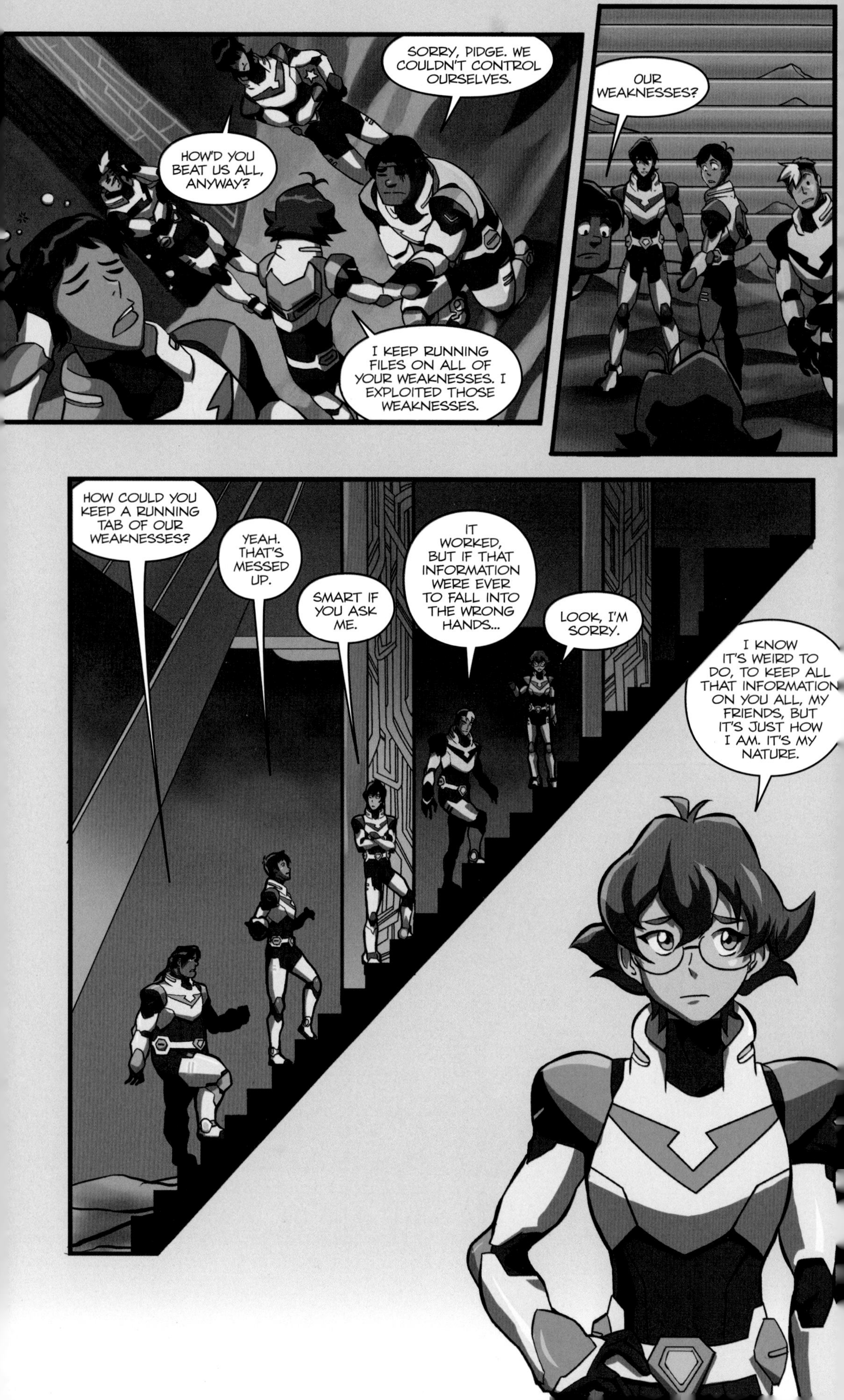
HOW'D YOU BEAT US ALL, ANYWAY?
SORRY, PIDGE. WE COULDN'T CONTROL OURSELVES.
I KEEP RUNNING FILES ON ALL OF YOUR WEAKNESSES. I EXPLOITED THOSE WEAKNESSES.
OUR WEAKNESSES?
HOW COULD YOU KEEP A RUNNING TAB OF OUR WEAKNESSES?
YEAH. THAT'S MESSED UP.
SMART IF YOU ASK ME.
IT WORKED, BUT IF THAT INFORMATION WERE EVER TO FALL INTO THE WRONG HANDS...
LOOK, I'M SORRY.
I KNOW IT'S WEIRD TO DO, TO KEEP ALL THAT INFORMATION ON YOU ALL, MY FRIENDS, BUT IT'S JUST HOW I AM. IT'S MY NATURE.

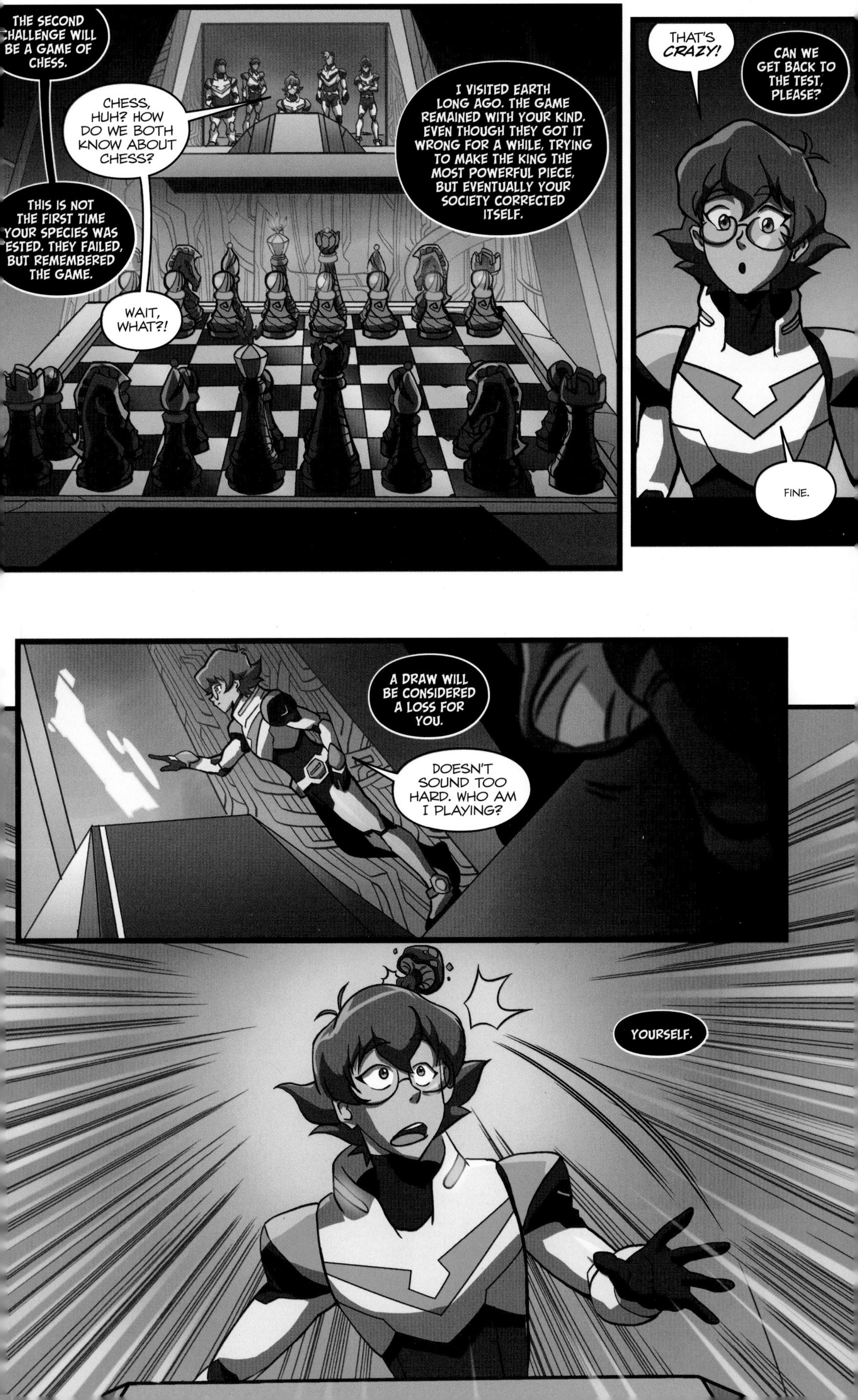
THE SECOND HALLENGE WILL BE A GAME OF CHESS.
CHESS, HUH? HOW DO WE BOTH KNOW ABOUT CHESS?
THIS IS NOT THE FIRST TIME YOUR SPECIES WAS ESTED. THEY FAILED, BUT REMEMBERED THE GAME.
WAIT, WHAT?!
I VISITED EARTH LONG AGO. THE GAME REMAINED WITH YOUR KIND. EVEN THOUGH THEY GOT IT WRONG FOR A WHILE, TRYING TO MAKE THE KING THE MOST POWERFUL PIECE, BUT EVENTUALLY YOUR SOCIETY CORRECTED ITSELF.
THAT'S *CRAZY!*
CAN WE GET BACK TO THE TEST, PLEASE?
FINE.
A DRAW WILL BE CONSIDERED A LOSS FOR YOU.
DOESN'T SOUND TOO HARD. WHO AM I PLAYING?
YOURSELF.

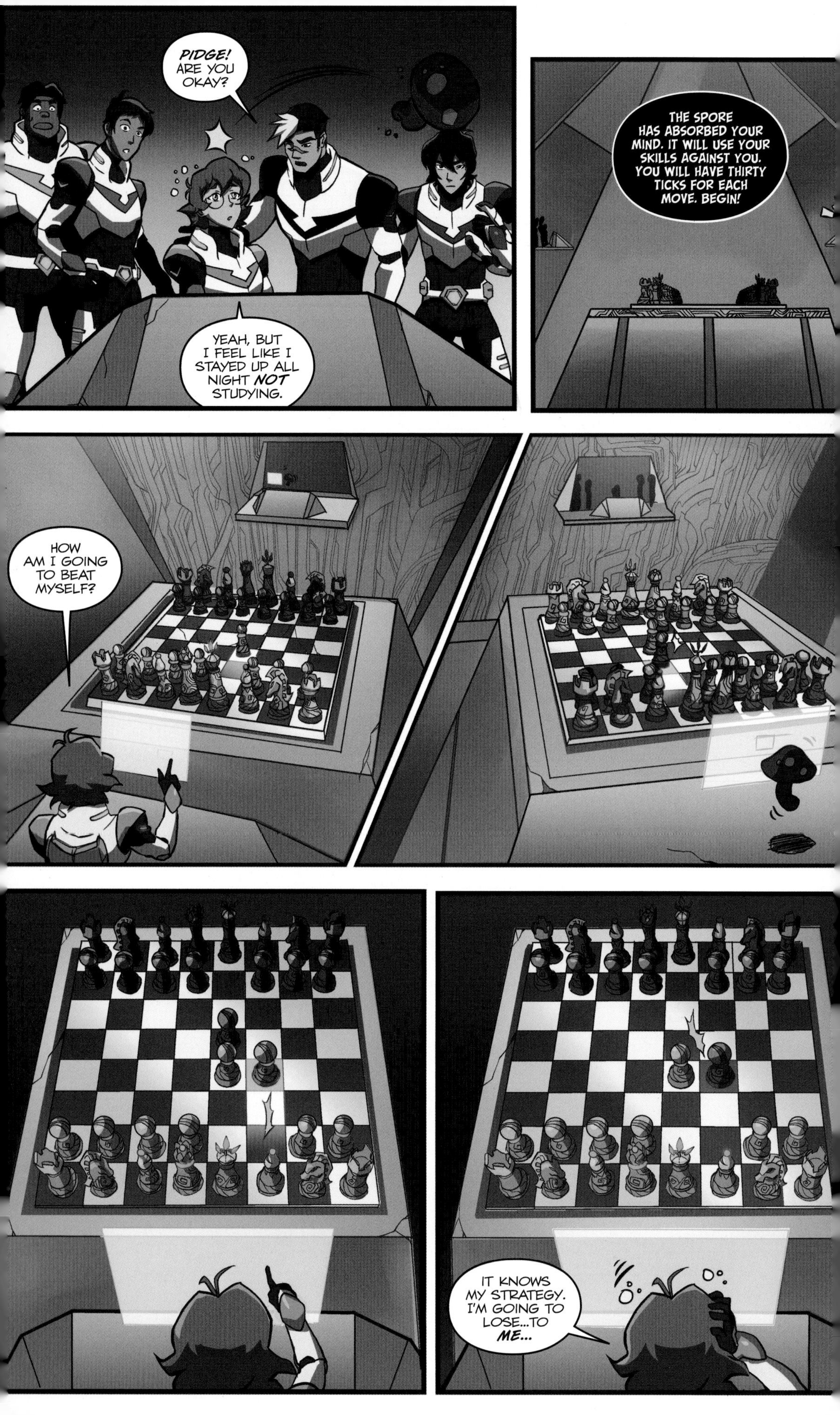
PIDGE! ARE YOU OKAY?
YEAH, BUT I FEEL LIKE I STAYED UP ALL NIGHT NOT STUDYING.
THE SPORE HAS ABSORBED YOUR MIND. IT WILL USE YOUR SKILLS AGAINST YOU. YOU WILL HAVE THIRTY TICKS FOR EACH MOVE. BEGIN!
HOW AM I GOING TO BEAT MYSELF?
IT KNOWS MY STRATEGY. I'M GOING TO LOSE...TO ME...

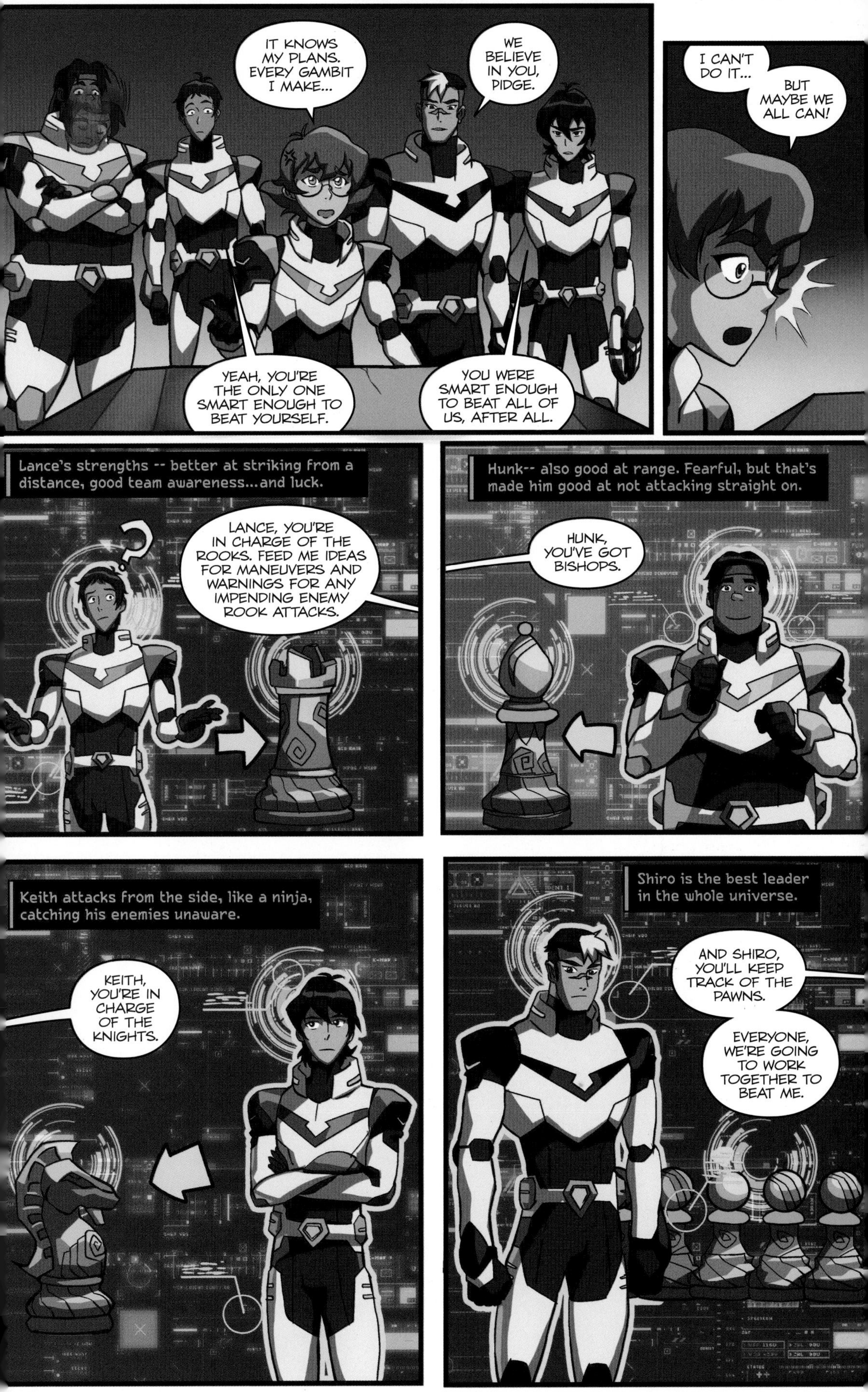
IT KNOWS MY PLANS. EVERY GAMBIT I MAKE...
WE BELIEVE IN YOU, PIDGE.
YEAH, YOU'RE THE ONLY ONE SMART ENOUGH TO BEAT YOURSELF.
YOU WERE SMART ENOUGH TO BEAT ALL OF US, AFTER ALL.
I CAN'T DO IT...
BUT MAYBE WE ALL CAN!
Lance's strengths -- better at striking from a distance, good team awareness...and luck.
LANCE, YOU'RE IN CHARGE OF THE ROOKS. FEED ME IDEAS FOR MANEUVERS AND WARNINGS FOR ANY IMPENDING ENEMY ROOK ATTACKS.
Hunk-- also good at range. Fearful, but that's made him good at not attacking straight on.
HUNK, YOU'VE GOT BISHOPS.
Keith attacks from the side, like a ninja, catching his enemies unaware.
KEITH, YOU'RE IN CHARGE OF THE KNIGHTS.
Shiro is the best leader in the whole universe.
AND SHIRO, YOU'LL KEEP TRACK OF THE PAWNS.
EVERYONE, WE'RE GOING TO WORK TOGETHER TO BEAT ME.

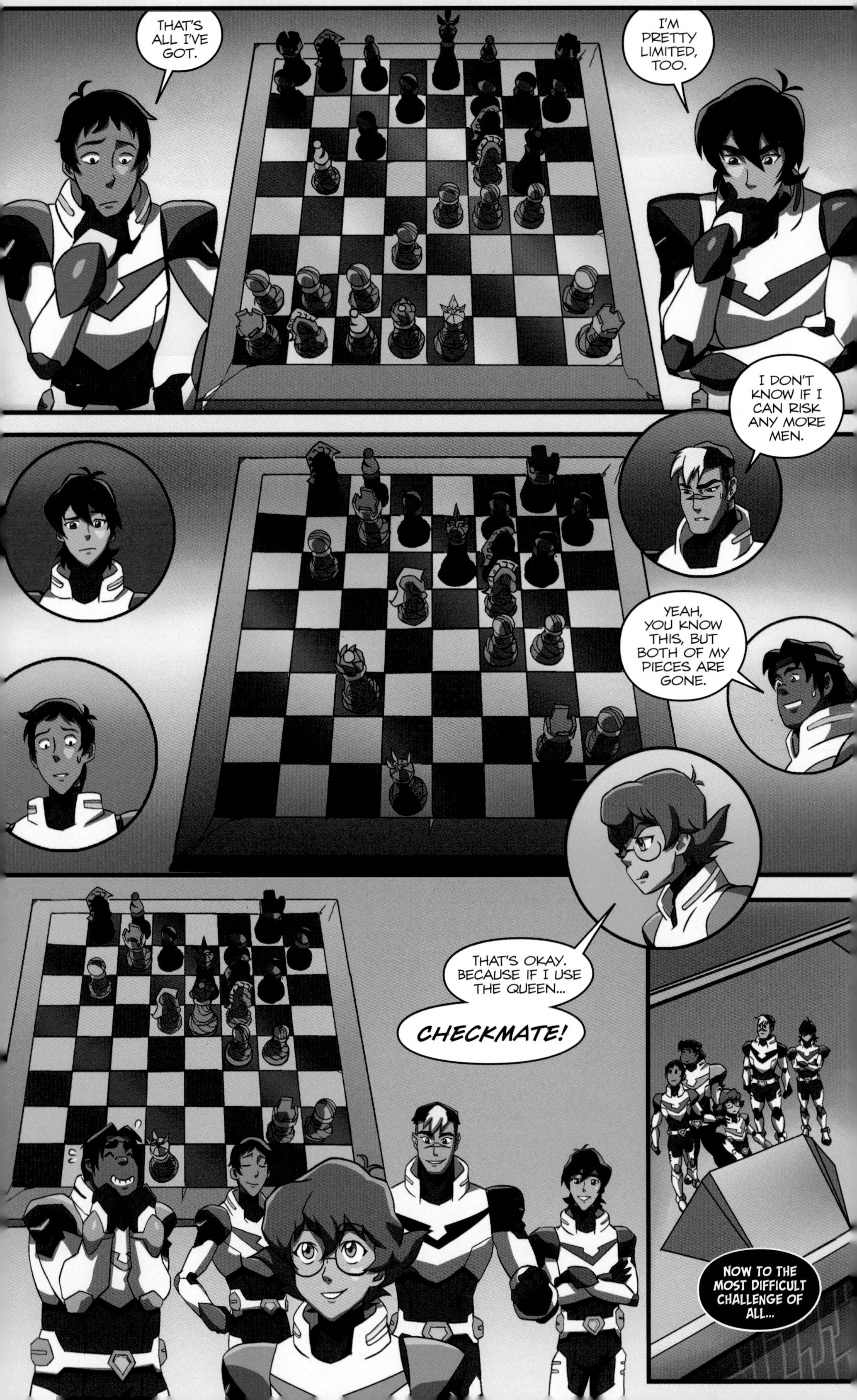

THAT'S ALL I'VE GOT.
I'M PRETTY LIMITED, TOO.
I DON'T KNOW IF I CAN RISK ANY MORE MEN.
YEAH, YOU KNOW THIS, BUT BOTH OF MY PIECES ARE GONE.
THAT'S OKAY. BECAUSE IF I USE THE QUEEN...
CHECKMATE!
NOW TO THE MOST DIFFICULT CHALLENGE OF ALL...

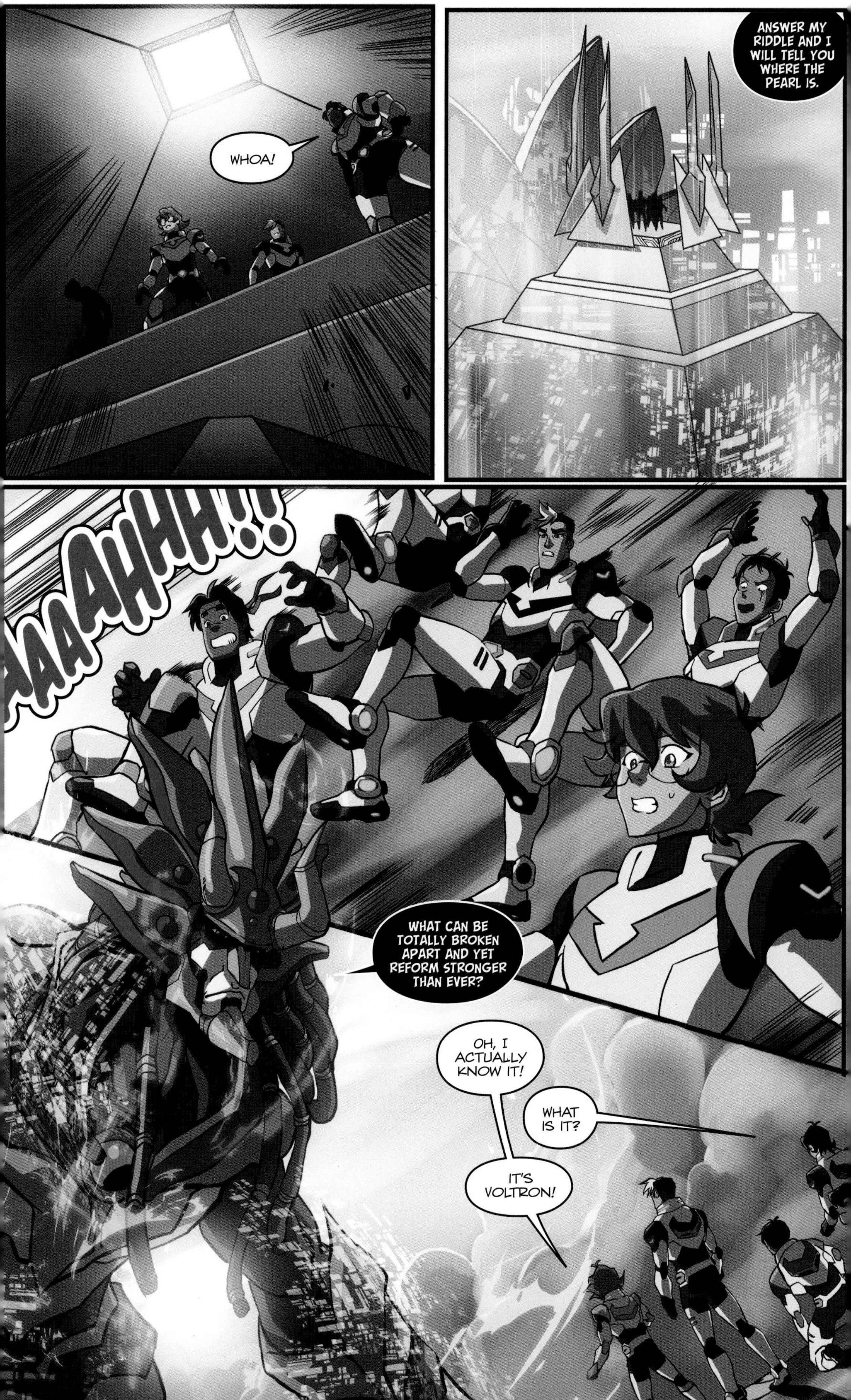
WHOA!
ANSWER MY RIDDLE AND I WILL TELL YOU WHERE THE PEARL IS.
AAAAHHH!!
WHAT CAN BE TOTALLY BROKEN APART AND YET REFORM STRONGER THAN EVER?
OH, I ACTUALLY KNOW IT!
WHAT IS IT?
IT'S VOLTRON!

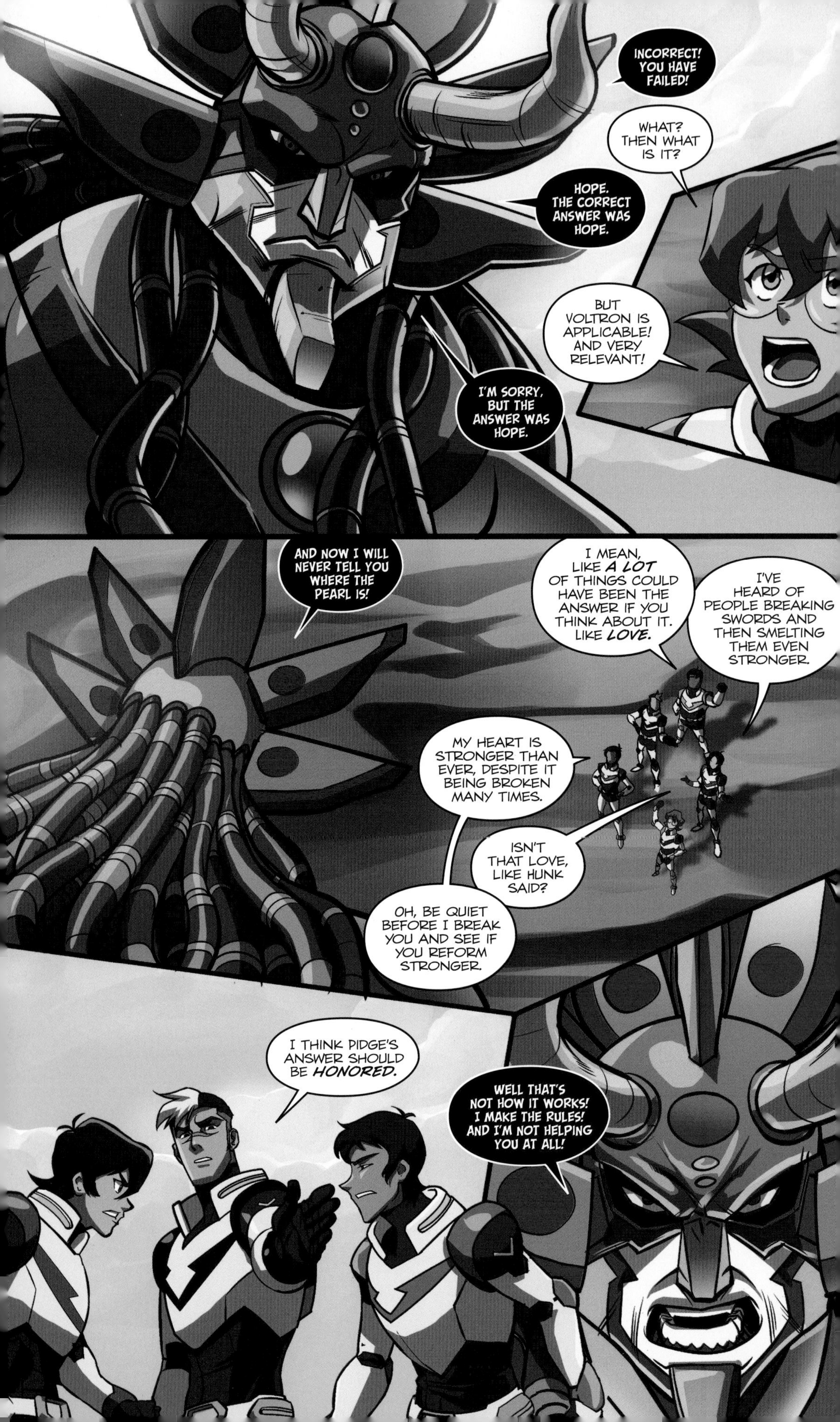
INCORRECT! YOU HAVE FAILED!
WHAT? THEN WHAT IS IT?
HOPE. THE CORRECT ANSWER WAS HOPE.
BUT VOLTRON IS APPLICABLE! AND VERY RELEVANT!
I'M SORRY, BUT THE ANSWER WAS HOPE.
AND NOW I WILL NEVER TELL YOU WHERE THE PEARL IS!
I MEAN, LIKE A LOT OF THINGS COULD HAVE BEEN THE ANSWER IF YOU THINK ABOUT IT. LIKE LOVE.
I'VE HEARD OF PEOPLE BREAKING SWORDS AND THEN SMELTING THEM EVEN STRONGER.
MY HEART IS STRONGER THAN EVER, DESPITE IT BEING BROKEN MANY TIMES.
ISN'T THAT LOVE, LIKE HUNK SAID?
OH, BE QUIET BEFORE I BREAK YOU AND SEE IF YOU REFORM STRONGER.
I THINK PIDGE'S ANSWER SHOULD BE HONORED.
WELL THAT'S NOT HOW IT WORKS! I MAKE THE RULES! AND I'M NOT HELPING YOU AT ALL!

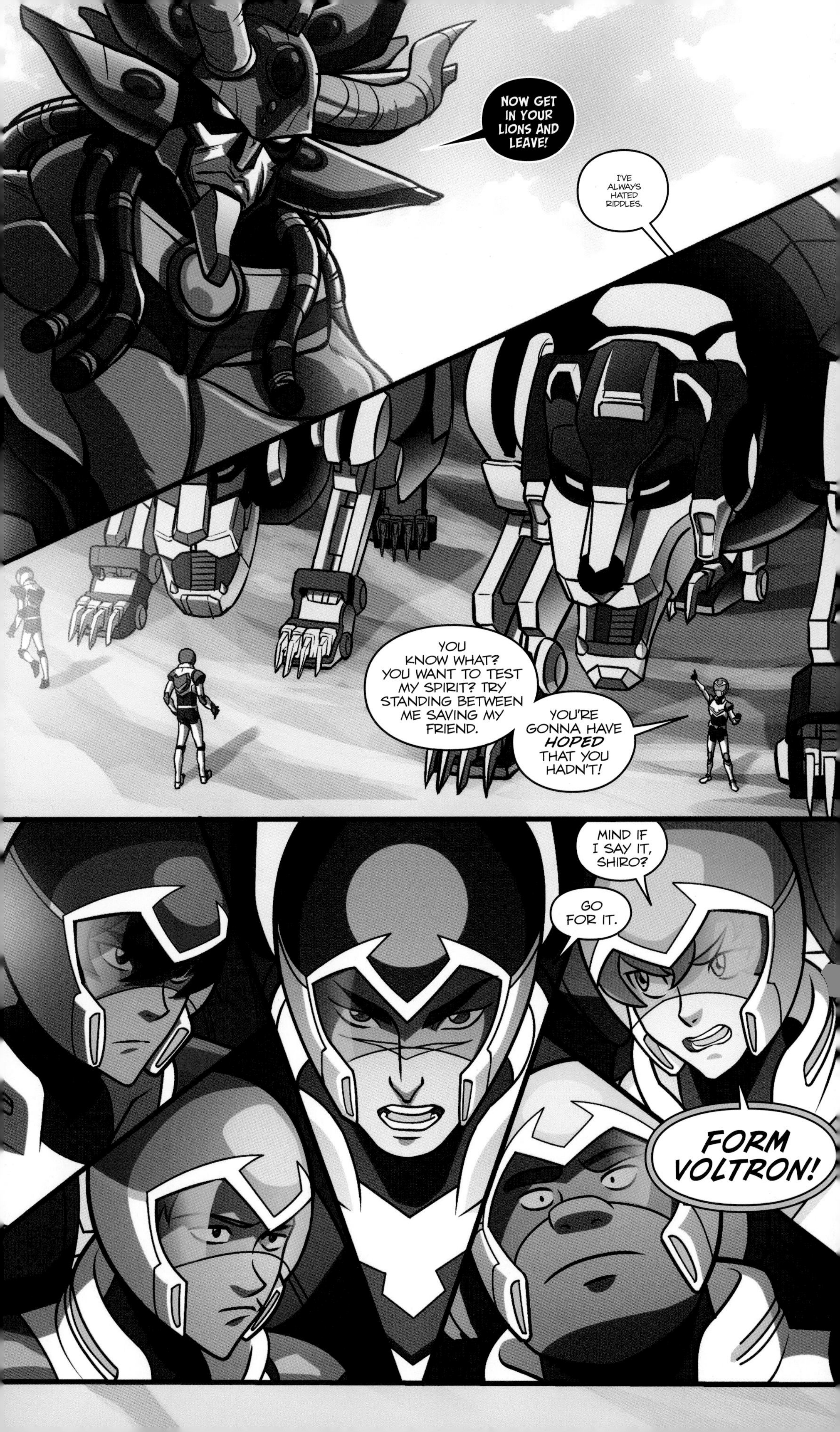
NOW GET IN YOUR LIONS AND LEAVE!
I'VE ALWAYS HATED RIDDLES.
YOU KNOW WHAT? YOU WANT TO TEST MY SPIRIT? TRY STANDING BETWEEN ME SAVING MY FRIEND.
YOU'RE GONNA HAVE HOPED THAT YOU HADN'T!
MIND IF I SAY IT, SHIRO?
GO FOR IT.
FORM VOLTRON!

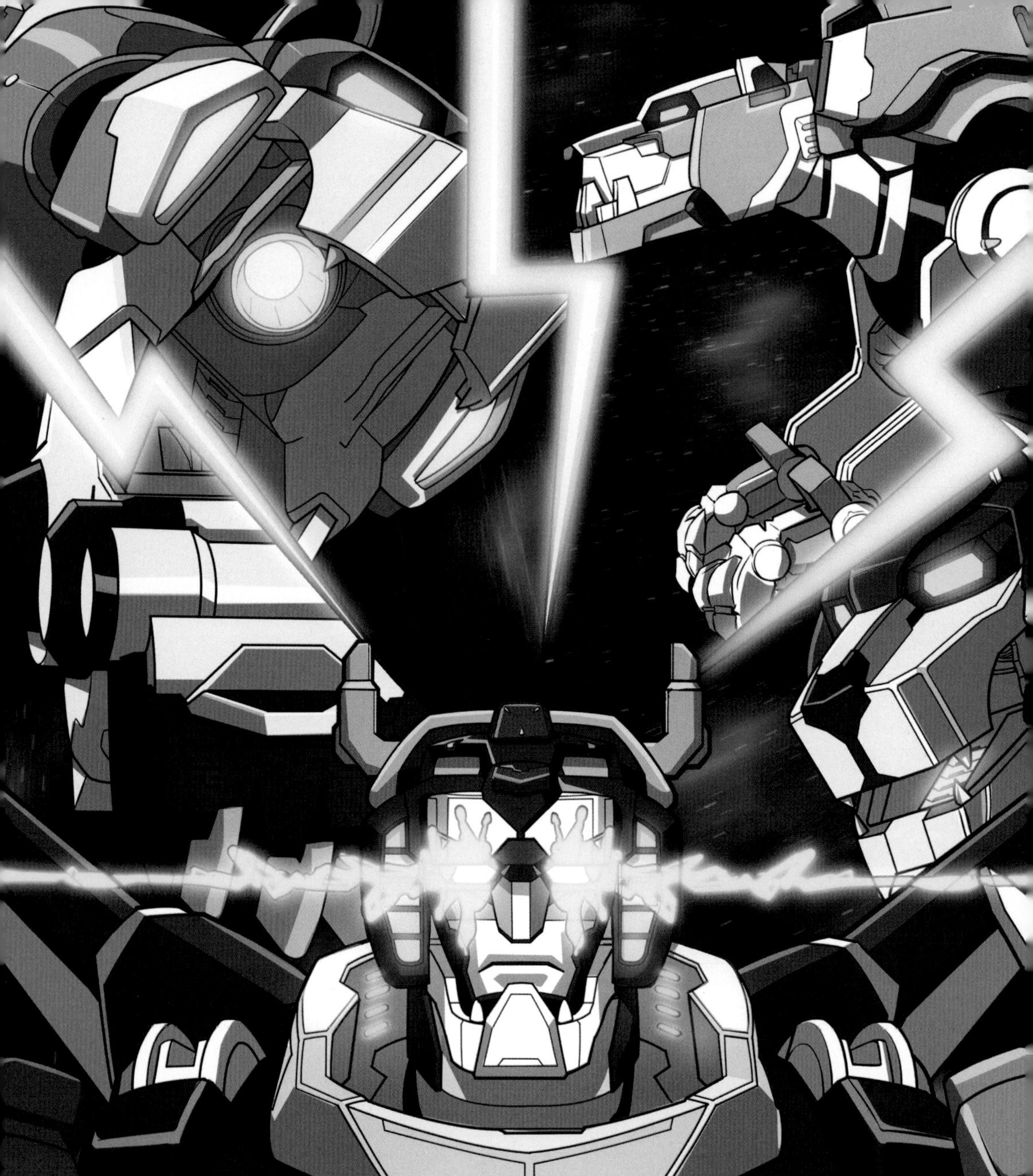

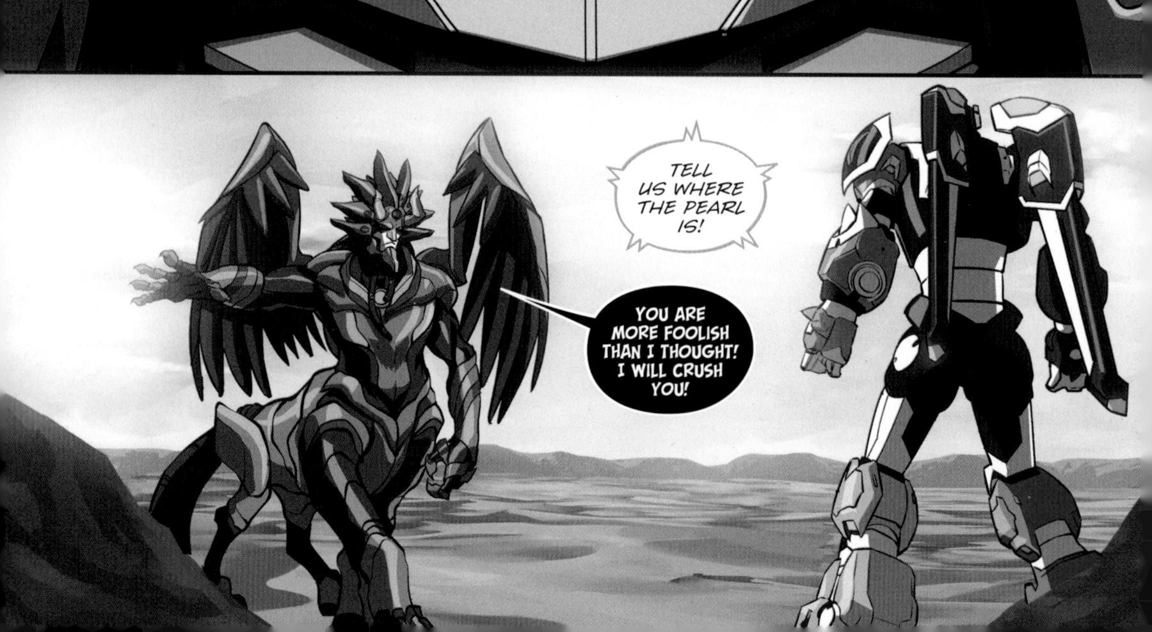
TELL US WHERE THE PEARL IS!
YOU ARE MORE FOOLISH THAN I THOUGHT! I WILL CRUSH YOU!

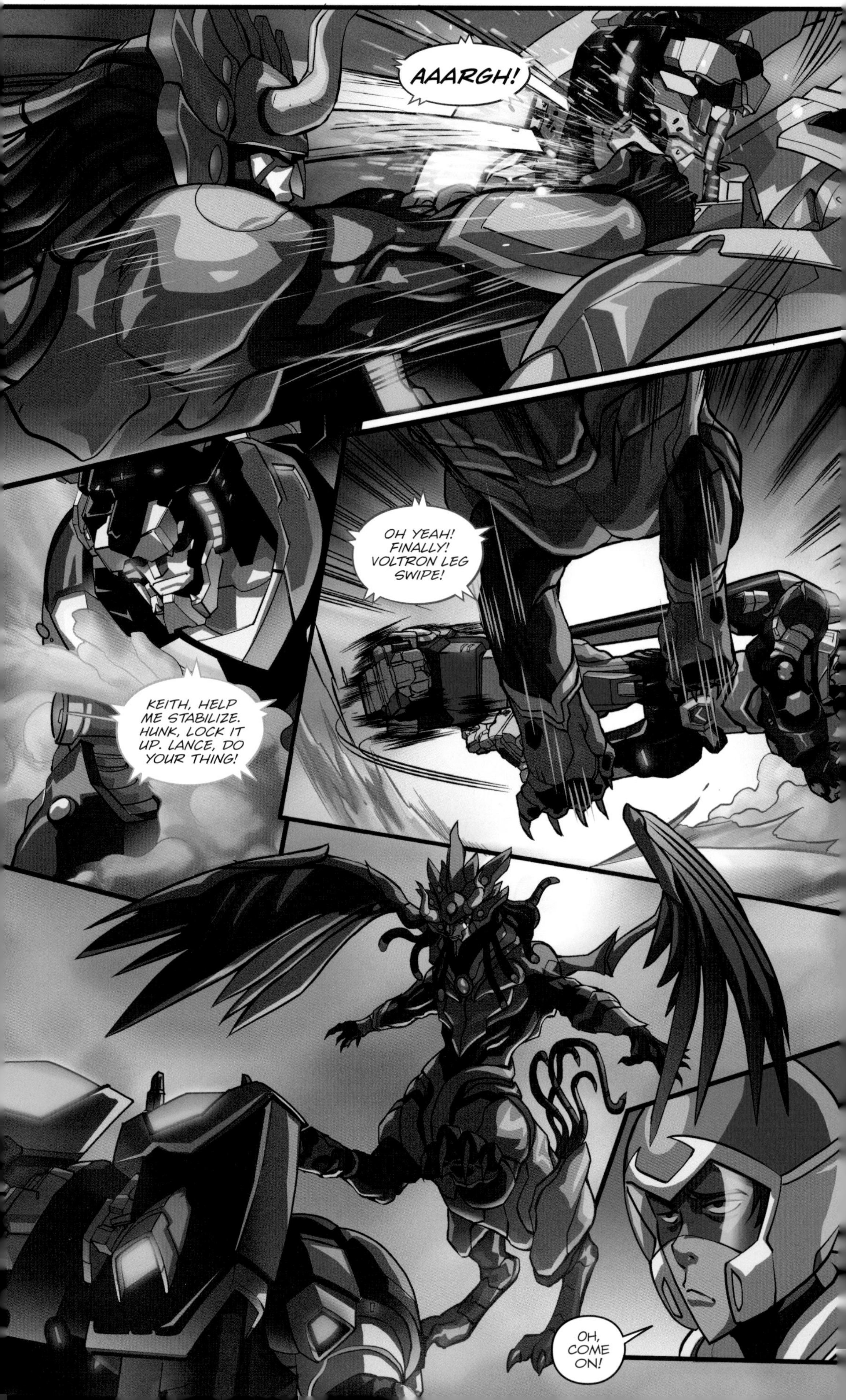
AAARGH!
OH YEAH! FINALLY! VOLTRON LEG SWIPE!
KEITH, HELP ME STABILIZE. HUNK, LOCK IT UP. LANCE, DO YOUR THING!
OH, COME ON!

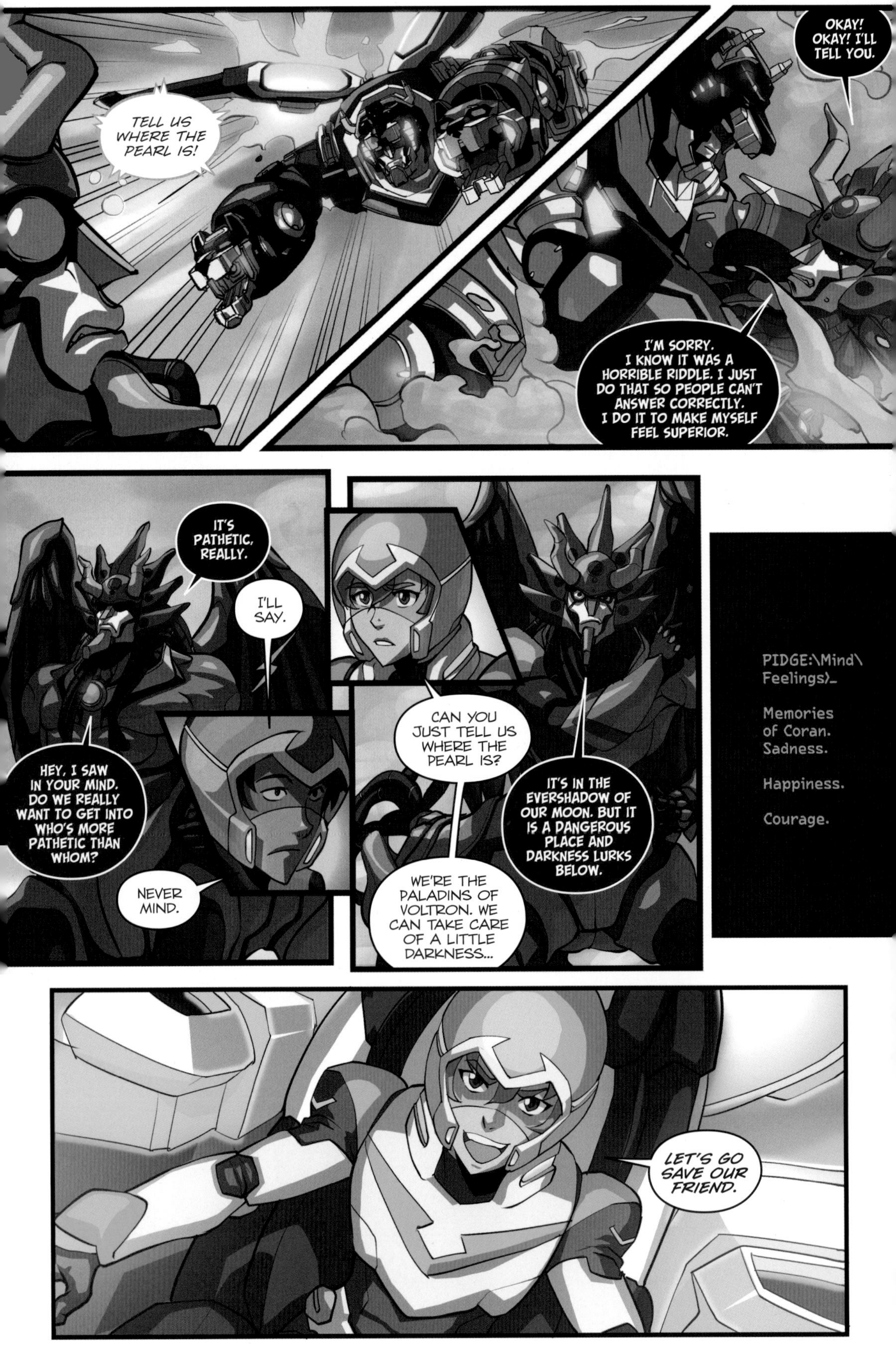
TELL US WHERE THE PEARL IS!
OKAY! OKAY! I'LL TELL YOU.
I'M SORRY. I KNOW IT WAS A HORRIBLE RIDDLE. I JUST DO THAT SO PEOPLE CAN'T ANSWER CORRECTLY. I DO IT TO MAKE MYSELF FEEL SUPERIOR.
IT'S PATHETIC, REALLY.
I'LL SAY.
HEY, I SAW IN YOUR MIND. DO WE REALLY WANT TO GET INTO WHO'S MORE PATHETIC THAN WHOM?
NEVER MIND.
CAN YOU JUST TELL US WHERE THE PEARL IS?
IT'S IN THE EVERSHADOW OF OUR MOON. BUT IT IS A DANGEROUS PLACE AND DARKNESS LURKS BELOW.
WE'RE THE PALADINS OF VOLTRON. WE CAN TAKE CARE OF A LITTLE DARKNESS...
PIDGE:\Mind\
Feelings>_
Memories of Coran. Sadness.
Happiness.
Courage.
LET'S GO SAVE OUR FRIEND.

CHAPTER FIVE:
THE INNER EYE

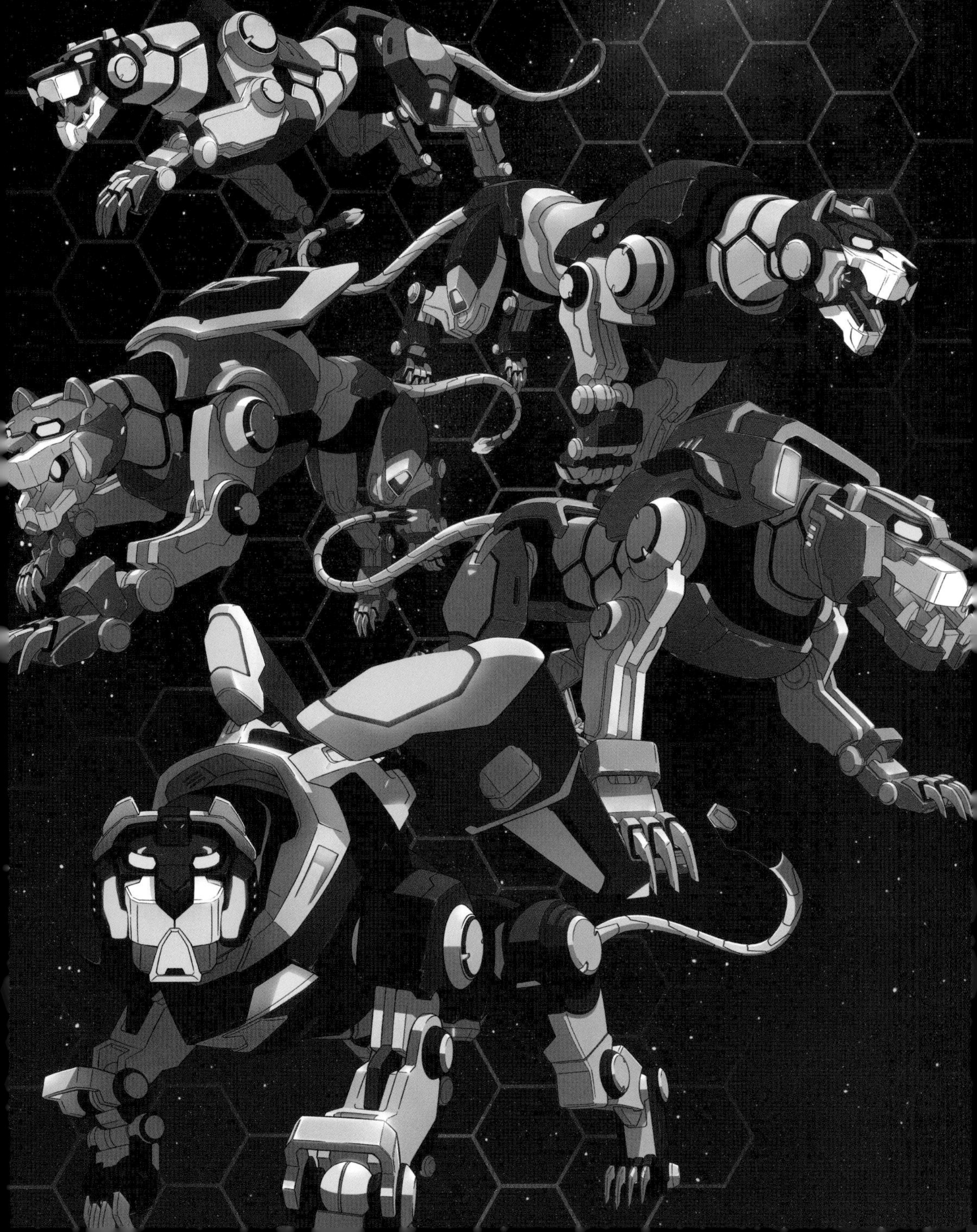

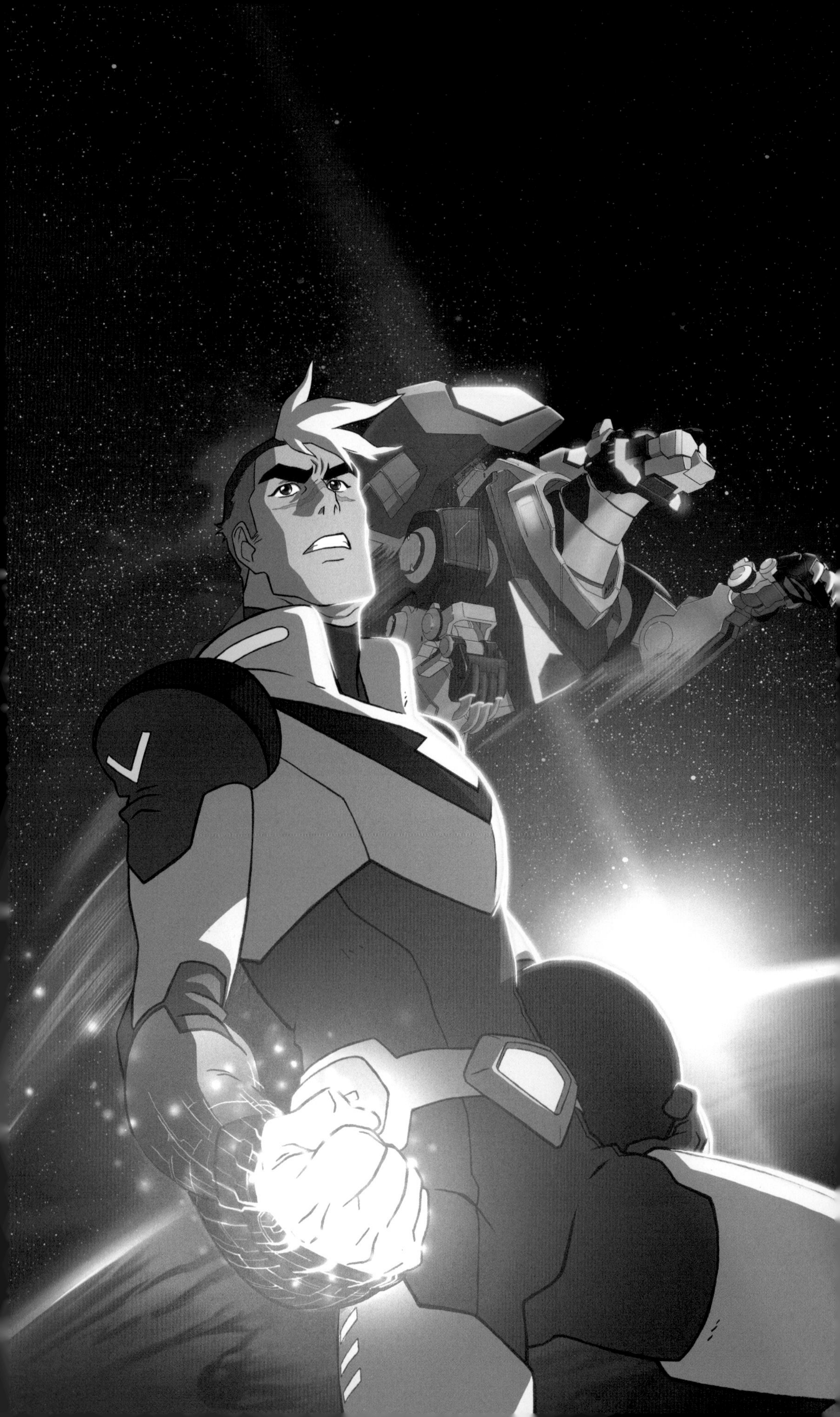

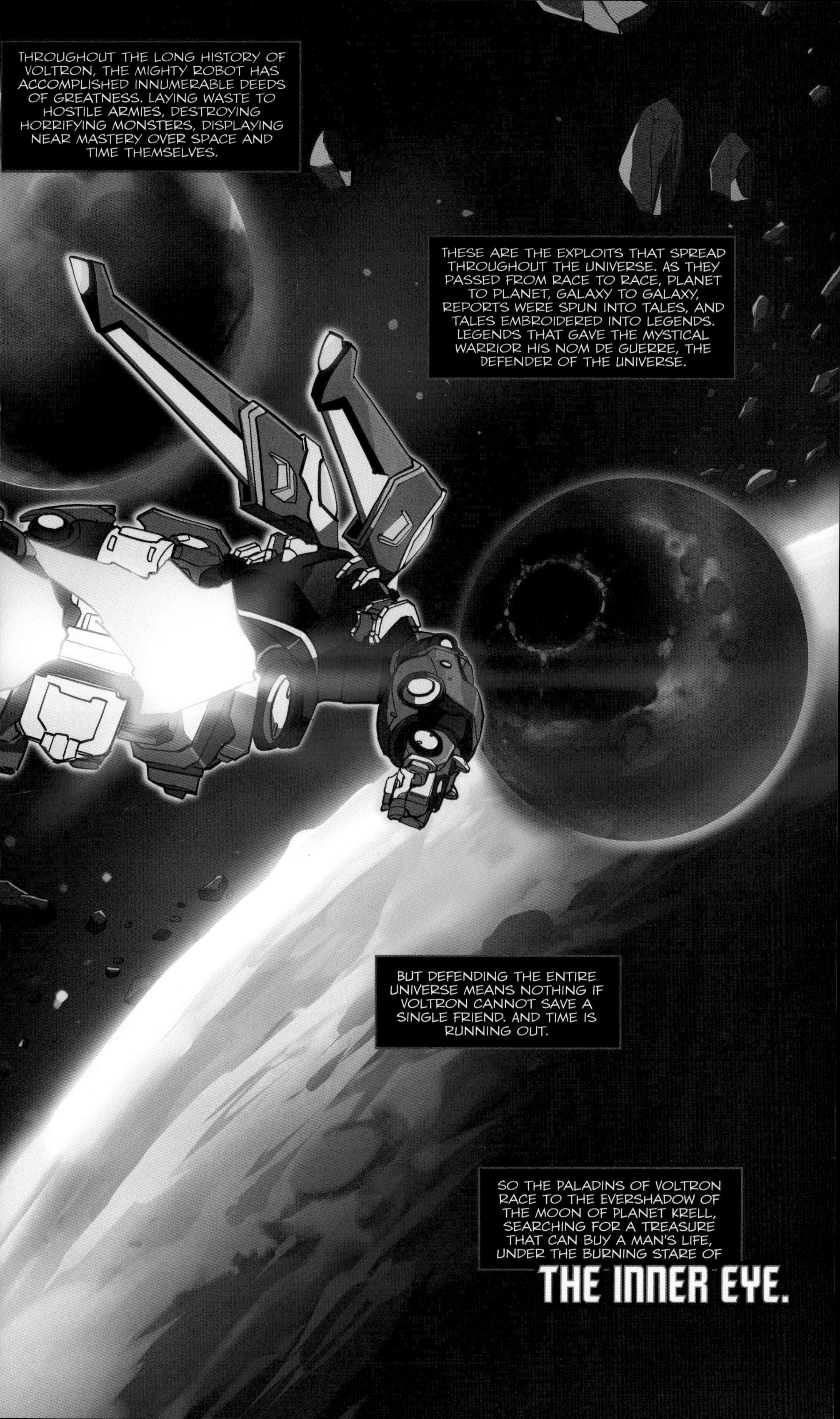
THROUGHOUT THE LONG HISTORY OF VOLTRON, THE MIGHTY ROBOT HAS ACCOMPLISHED INNUMERABLE DEEDS OF GREATNESS. LAYING WASTE TO HOSTILE ARMIES, DESTROYING HORRIFYING MONSTERS, DISPLAYING NEAR MASTERY OVER SPACE AND TIME THEMSELVES.
THESE ARE THE EXPLOITS THAT SPREAD THROUGHOUT THE UNIVERSE. AS THEY PASSED FROM RACE TO RACE, PLANET TO PLANET, GALAXY TO GALAXY, REPORTS WERE SPUN INTO TALES, AND TALES EMBROIDERED INTO LEGENDS. LEGENDS THAT GAVE THE MYSTICAL WARRIOR HIS NOM DE GUERRE, THE DEFENDER OF THE UNIVERSE.
BUT DEFENDING THE ENTIRE UNIVERSE MEANS NOTHING IF VOLTRON CANNOT SAVE A SINGLE FRIEND. AND TIME IS RUNNING OUT.
SO THE PALADINS OF VOLTRON RACE TO THE EVERSHADOW OF THE MOON OF PLANET KRELL, SEARCHING FOR A TREASURE THAT CAN BUY A MAN'S LIFE, UNDER THE BURNING STARE OF
THE INNER EYE.

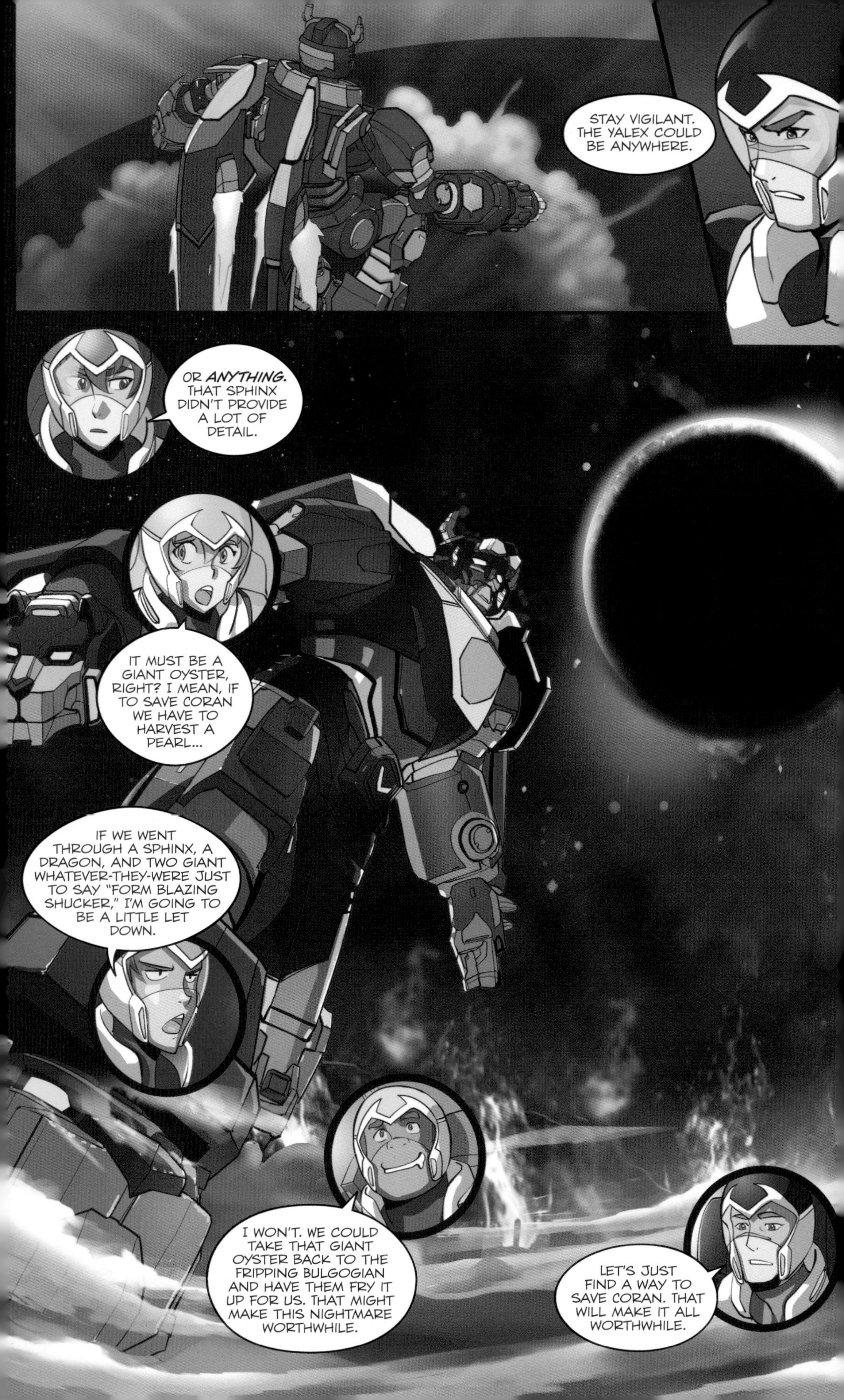
STAY VIGILANT. THE YALEX COULD BE ANYWHERE.
OR *ANYTHING.* THAT SPHINX DIDN'T PROVIDE A LOT OF DETAIL.
IT MUST BE A GIANT OYSTER, RIGHT? I MEAN, IF TO SAVE CORAN WE HAVE TO HARVEST A PEARL...
IF WE WENT THROUGH A SPHINX, A DRAGON, AND TWO GIANT WHATEVER-THEY-WERE JUST TO SAY "FORM BLAZING SHUCKER," I'M GOING TO BE A LITTLE LET DOWN.
I WON'T. WE COULD TAKE THAT GIANT OYSTER BACK TO THE FRIPPING BULGOGIAN AND HAVE THEM FRY IT UP FOR US. THAT MIGHT MAKE THIS NIGHTMARE WORTHWHILE.
LET'S JUST FIND A WAY TO SAVE CORAN. THAT WILL MAKE IT ALL WORTHWHILE.

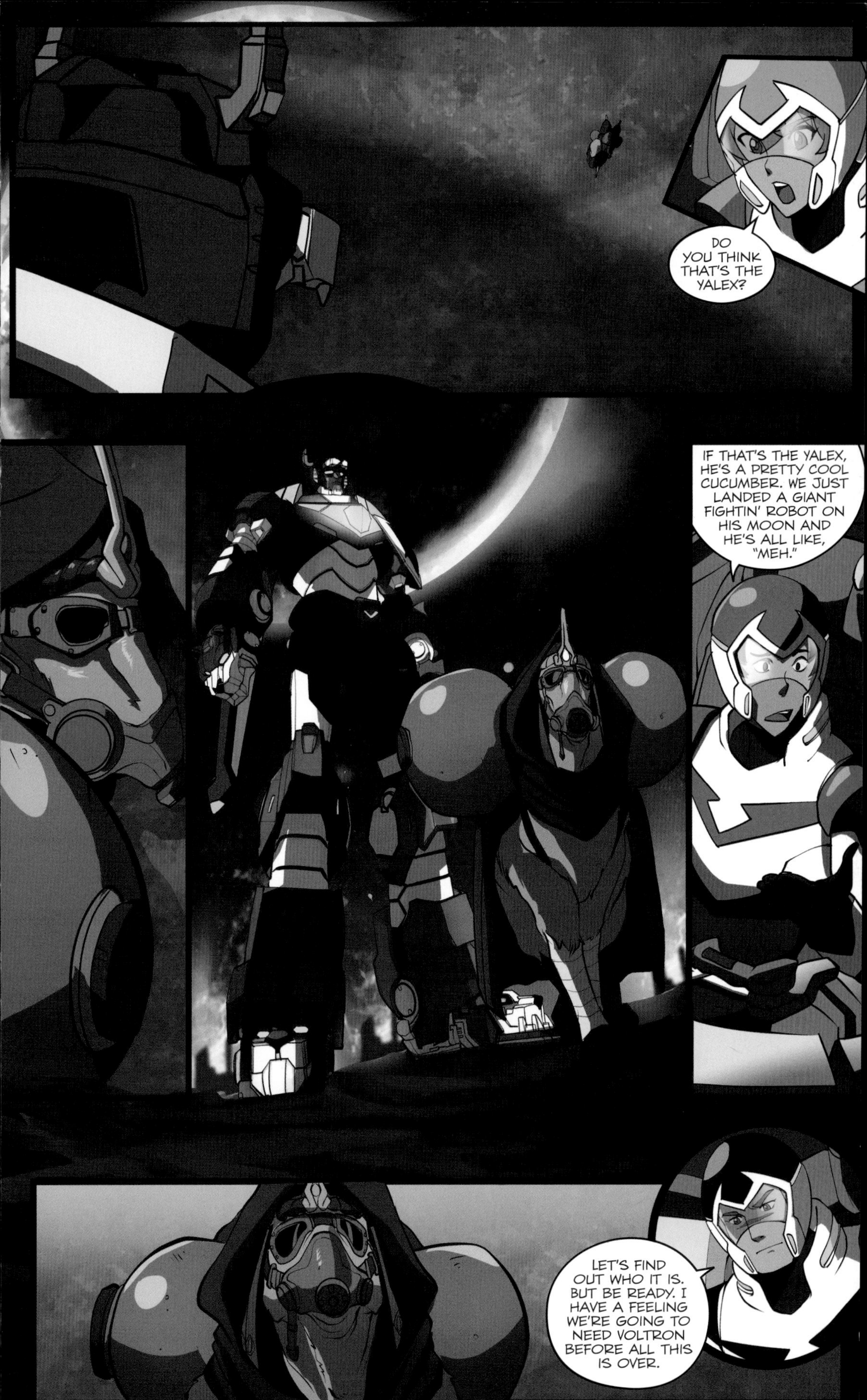
DO YOU THINK THAT'S THE YALEX?
IF THAT'S THE YALEX, HE'S A PRETTY COOL CUCUMBER. WE JUST LANDED A GIANT FIGHTIN' ROBOT ON HIS MOON AND HE'S ALL LIKE, "MEH."
LET'S FIND OUT WHO IT IS. BUT BE READY. I HAVE A FEELING WE'RE GOING TO NEED VOLTRON BEFORE ALL THIS IS OVER.

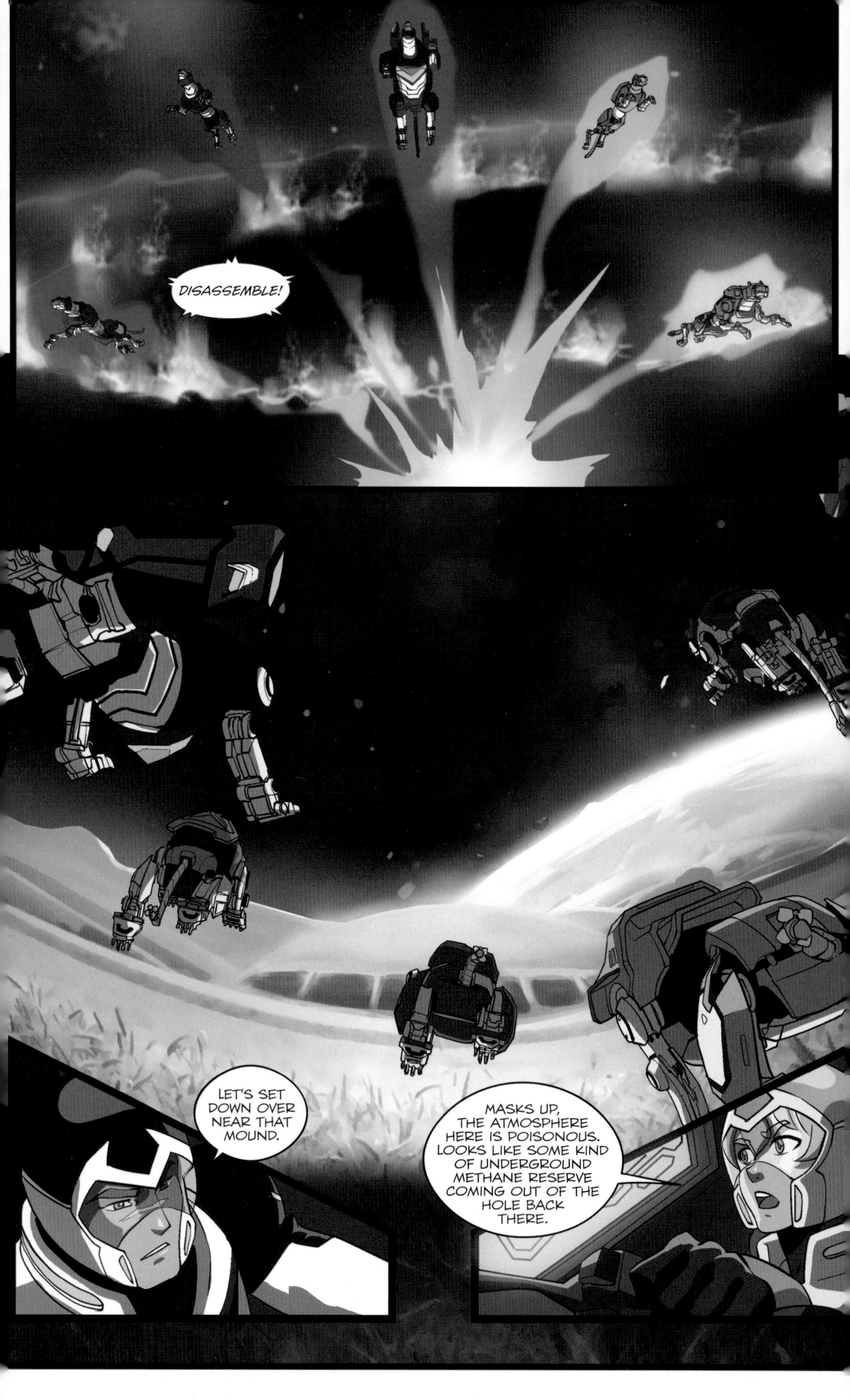
DISASSEMBLE!
LET'S SET DOWN OVER NEAR THAT MOUND.
MASKS UP, THE ATMOSPHERE HERE IS POISONOUS. LOOKS LIKE SOME KIND OF UNDERGROUND METHANE RESERVE COMING OUT OF THE HOLE BACK THERE.

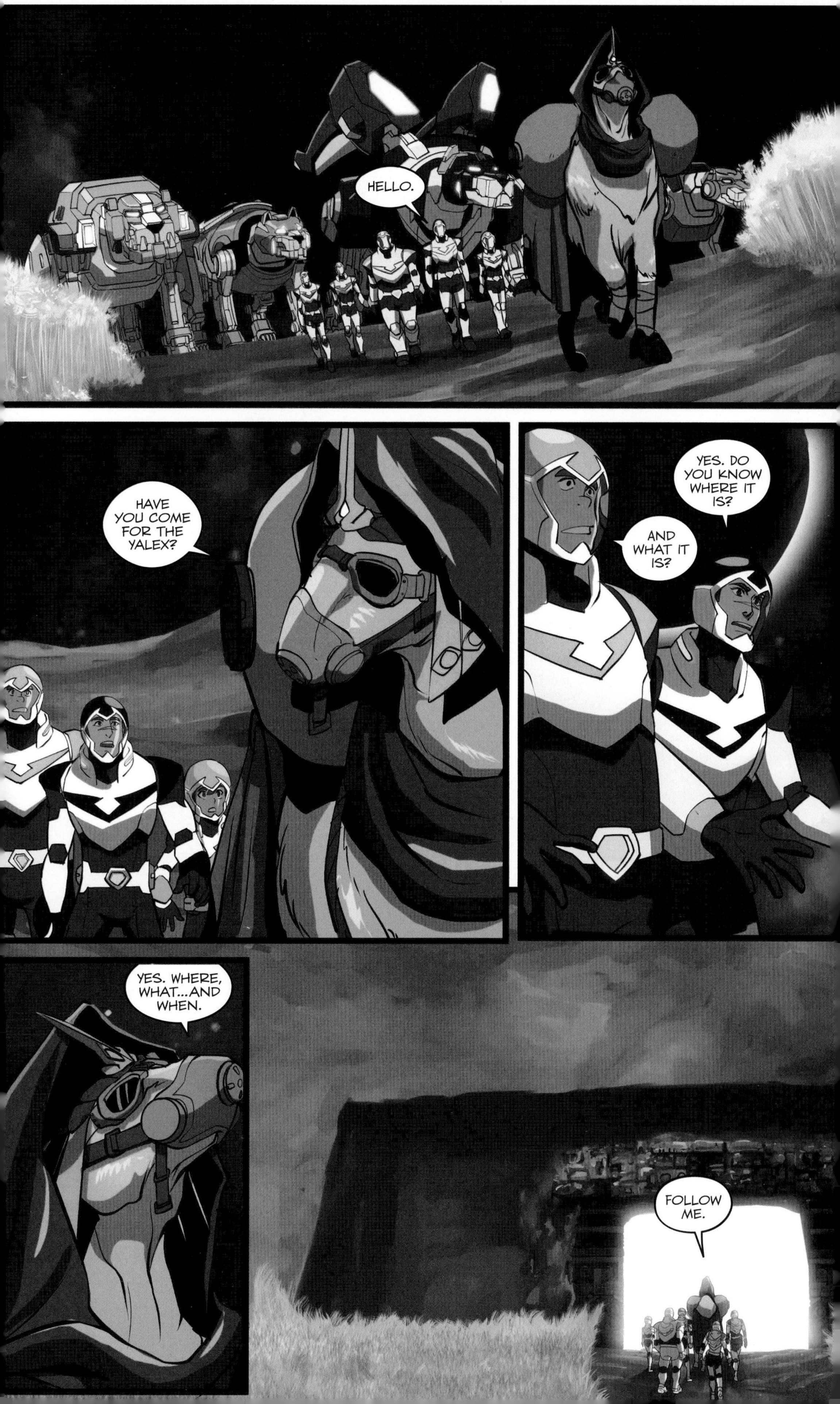
HELLO.
HAVE YOU COME FOR THE YALEX?
YES. DO YOU KNOW WHERE IT IS?
AND WHAT IT IS?
YES. WHERE, WHAT...AND WHEN.
FOLLOW ME.

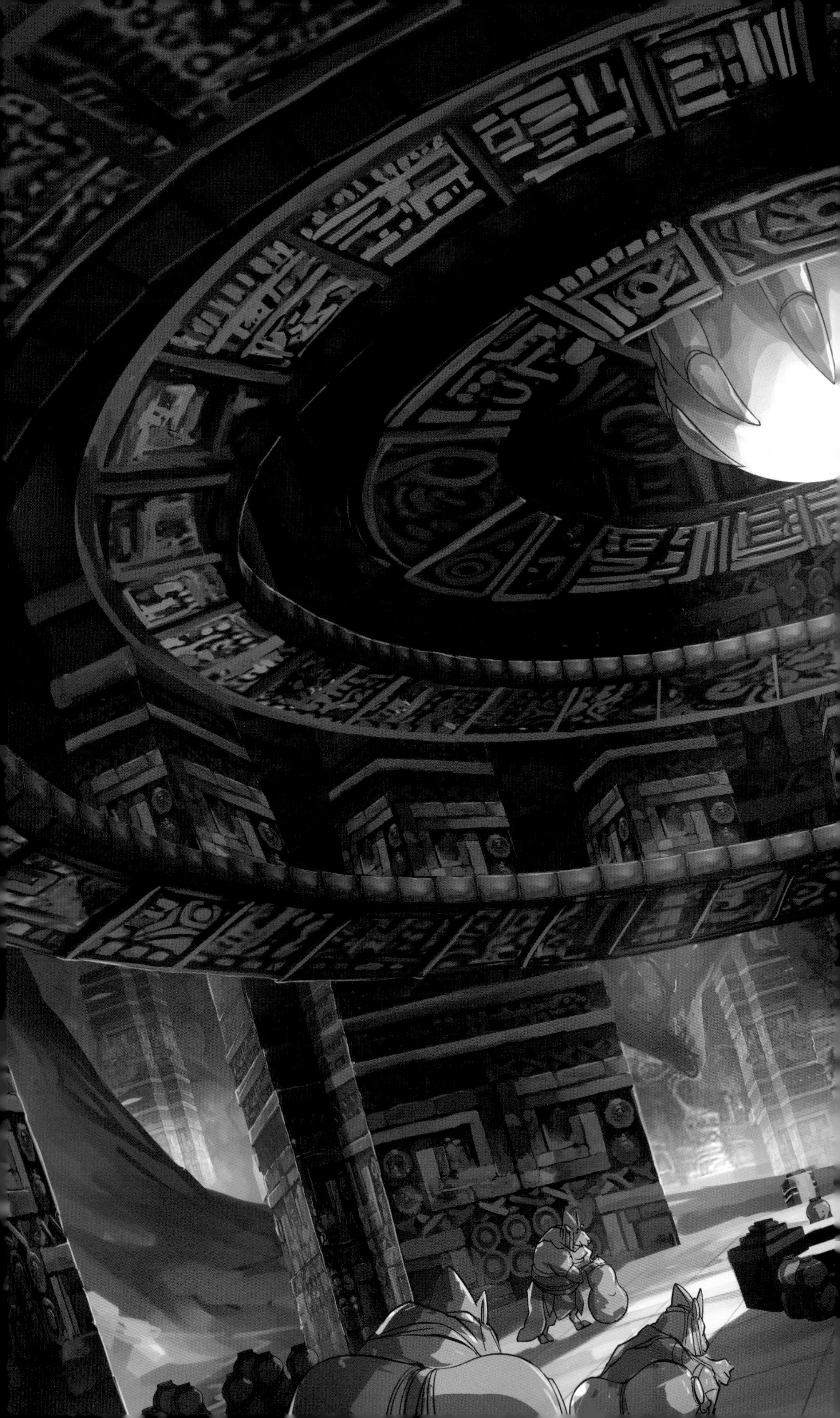

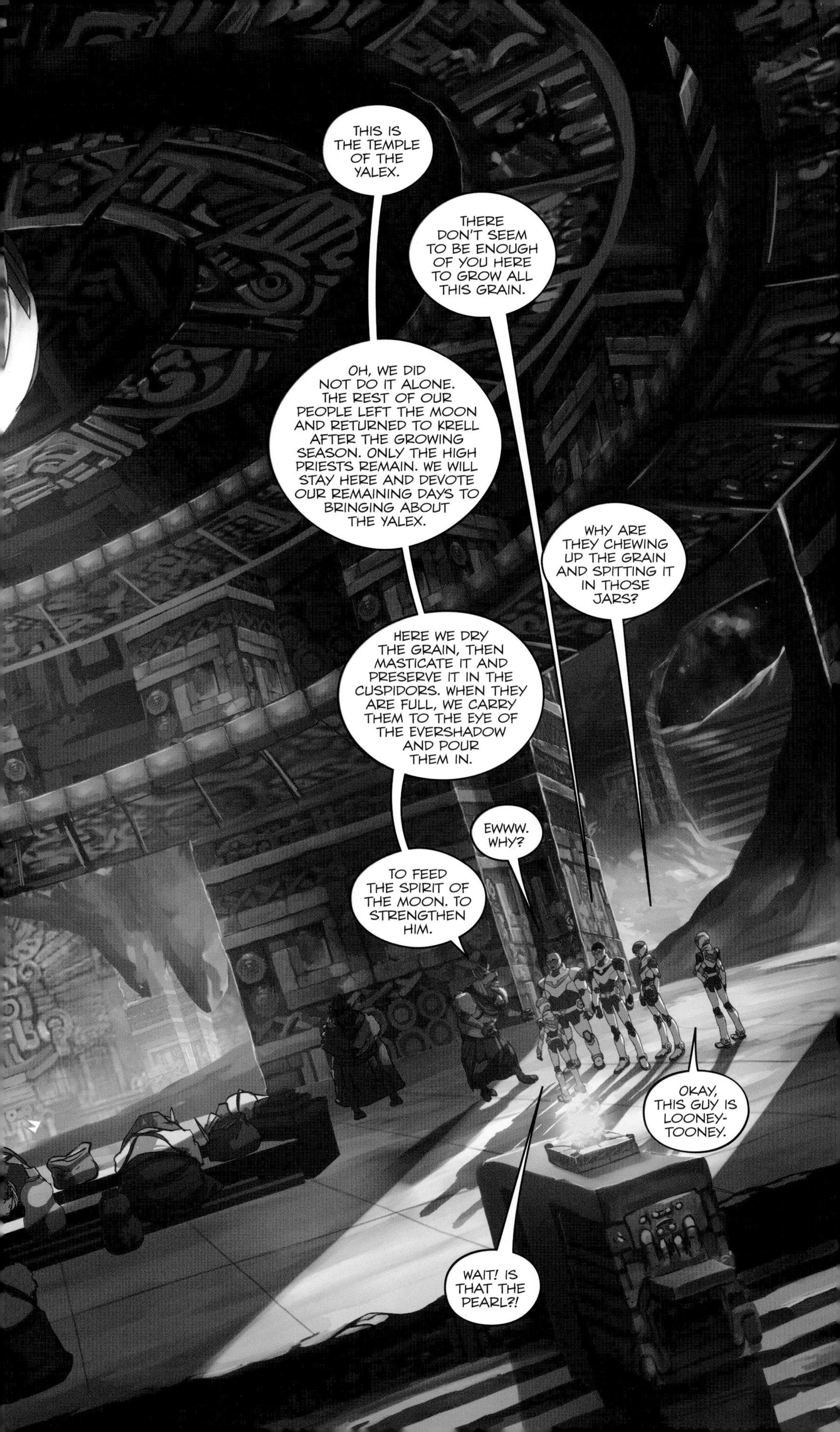
THIS IS THE TEMPLE OF THE YALEX.
THERE DON'T SEEM TO BE ENOUGH OF YOU HERE TO GROW ALL THIS GRAIN.
OH, WE DID NOT DO IT ALONE. THE REST OF OUR PEOPLE LEFT THE MOON AND RETURNED TO KRELL AFTER THE GROWING SEASON. ONLY THE HIGH PRIESTS REMAIN. WE WILL STAY HERE AND DEVOTE OUR REMAINING DAYS TO BRINGING ABOUT THE YALEX.
WHY ARE THEY CHEWING UP THE GRAIN AND SPITTING IT IN THOSE JARS?
HERE WE DRY THE GRAIN, THEN MASTICATE IT AND PRESERVE IT IN THE CUSPIDORS. WHEN THEY ARE FULL, WE CARRY THEM TO THE EYE OF THE EVERSHADOW AND POUR THEM IN.
EWWW. WHY?
TO FEED THE SPIRIT OF THE MOON. TO STRENGTHEN HIM.
OKAY, THIS GUY IS LOONEY-TOONEY.
WAIT! IS THAT THE PEARL?!

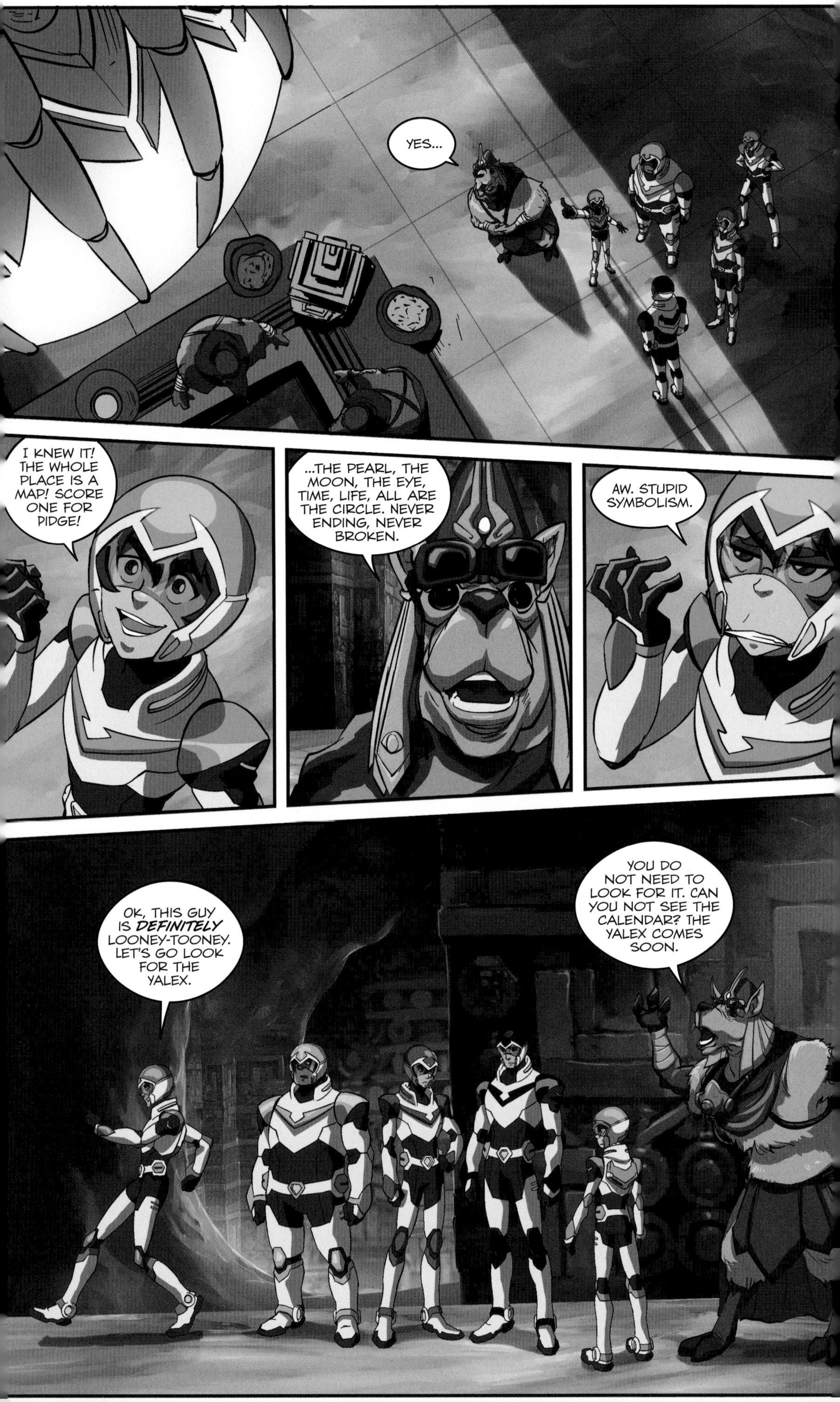
YES...
I KNEW IT! THE WHOLE PLACE IS A MAP! SCORE ONE FOR PIDGE!
...THE PEARL, THE MOON, THE EYE, TIME, LIFE, ALL ARE THE CIRCLE. NEVER ENDING, NEVER BROKEN.
AW. STUPID SYMBOLISM.
OK, THIS GUY IS ***DEFINITELY*** LOONEY-TOONEY. LET'S GO LOOK FOR THE YALEX.
YOU DO NOT NEED TO LOOK FOR IT. CAN YOU NOT SEE THE CALENDAR? THE YALEX COMES SOON.

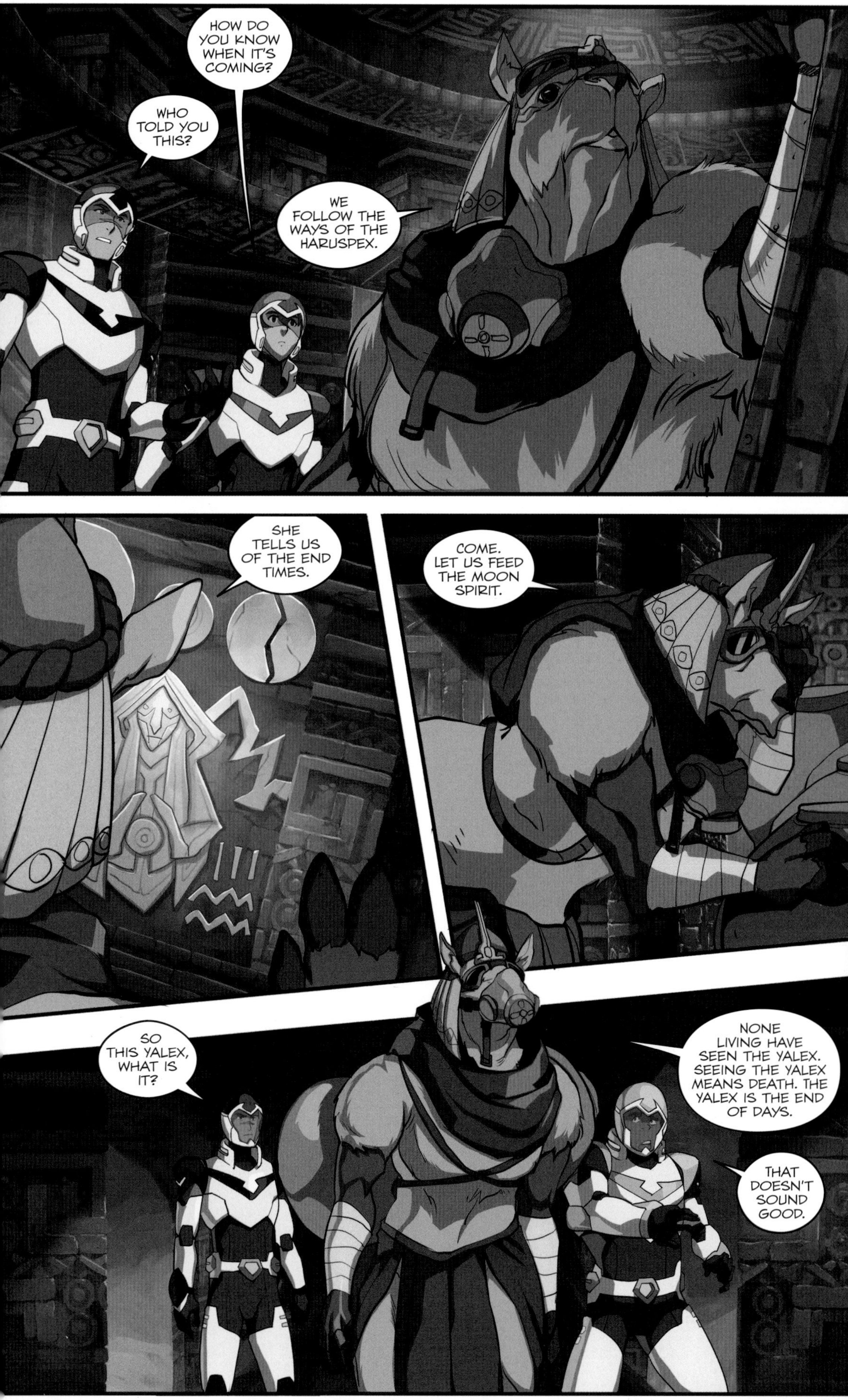
WHO TOLD YOU THIS?
HOW DO YOU KNOW WHEN IT'S COMING?
WE FOLLOW THE WAYS OF THE HARUSPEX.
SHE TELLS US OF THE END TIMES.
COME. LET US FEED THE MOON SPIRIT.
SO THIS YALEX, WHAT IS IT?
NONE LIVING HAVE SEEN THE YALEX. SEEING THE YALEX MEANS DEATH. THE YALEX IS THE END OF DAYS.
THAT DOESN'T SOUND GOOD.

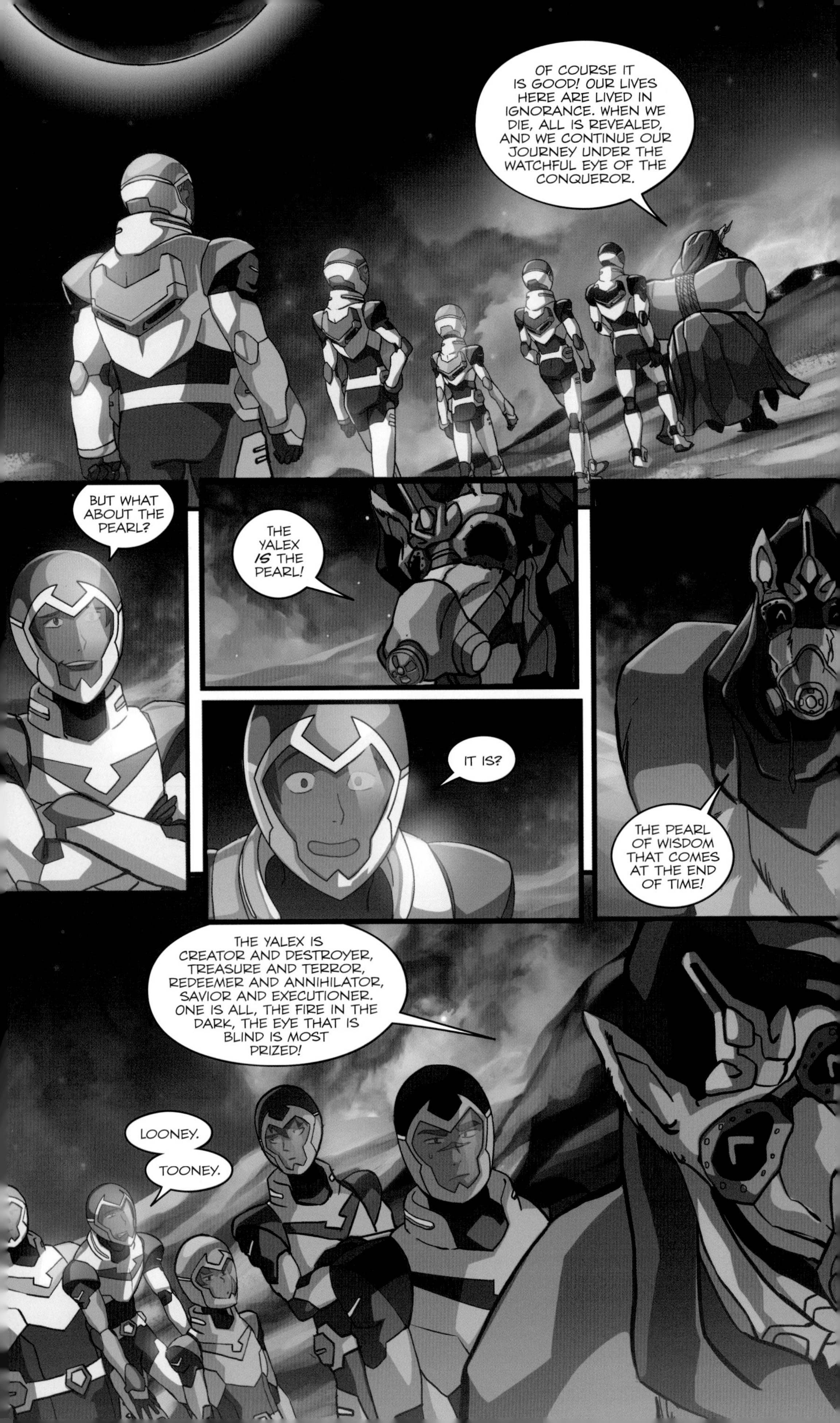
OF COURSE IT IS GOOD! OUR LIVES HERE ARE LIVED IN IGNORANCE. WHEN WE DIE, ALL IS REVEALED, AND WE CONTINUE OUR JOURNEY UNDER THE WATCHFUL EYE OF THE CONQUEROR.
BUT WHAT ABOUT THE PEARL?
THE YALEX ***IS*** THE PEARL!
IT IS?
THE PEARL OF WISDOM THAT COMES AT THE END OF TIME!
THE YALEX IS CREATOR AND DESTROYER, TREASURE AND TERROR, REDEEMER AND ANNIHILATOR, SAVIOR AND EXECUTIONER. ONE IS ALL, THE FIRE IN THE DARK, THE EYE THAT IS BLIND IS MOST PRIZED!
LOONEY.
TOONEY.

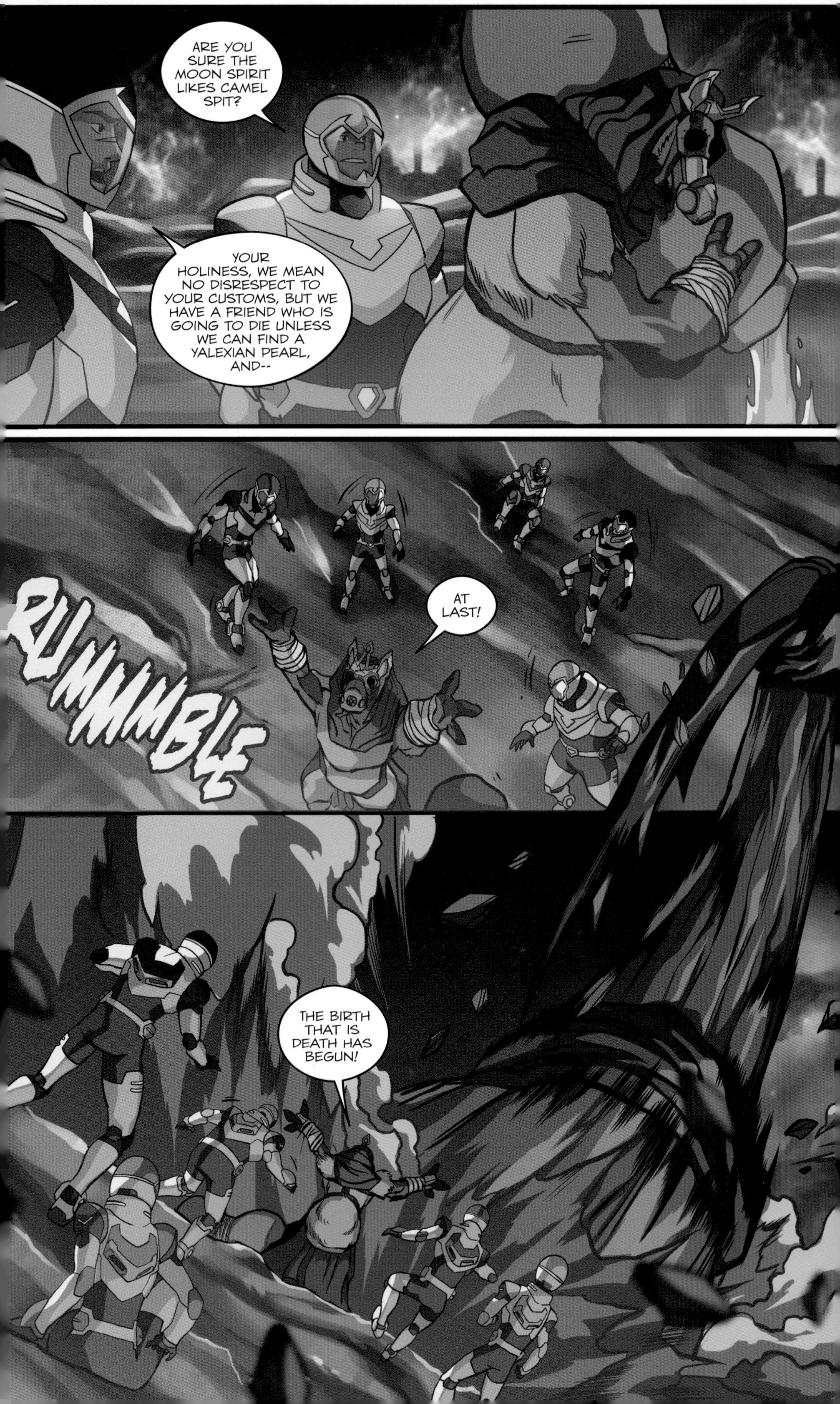
ARE YOU SURE THE MOON SPIRIT LIKES CAMEL SPIT?
YOUR HOLINESS, WE MEAN NO DISRESPECT TO YOUR CUSTOMS, BUT WE HAVE A FRIEND WHO IS GOING TO DIE UNLESS WE CAN FIND A YALEXIAN PEARL, AND--
RUMMMBLE
AT LAST!
THE BIRTH THAT IS DEATH HAS BEGUN!

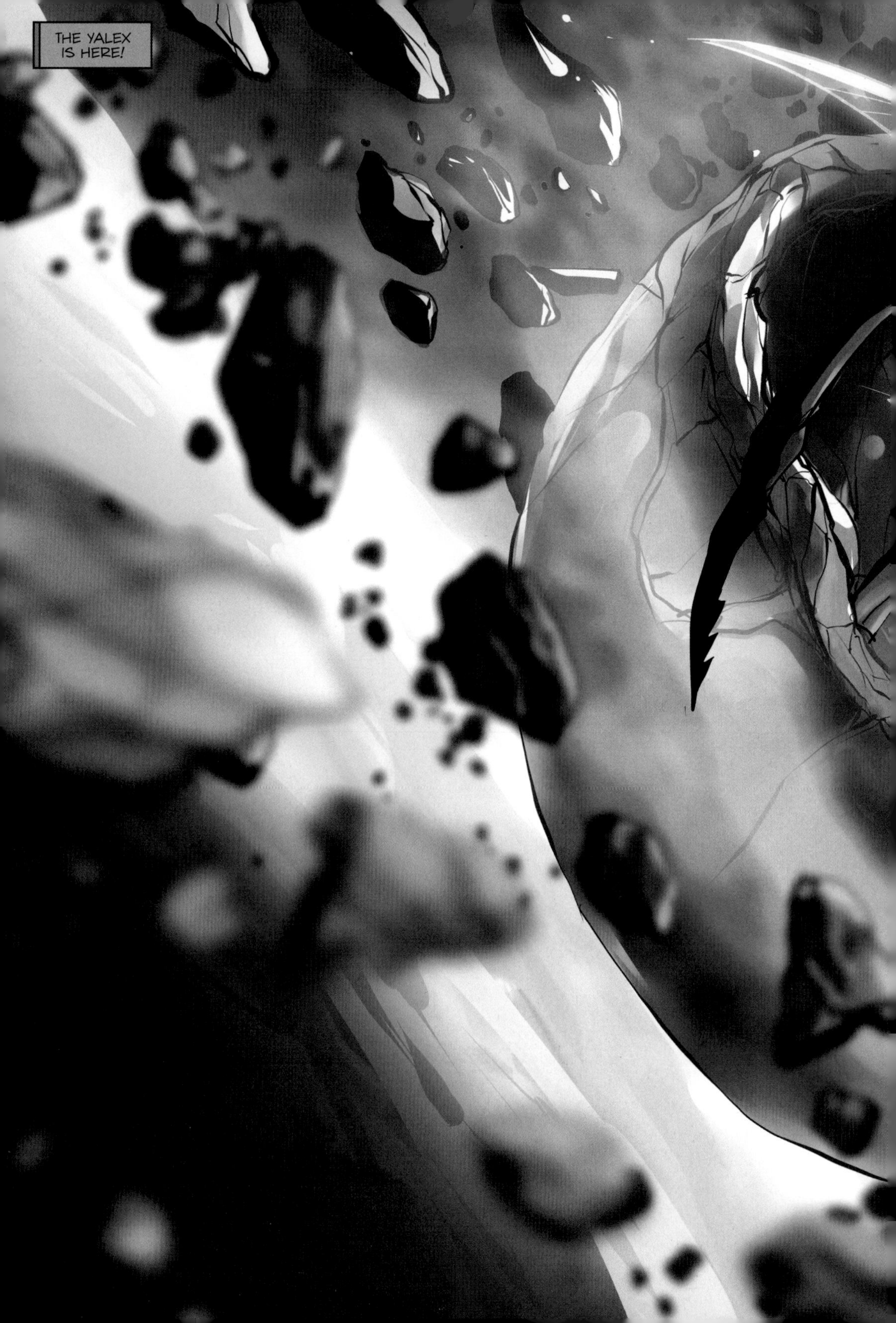
THE YALEX IS HERE!

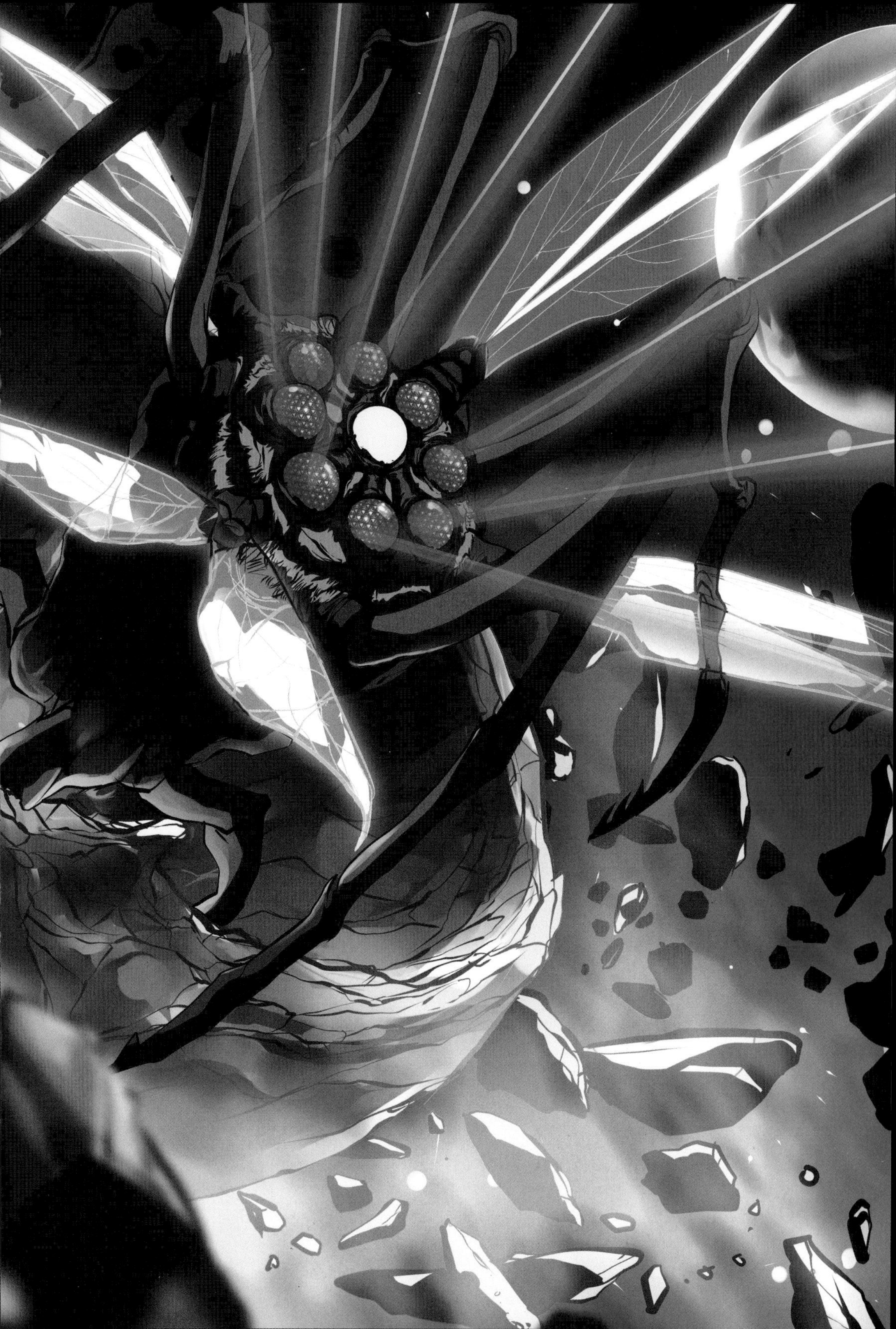

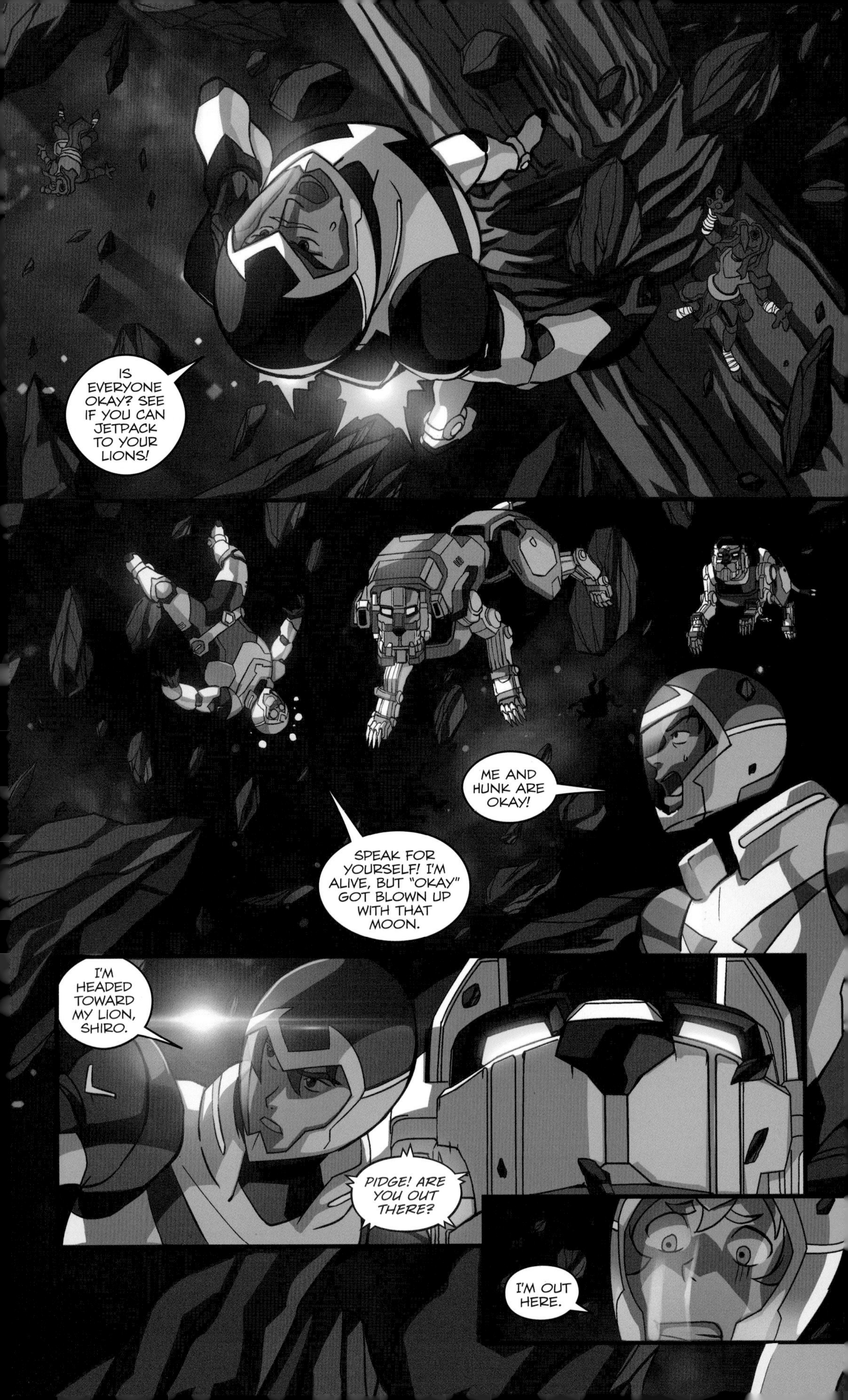
IS EVERYONE OKAY? SEE IF YOU CAN JETPACK TO YOUR LIONS!
ME AND HUNK ARE OKAY!
SPEAK FOR YOURSELF! I'M ALIVE, BUT "OKAY" GOT BLOWN UP WITH THAT MOON.
I'M HEADED TOWARD MY LION, SHIRO.
PIDGE! ARE YOU OUT THERE?
I'M OUT HERE.

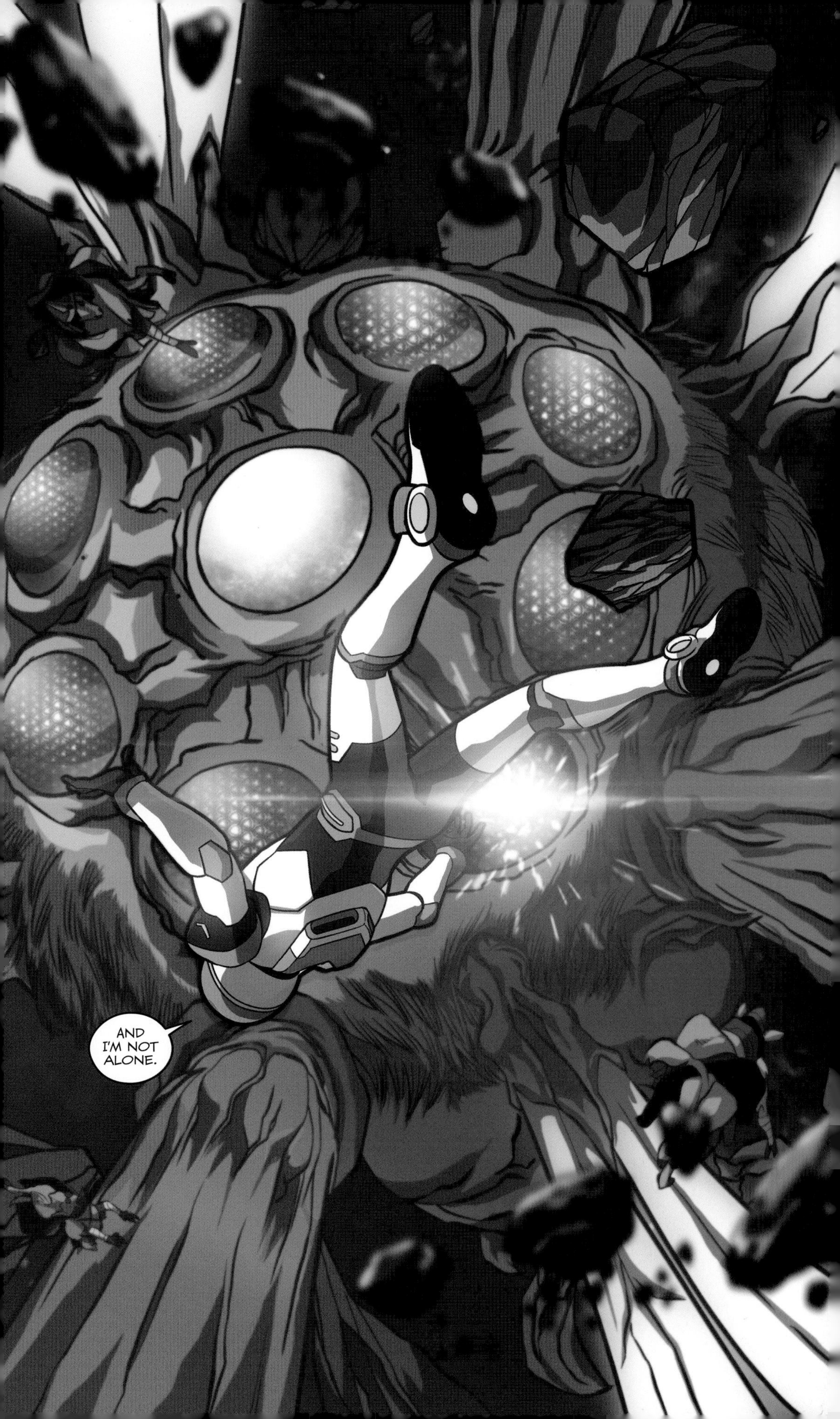
AND I'M NOT ALONE.

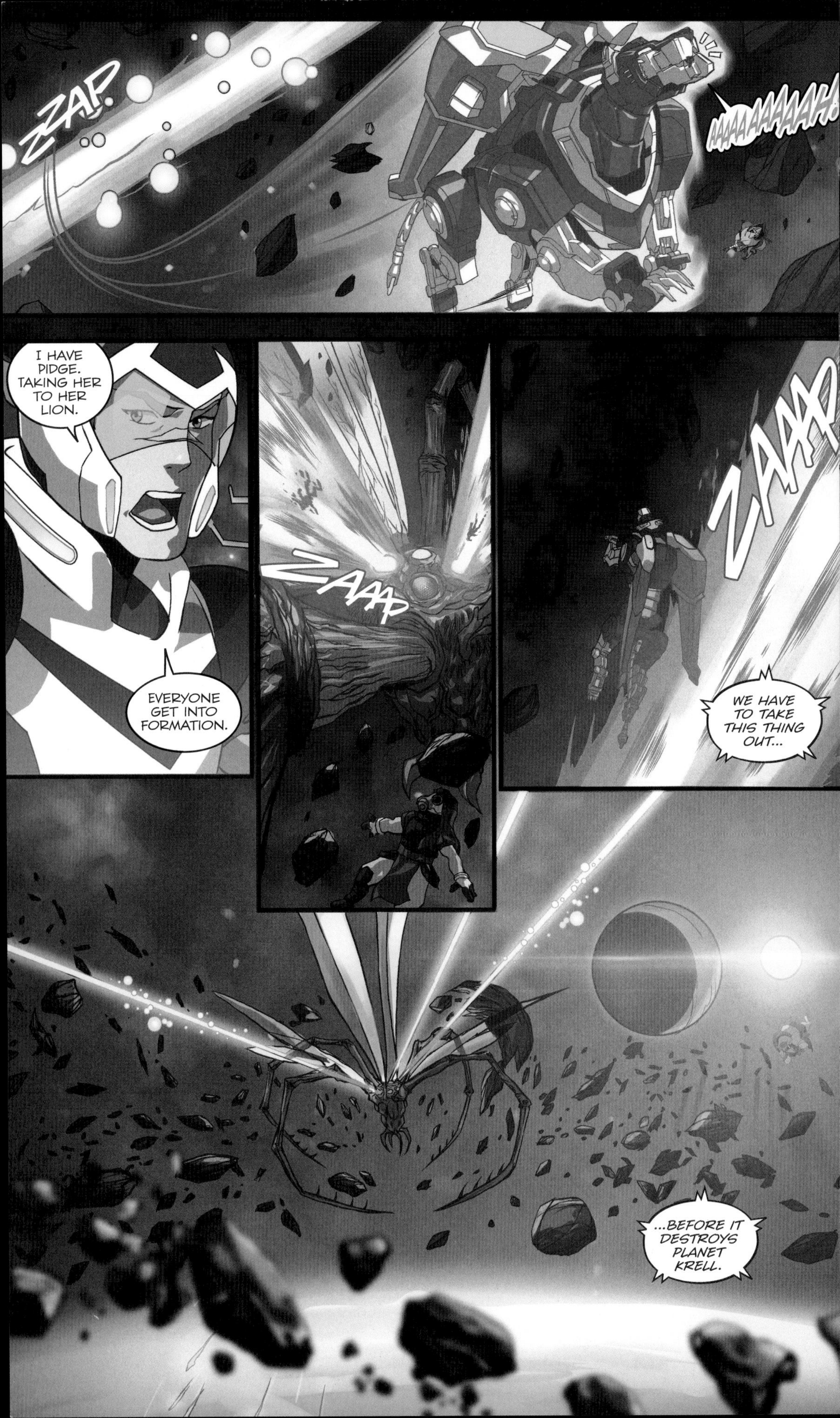
ZZAP
AAAAAAAAAAH!
I HAVE PIDGE. TAKING HER TO HER LION.
EVERYONE GET INTO FORMATION.
ZAAAP
ZAAAP
WE HAVE TO TAKE THIS THING OUT...
...BEFORE IT DESTROYS PLANET KRELL.

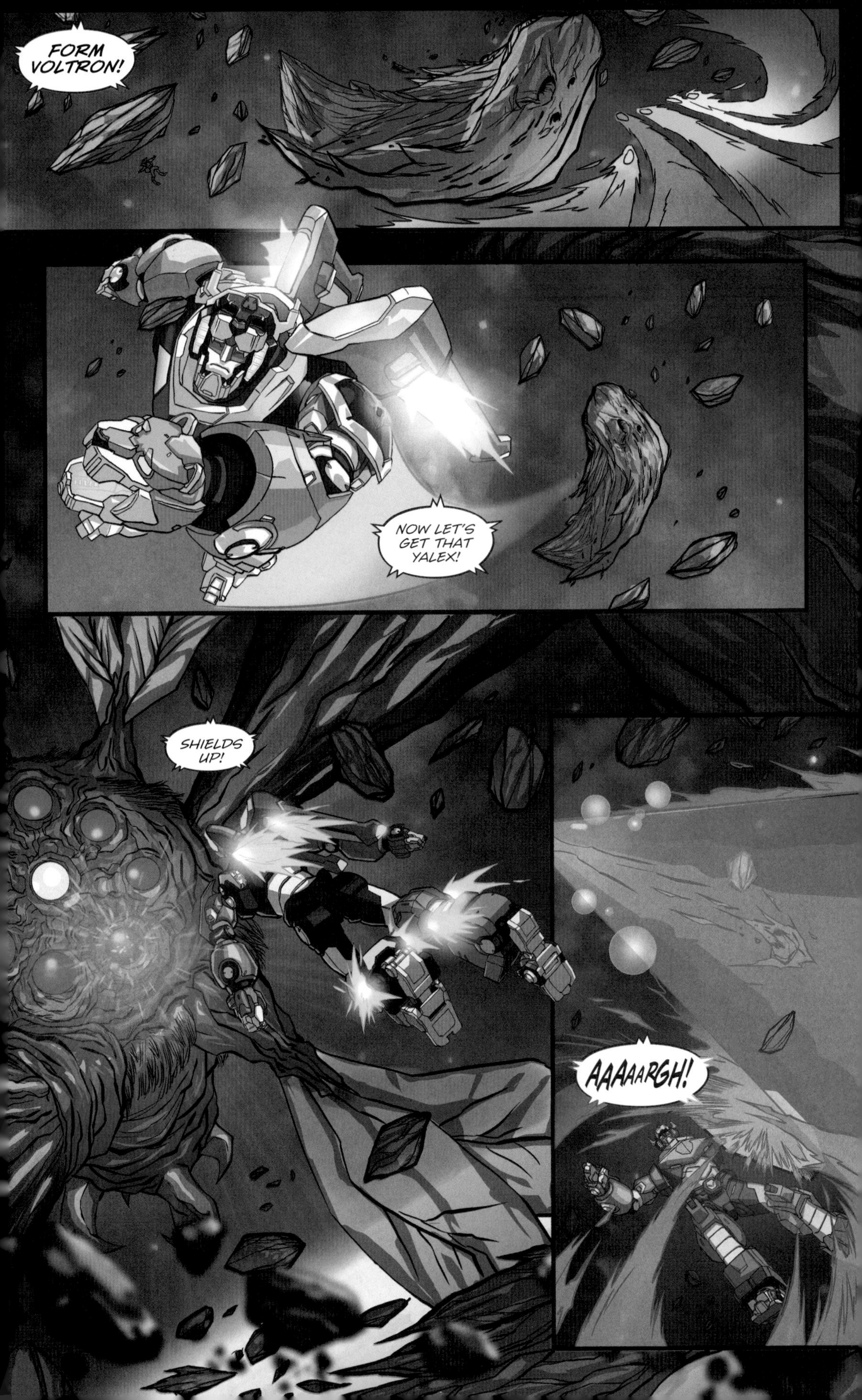
FORM VOLTRON!
NOW LET'S GET THAT YALEX!
SHIELDS UP!
AAAAARGH!

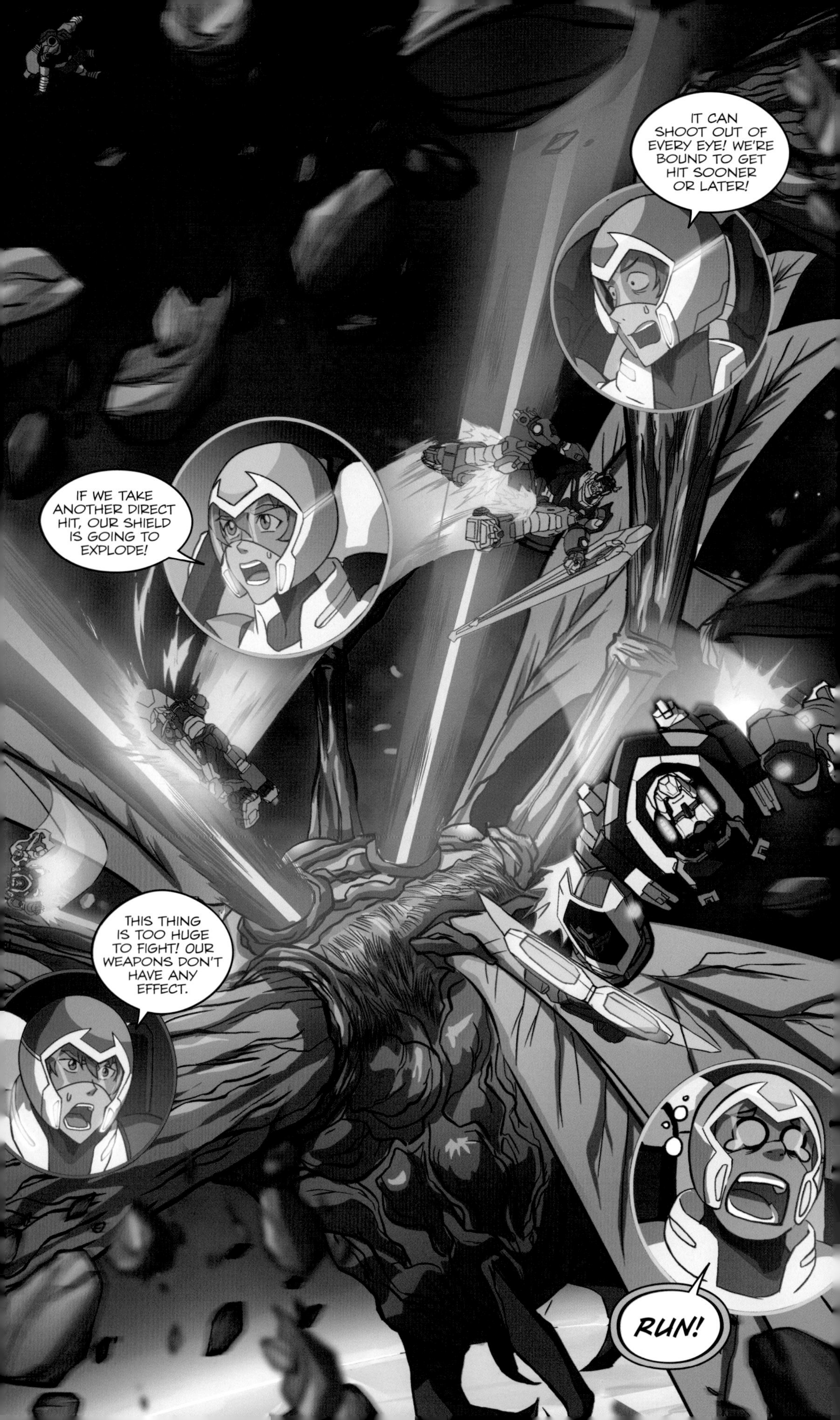
IT CAN SHOOT OUT OF EVERY EYE! WE'RE BOUND TO GET HIT SOONER OR LATER!
IF WE TAKE ANOTHER DIRECT HIT, OUR SHIELD IS GOING TO EXPLODE!
THIS THING IS TOO HUGE TO FIGHT! OUR WEAPONS DON'T HAVE ANY EFFECT.
RUN!

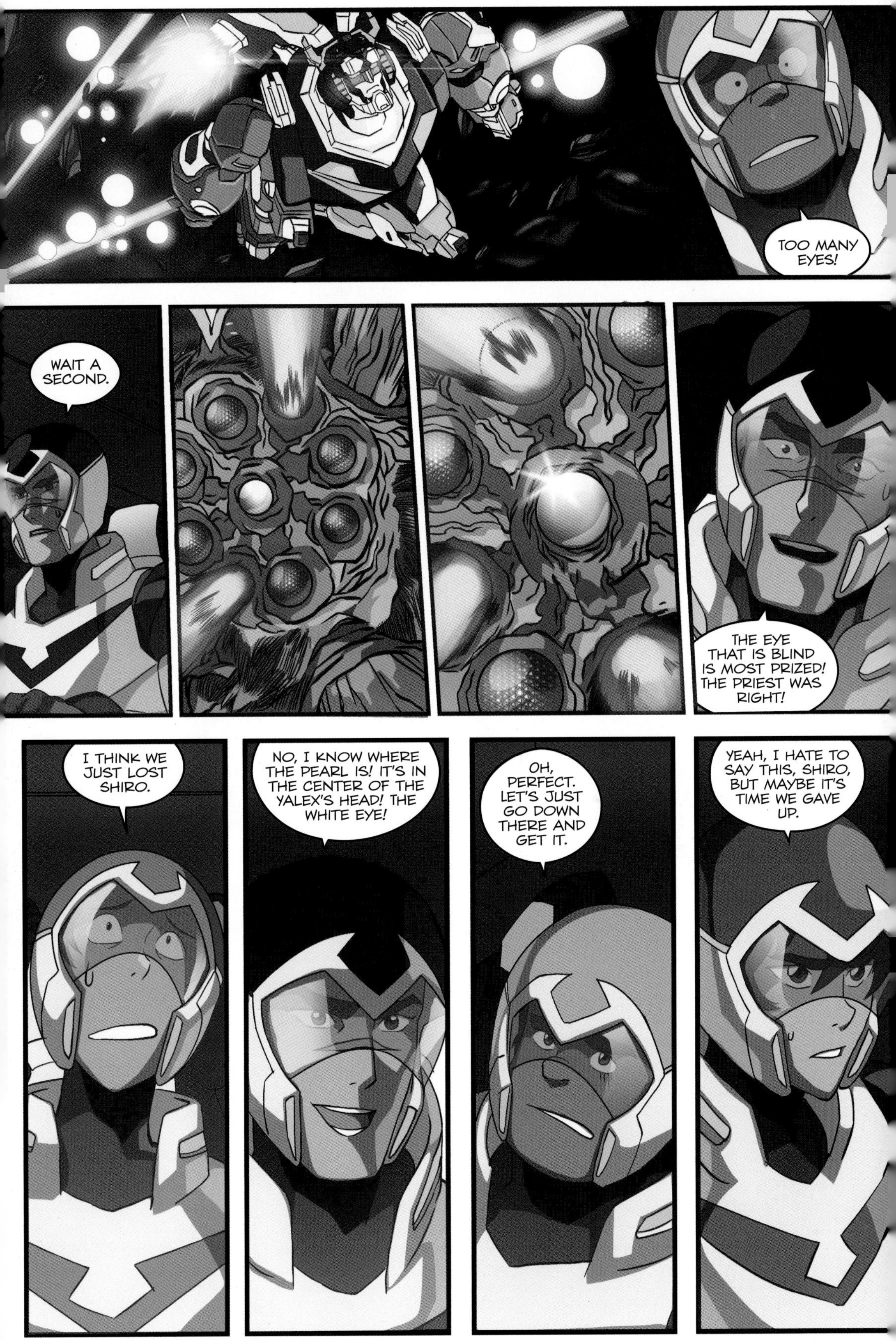
TOO MANY EYES!
WAIT A SECOND.
THE EYE THAT IS BLIND IS MOST PRIZED! THE PRIEST WAS RIGHT!
I THINK WE JUST LOST SHIRO.
NO, I KNOW WHERE THE PEARL IS! IT'S IN THE CENTER OF THE YALEX'S HEAD! THE WHITE EYE!
OH, PERFECT. LET'S JUST GO DOWN THERE AND GET IT.
YEAH, I HATE TO SAY THIS, SHIRO, BUT MAYBE IT'S TIME WE GAVE UP.

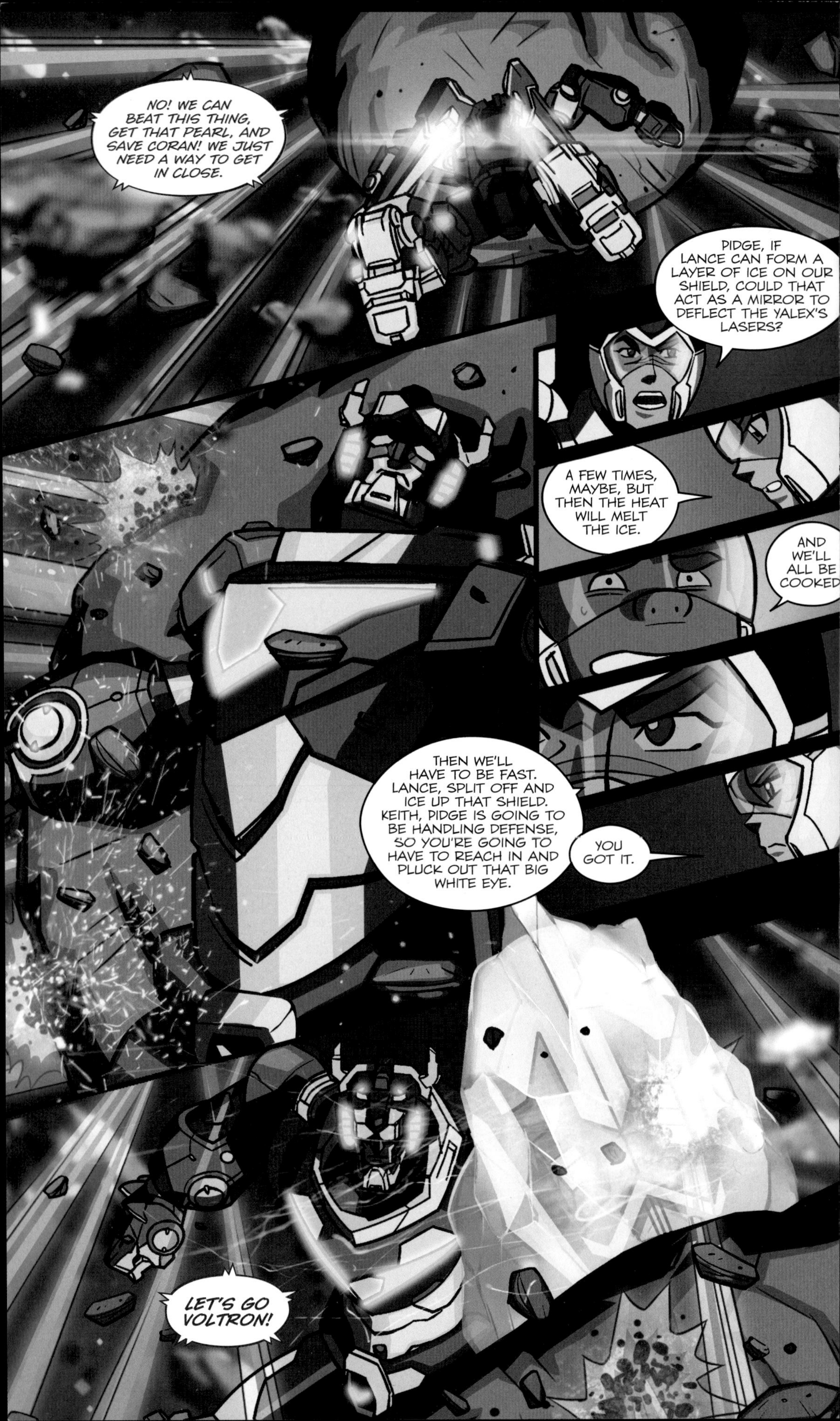
NO! WE CAN BEAT THIS THING, GET THAT PEARL, AND SAVE CORAN! WE JUST NEED A WAY TO GET IN CLOSE.
PIDGE, IF LANCE CAN FORM A LAYER OF ICE ON OUR SHIELD, COULD THAT ACT AS A MIRROR TO DEFLECT THE YALEX'S LASERS?
A FEW TIMES, MAYBE, BUT THEN THE HEAT WILL MELT THE ICE.
AND WE'LL ALL BE COOKED
THEN WE'LL HAVE TO BE FAST. LANCE, SPLIT OFF AND ICE UP THAT SHIELD. KEITH, PIDGE IS GOING TO BE HANDLING DEFENSE, SO YOU'RE GOING TO HAVE TO REACH IN AND PLUCK OUT THAT BIG WHITE EYE.
YOU GOT IT.
LET'S GO VOLTRON!

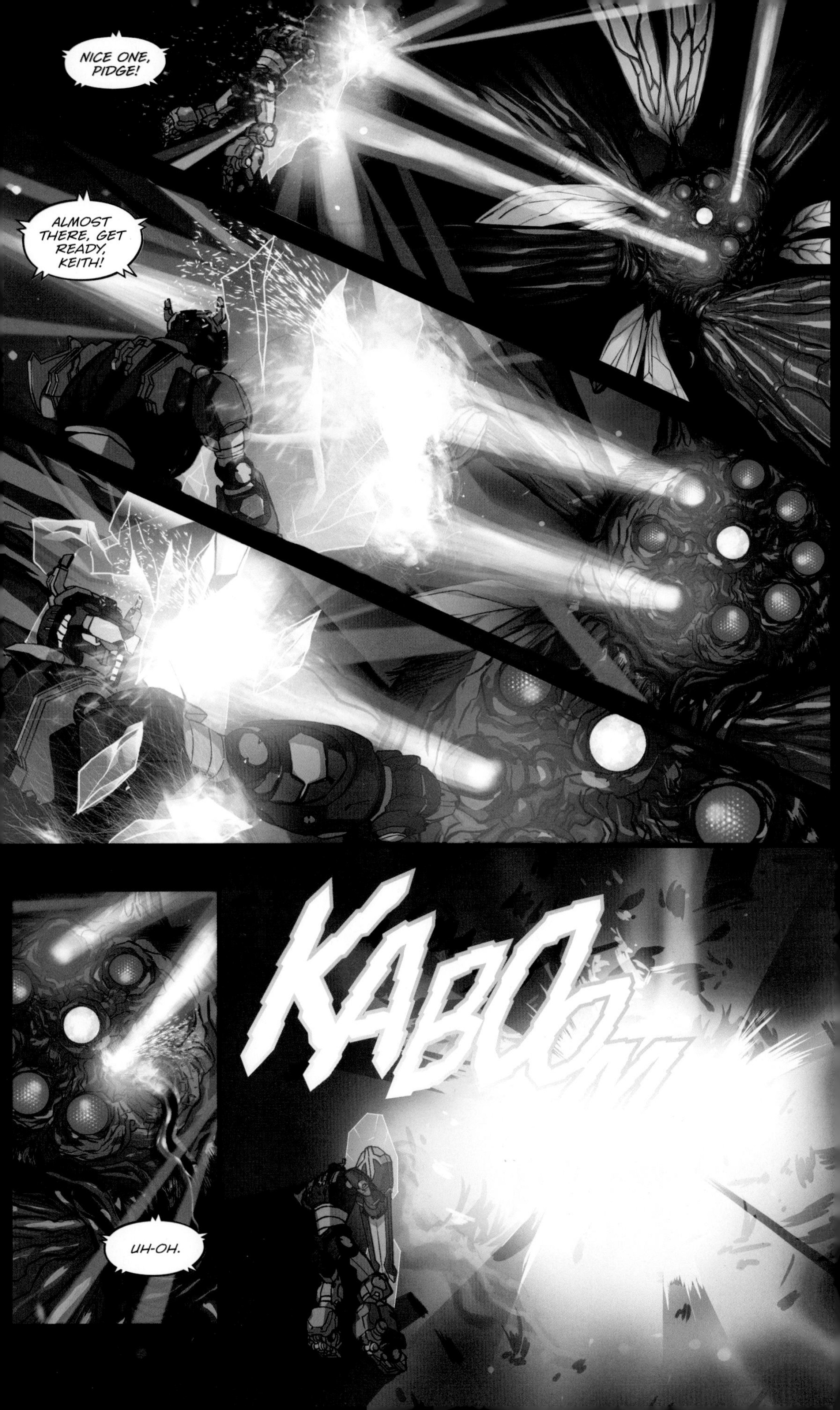
NICE ONE, PIDGE!
ALMOST THERE, GET READY, KEITH!
KABOOM
UH-OH.

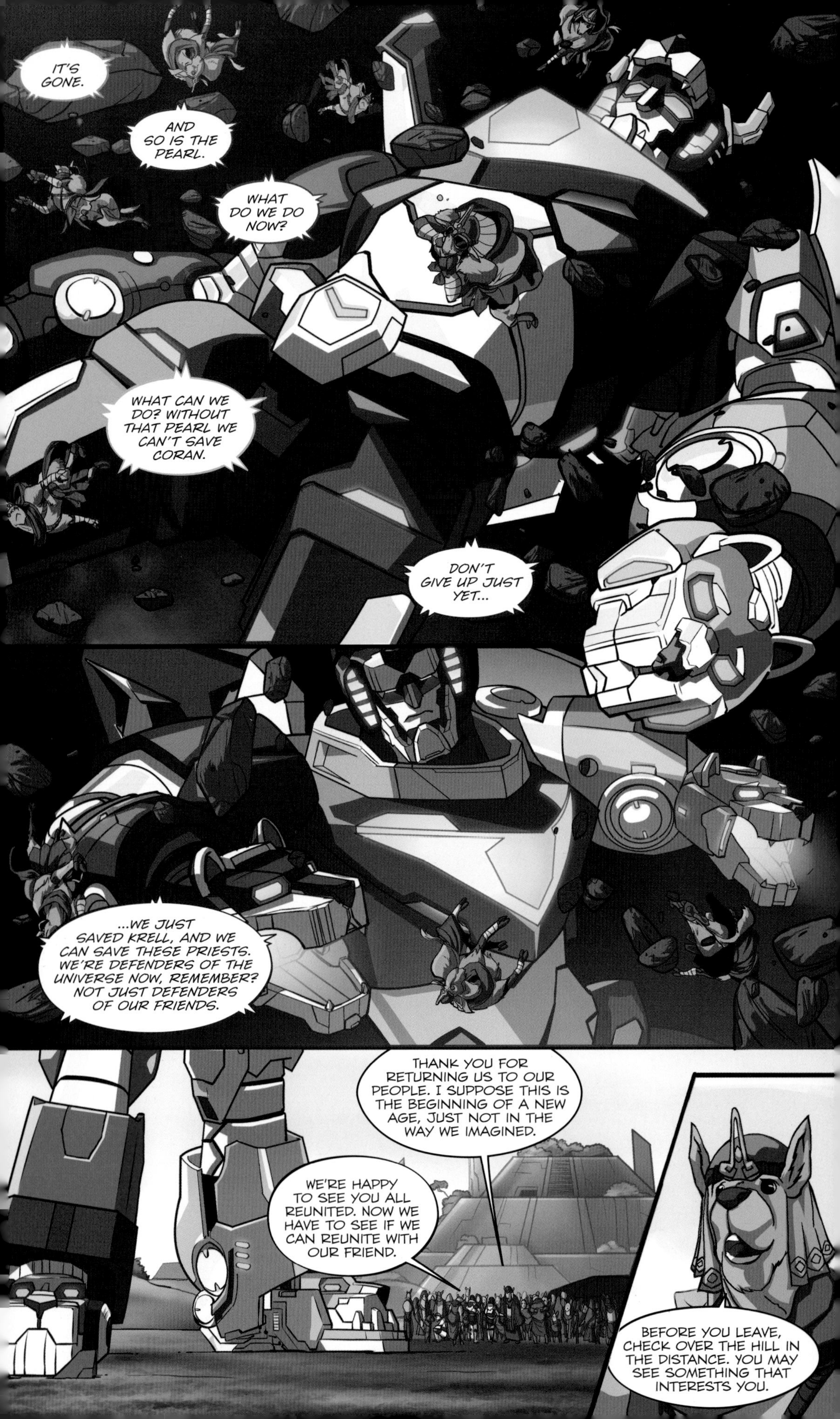
IT'S GONE.
AND SO IS THE PEARL.
WHAT DO WE DO NOW?
WHAT CAN WE DO? WITHOUT THAT PEARL WE CAN'T SAVE CORAN.
DON'T GIVE UP JUST YET...
...WE JUST SAVED KRELL, AND WE CAN SAVE THESE PRIESTS. WE'RE DEFENDERS OF THE UNIVERSE NOW, REMEMBER? NOT JUST DEFENDERS OF OUR FRIENDS.
THANK YOU FOR RETURNING US TO OUR PEOPLE. I SUPPOSE THIS IS THE BEGINNING OF A NEW AGE, JUST NOT IN THE WAY WE IMAGINED.
WE'RE HAPPY TO SEE YOU ALL REUNITED. NOW WE HAVE TO SEE IF WE CAN REUNITE WITH OUR FRIEND.
BEFORE YOU LEAVE, CHECK OVER THE HILL IN THE DISTANCE. YOU MAY SEE SOMETHING THAT INTERESTS YOU.

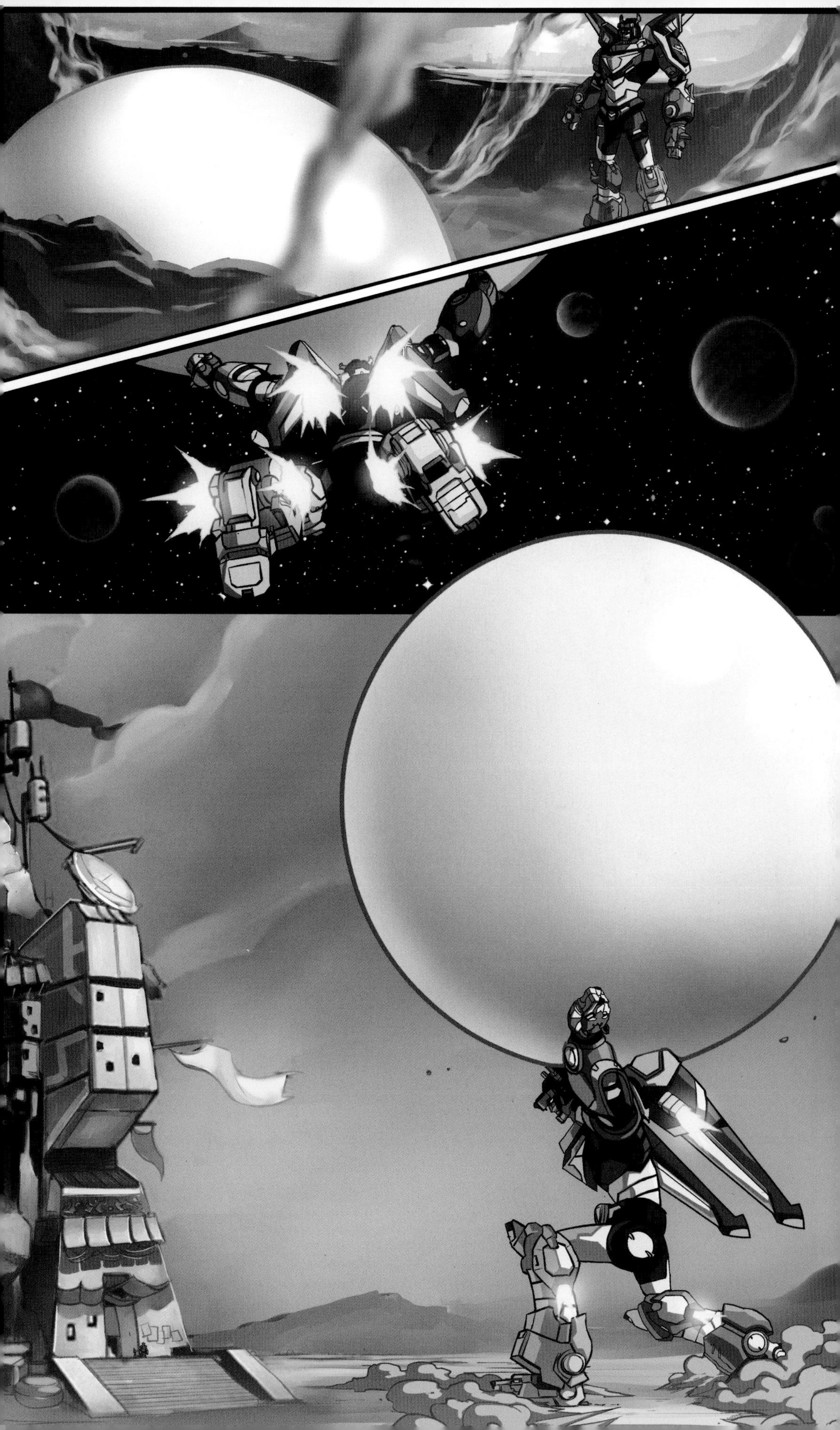

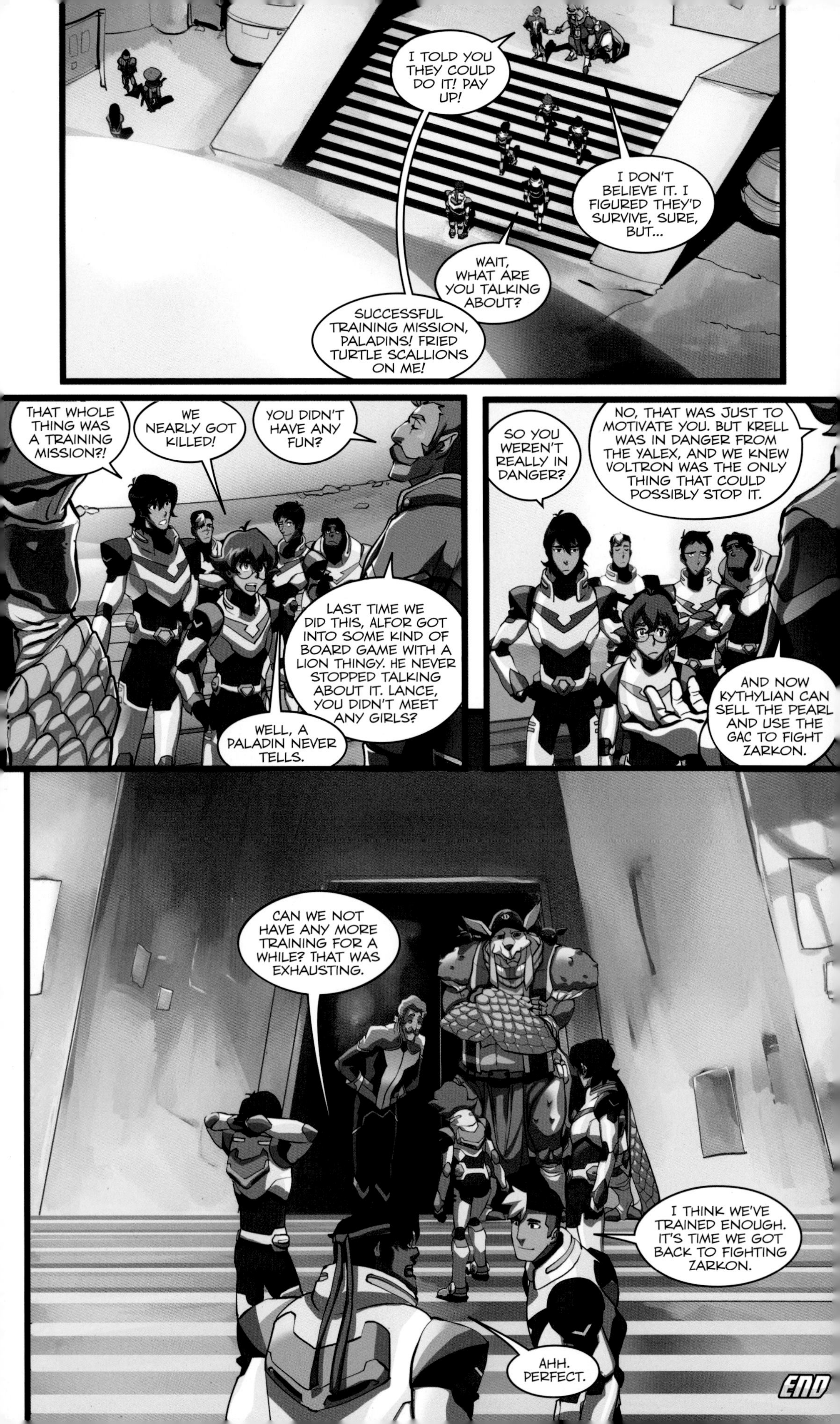
I TOLD YOU THEY COULD DO IT! PAY UP!
I DON'T BELIEVE IT. I FIGURED THEY'D SURVIVE, SURE, BUT...
WAIT, WHAT ARE YOU TALKING ABOUT?
SUCCESSFUL TRAINING MISSION, PALADINS! FRIED TURTLE SCALLIONS ON ME!
THAT WHOLE THING WAS A TRAINING MISSION?!
WE NEARLY GOT KILLED!
YOU DIDN'T HAVE ANY FUN?
LAST TIME WE DID THIS, ALFOR GOT INTO SOME KIND OF BOARD GAME WITH A LION THINGY. HE NEVER STOPPED TALKING ABOUT IT. LANCE, YOU DIDN'T MEET ANY GIRLS?
WELL, A PALADIN NEVER TELLS.
SO YOU WEREN'T REALLY IN DANGER?
NO, THAT WAS JUST TO MOTIVATE YOU. BUT KRELL WAS IN DANGER FROM THE YALEX, AND WE KNEW VOLTRON WAS THE ONLY THING THAT COULD POSSIBLY STOP IT.
AND NOW KYTHYLIAN CAN SELL THE PEARL AND USE THE GAC TO FIGHT ZARKON.
CAN WE NOT HAVE ANY MORE TRAINING FOR A WHILE? THAT WAS EXHAUSTING.
I THINK WE'VE TRAINED ENOUGH. IT'S TIME WE GOT BACK TO FIGHTING ZARKON.
AHH. PERFECT.
END

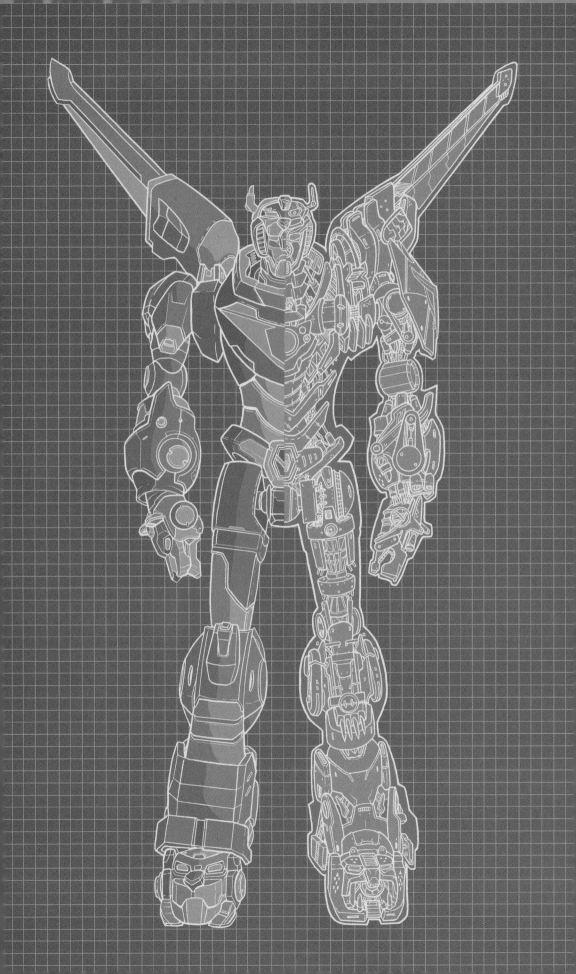

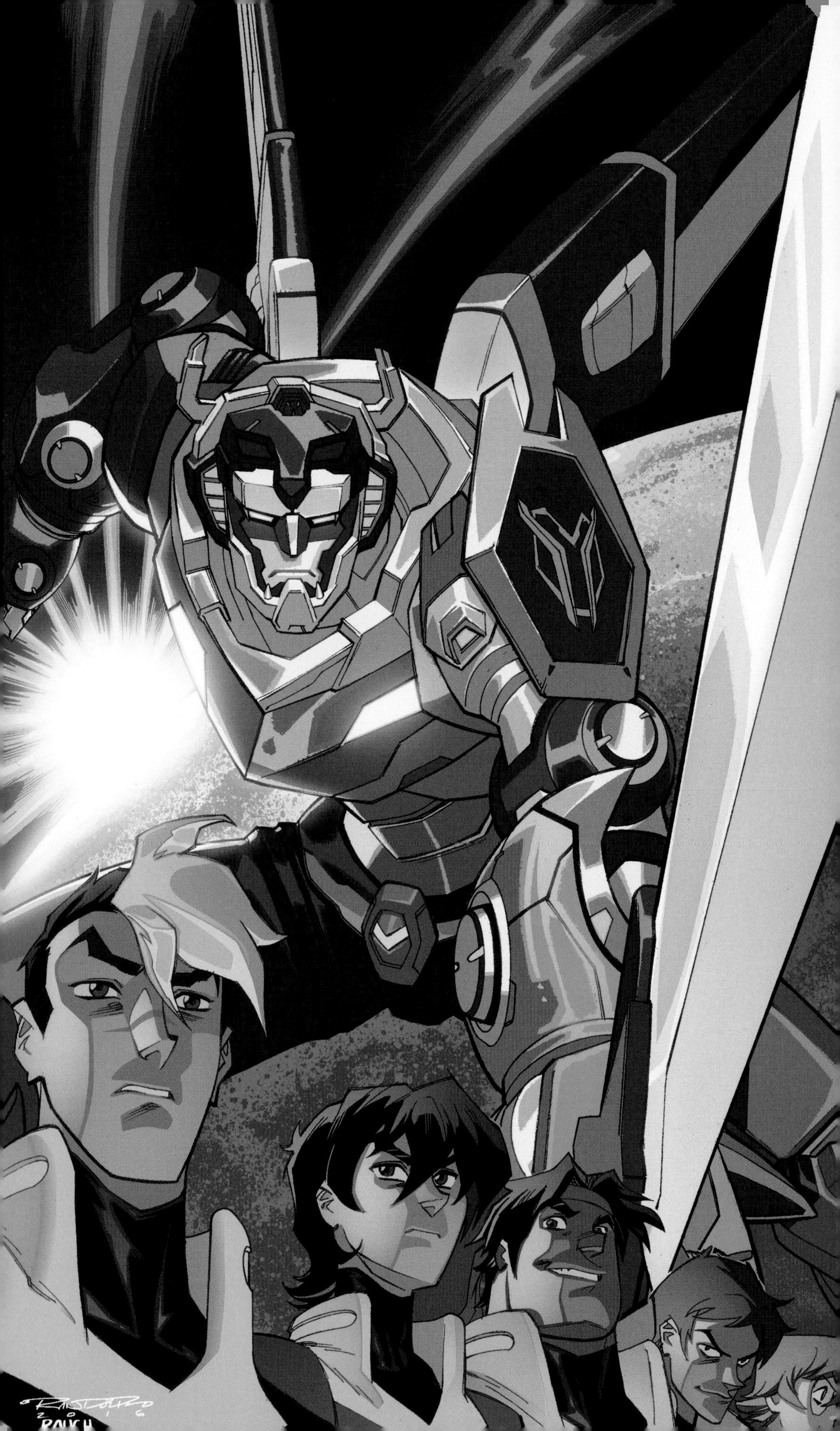

CREATOR **BIOS**

***TIM HEDRICK** is an Emmy and Peabody Award-winning writer and producer. Over the past decade he has written or produced shows for networks including NBC, CBS, ESPN, HBO, Nickelodeon, Disney Channel and MTV. He wrote on* Nickelodeon's Avatar: The Last Airbender *and* The Legend of Korra *and is currently head writer of DreamWorks Animation's VOLTRON LEGENDARY DEFENDER, debuting exclusively on Netflix in 2016. He is an alumnus of the Graduate Screenwriting Program at the University of Southern California. He lives in Los Angeles.*

***MITCH IVERSON** is a staff writer on DreamWorks Animation's VOLTRON LEGENDARY DEFENDER. He loves comic books, giant robots, and all things sci-fi. He lives with his fiancee, Trish, and his dog, Elway, in Hollywood, California. He can frequently be seen browsing the aisles of his local comic book store in Hollywood. Support your local comic book store!*

***DIGITAL ART CHEFS** (digitalartchefs.com) was founded in 2010 by a group of creative and versatile professionals who also happened to be friends led by James L. Palabay. DAC has had the opportunity to work with a wide variety of clients, from visionary startup game companies to well-known entertainment companies and brands, including: DC Comics, Lego, Warner Bros., Harmony Gold USA, Capcom, TOEI Japan, EA Bioware Casual, Cartoon Network and Disney. The group has done extensive creative work including the full production and creation of customized comics, concept designs, character designs, storyboards, and ad campaigns, as well as full art development for game apps including animation.*

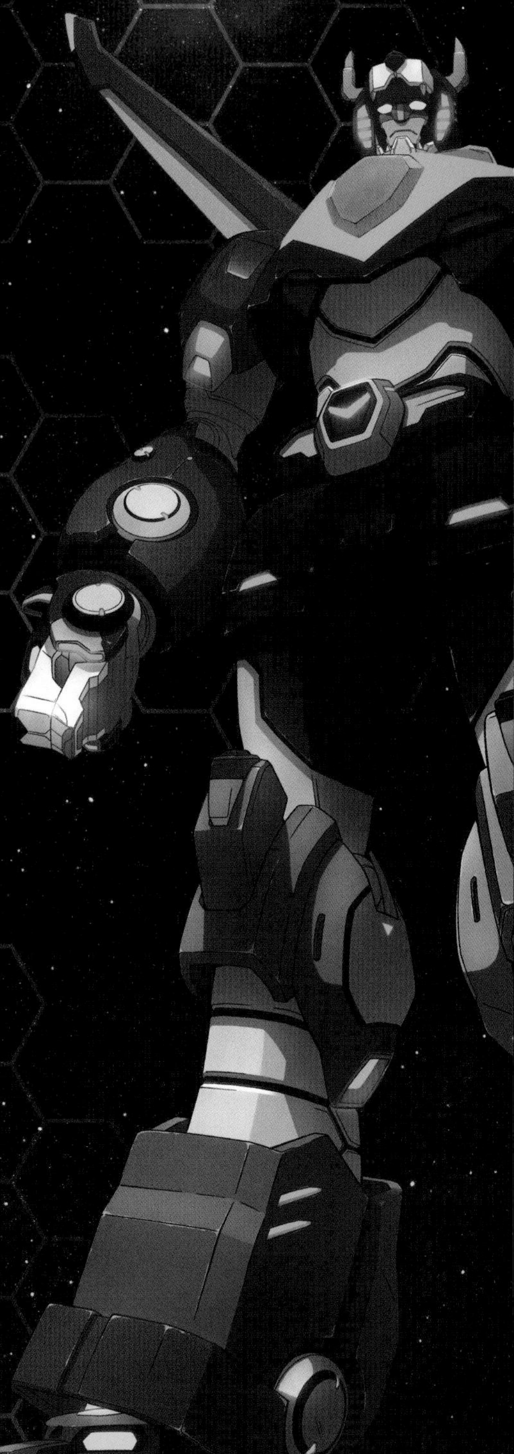

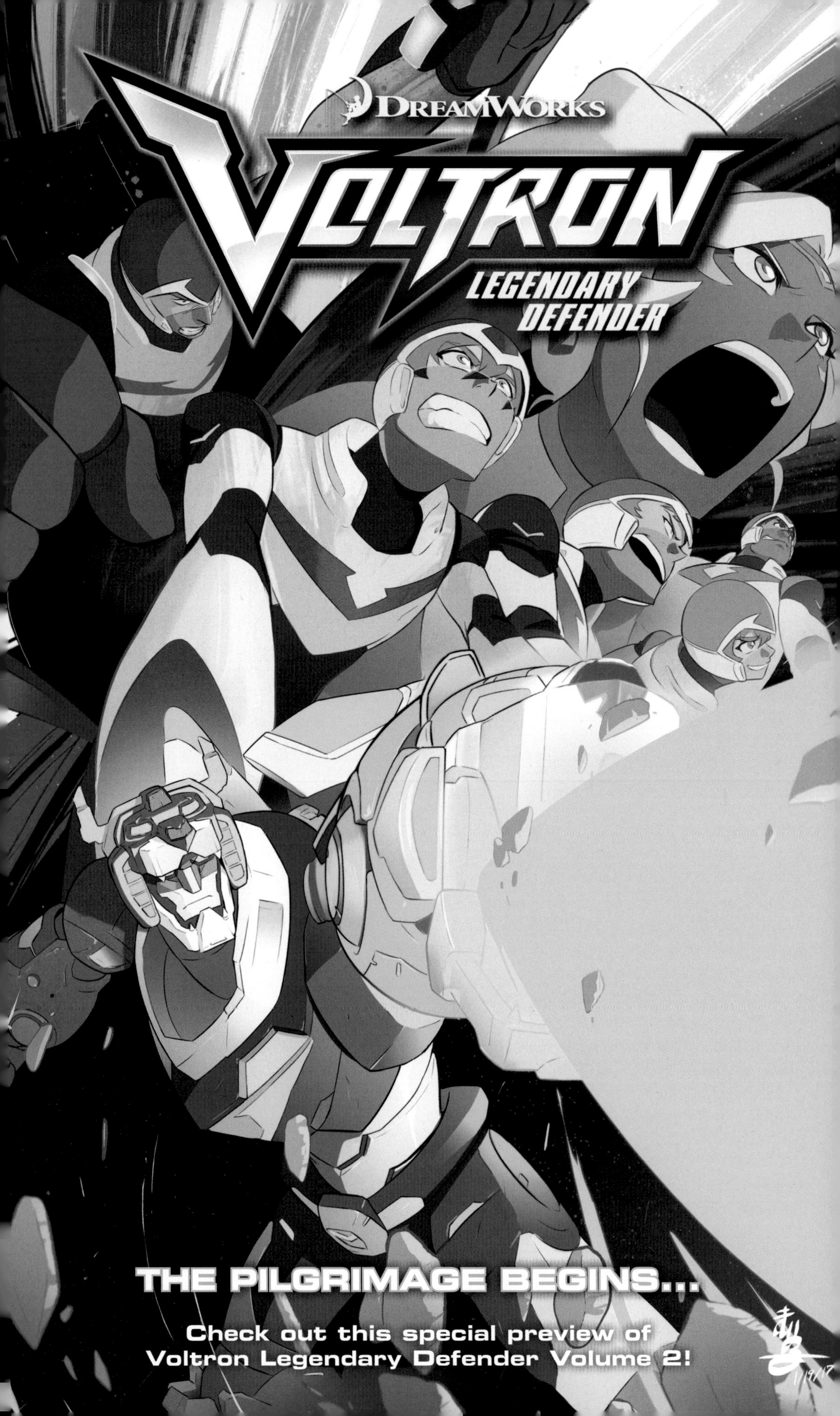
DreamWorks
Voltron
Legendary Defender
THE PILGRIMAGE BEGINS...
Check out this special preview of
Voltron Legendary Defender Volume 2!

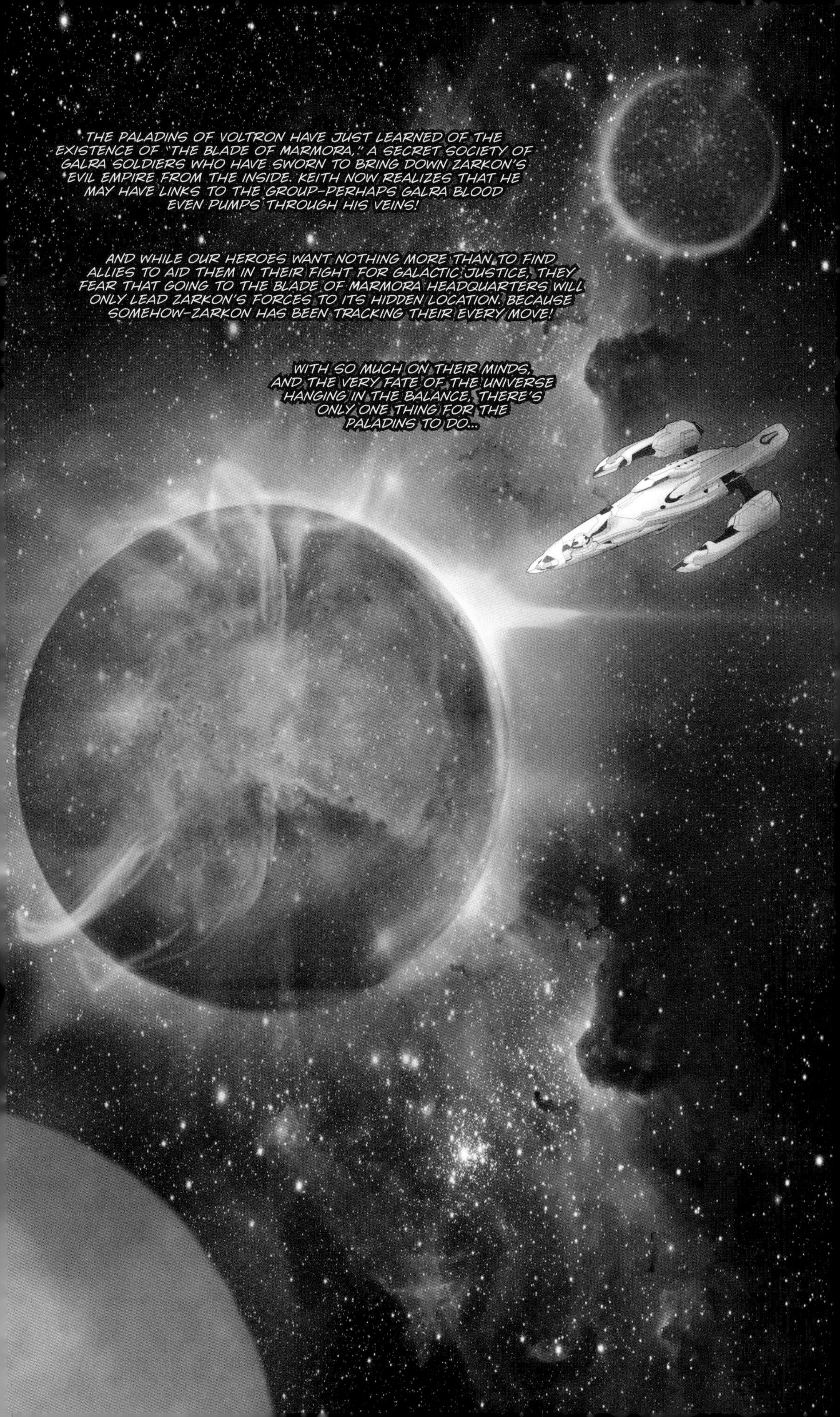
THE PALADINS OF VOLTRON HAVE JUST LEARNED OF THE EXISTENCE OF "THE BLADE OF MARMORA," A SECRET SOCIETY OF GALRA SOLDIERS WHO HAVE SWORN TO BRING DOWN ZARKON'S EVIL EMPIRE FROM THE INSIDE. KEITH NOW REALIZES THAT HE MAY HAVE LINKS TO THE GROUP-PERHAPS GALRA BLOOD EVEN PUMPS THROUGH HIS VEINS!
AND WHILE OUR HEROES WANT NOTHING MORE THAN TO FIND ALLIES TO AID THEM IN THEIR FIGHT FOR GALACTIC JUSTICE, THEY FEAR THAT GOING TO THE BLADE OF MARMORA HEADQUARTERS WILL ONLY LEAD ZARKON'S FORCES TO ITS HIDDEN LOCATION. BECAUSE SOMEHOW-ZARKON HAS BEEN TRACKING THEIR EVERY MOVE!
WITH SO MUCH ON THEIR MINDS, AND THE VERY FATE OF THE UNIVERSE HANGING IN THE BALANCE, THERE'S ONLY ONE THING FOR THE PALADINS TO DO...

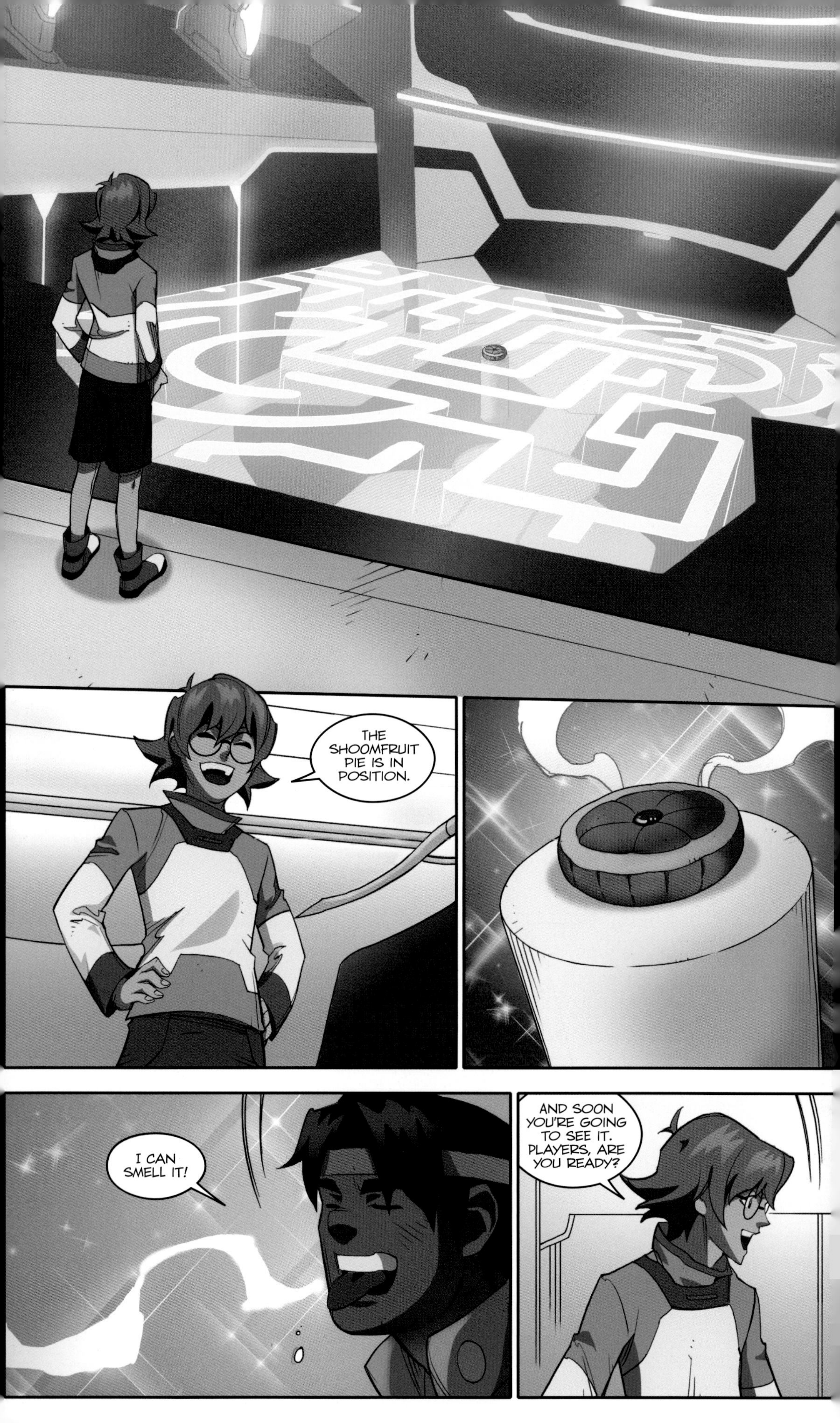
THE SHOOMFRUIT PIE IS IN POSITION.
I CAN SMELL IT!
AND SOON YOU'RE GOING TO SEE IT. PLAYERS, ARE YOU READY?

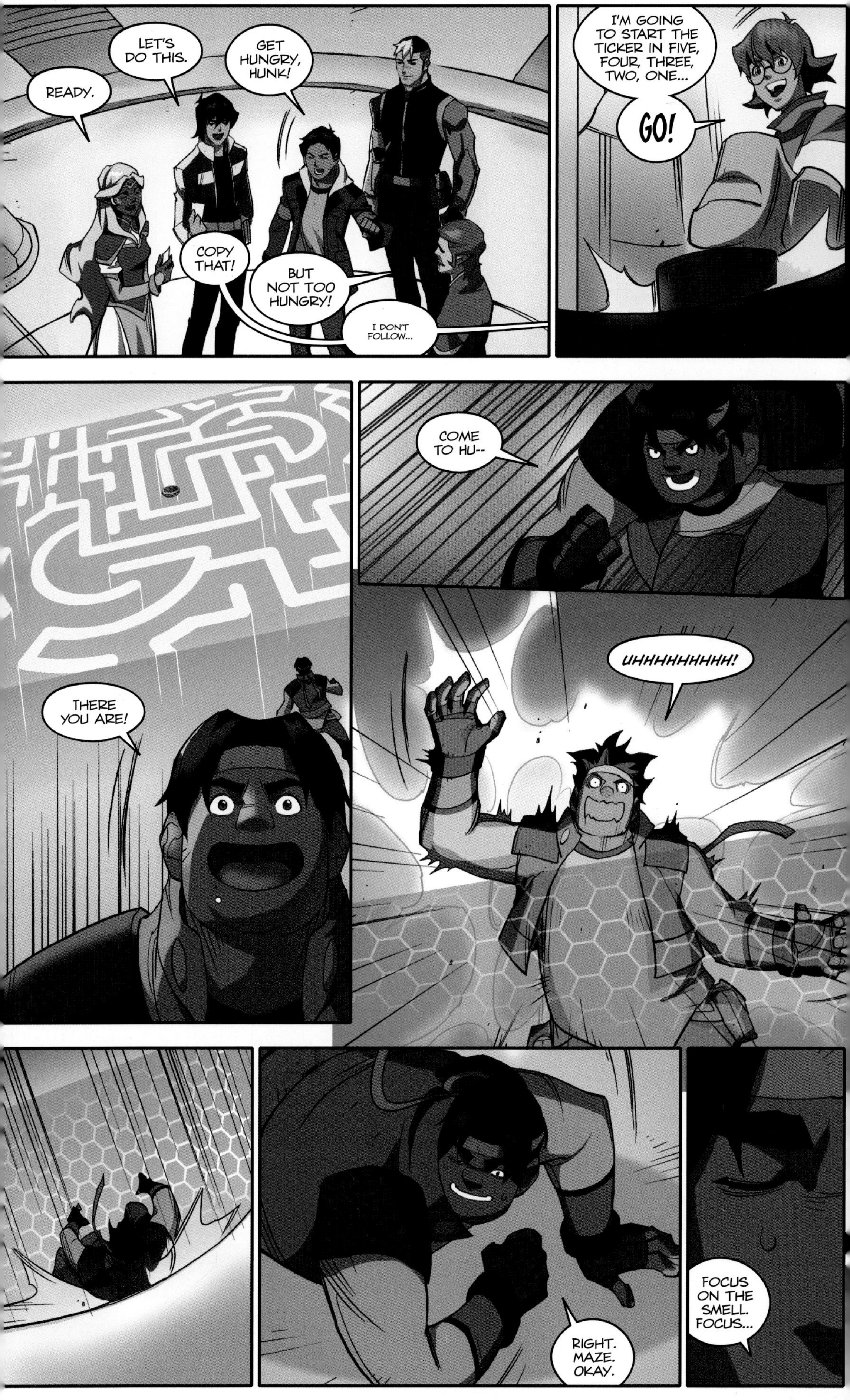
READY.
LET'S DO THIS.
GET HUNGRY, HUNK!
COPY THAT!
BUT NOT TOO HUNGRY!
I DON'T FOLLOW...
I'M GOING TO START THE TICKER IN FIVE, FOUR, THREE, TWO, ONE...
GO!
COME TO HU--
THERE YOU ARE!
UHHHHHHHHH!
RIGHT. MAZE. OKAY.
FOCUS ON THE SMELL. FOCUS...

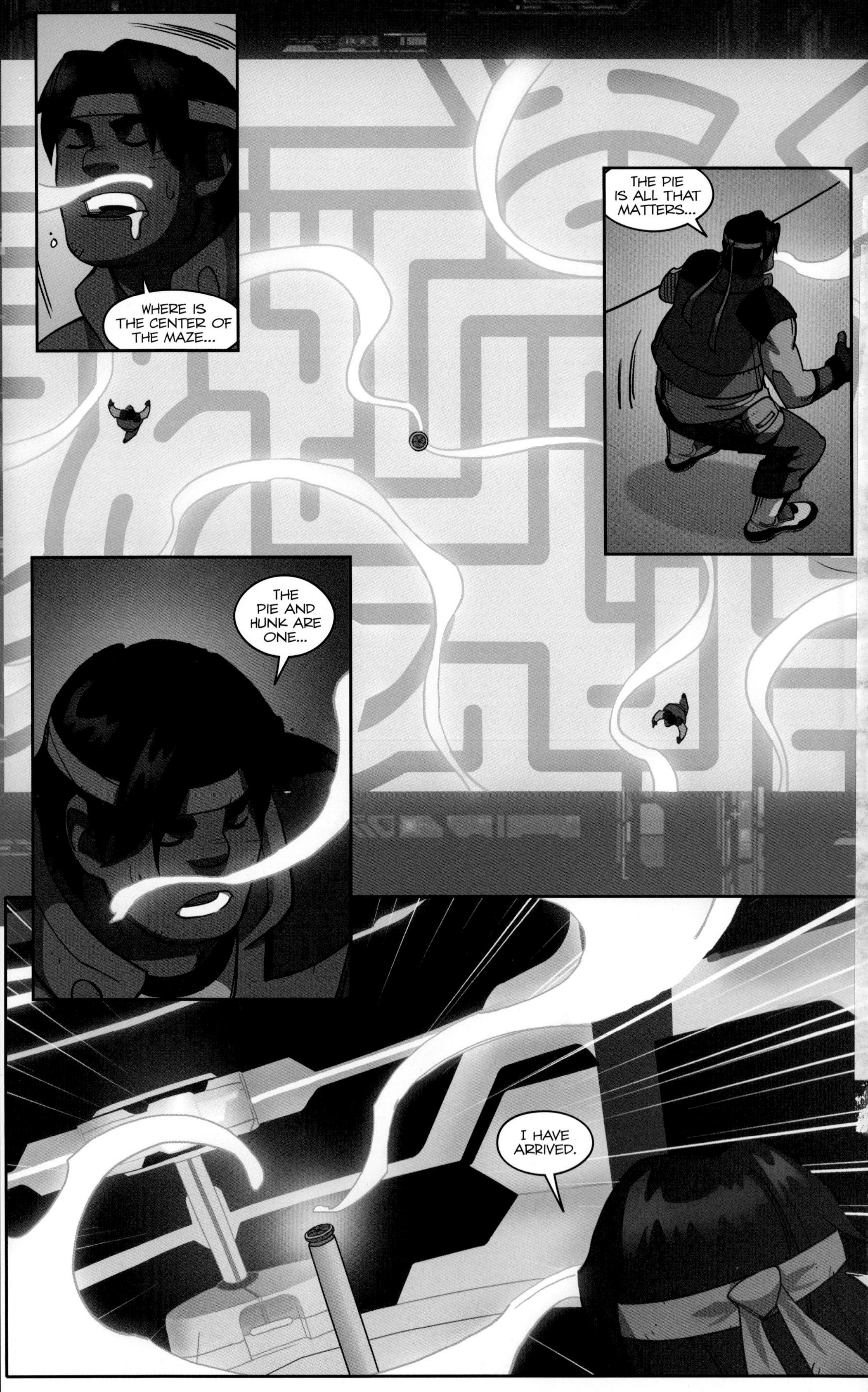
WHERE IS THE CENTER OF THE MAZE...
THE PIE IS ALL THAT MATTERS...
THE PIE AND HUNK ARE ONE...
I HAVE ARRIVED.

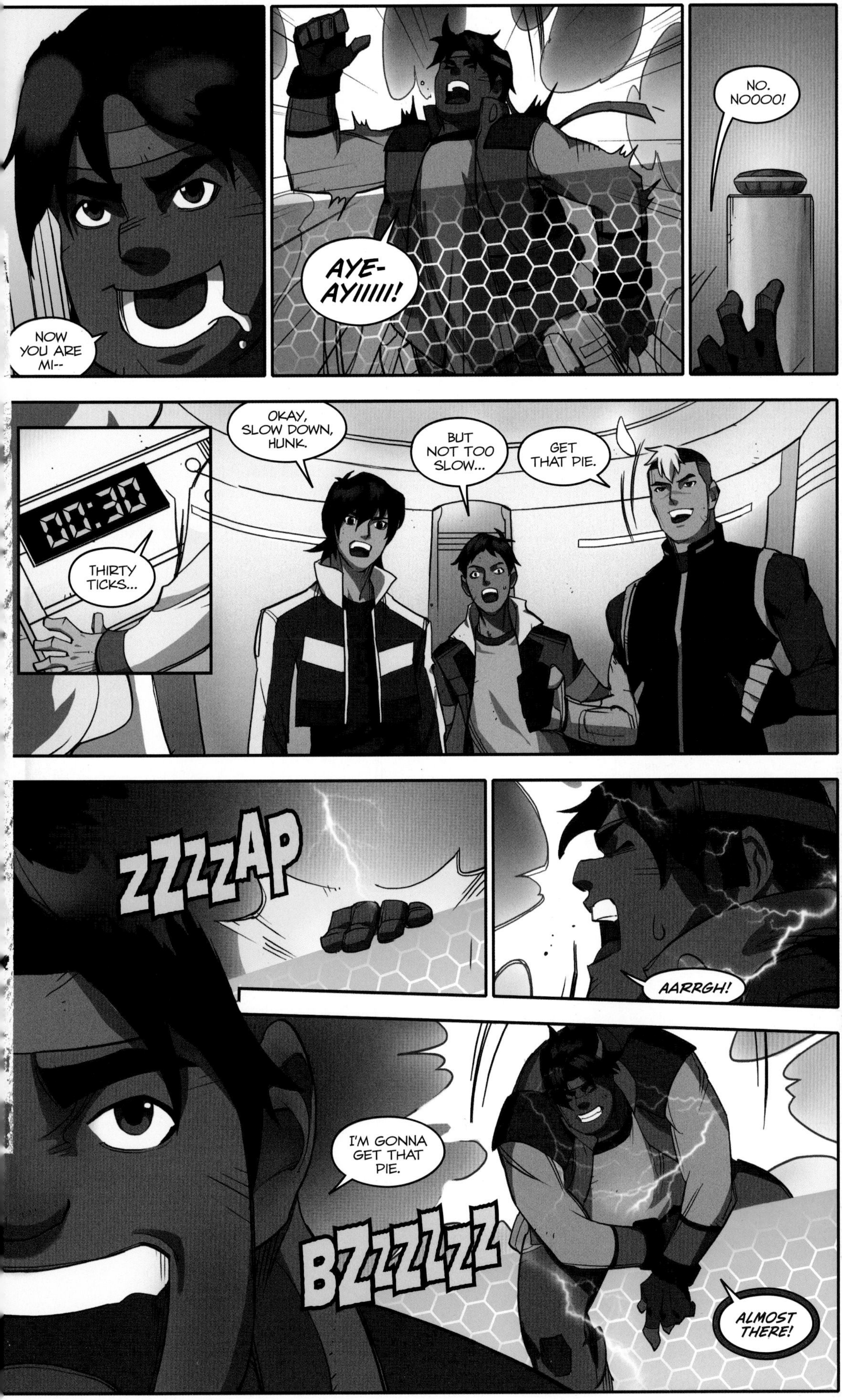
NOW YOU ARE MI--
AYE-AYIIIIII!
NO. NOOOO!
00:30
THIRTY TICKS...
OKAY, SLOW DOWN, HUNK.
BUT NOT TOO SLOW...
GET THAT PIE.
ZZZZZAP
AARRGH!
I'M GONNA GET THAT PIE.
BZZZZZZ
ALMOST THERE!

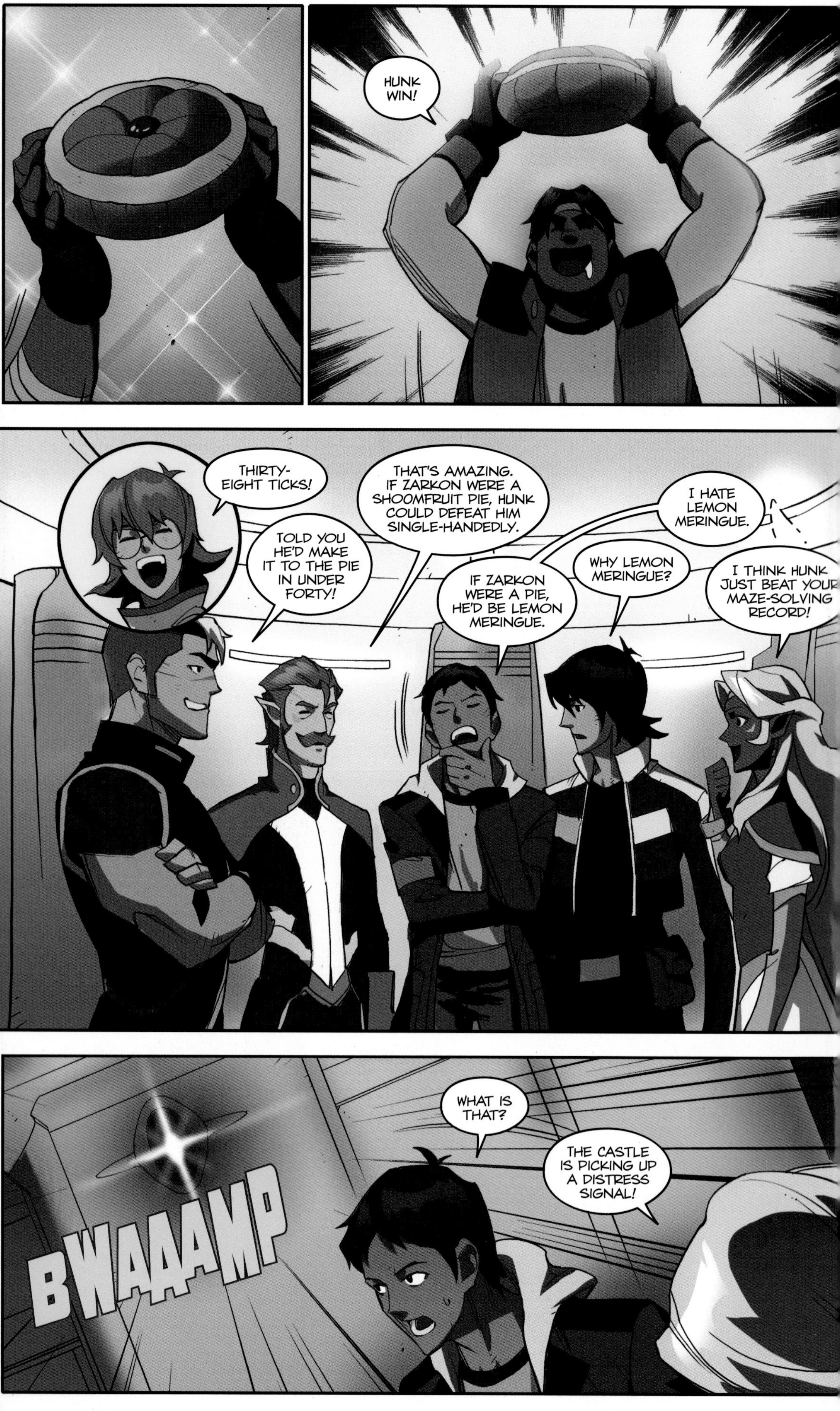
HUNK WIN!
THIRTY-EIGHT TICKS!
TOLD YOU HE'D MAKE IT TO THE PIE IN UNDER FORTY!
THAT'S AMAZING. IF ZARKON WERE A SHOOMFRUIT PIE, HUNK COULD DEFEAT HIM SINGLE-HANDEDLY.
IF ZARKON WERE A PIE, HE'D BE LEMON MERINGUE.
I HATE LEMON MERINGUE.
WHY LEMON MERINGUE?
I THINK HUNK JUST BEAT YOUR MAZE-SOLVING RECORD!
WHAT IS THAT?
BWAAAMP
THE CASTLE IS PICKING UP A DISTRESS SIGNAL!

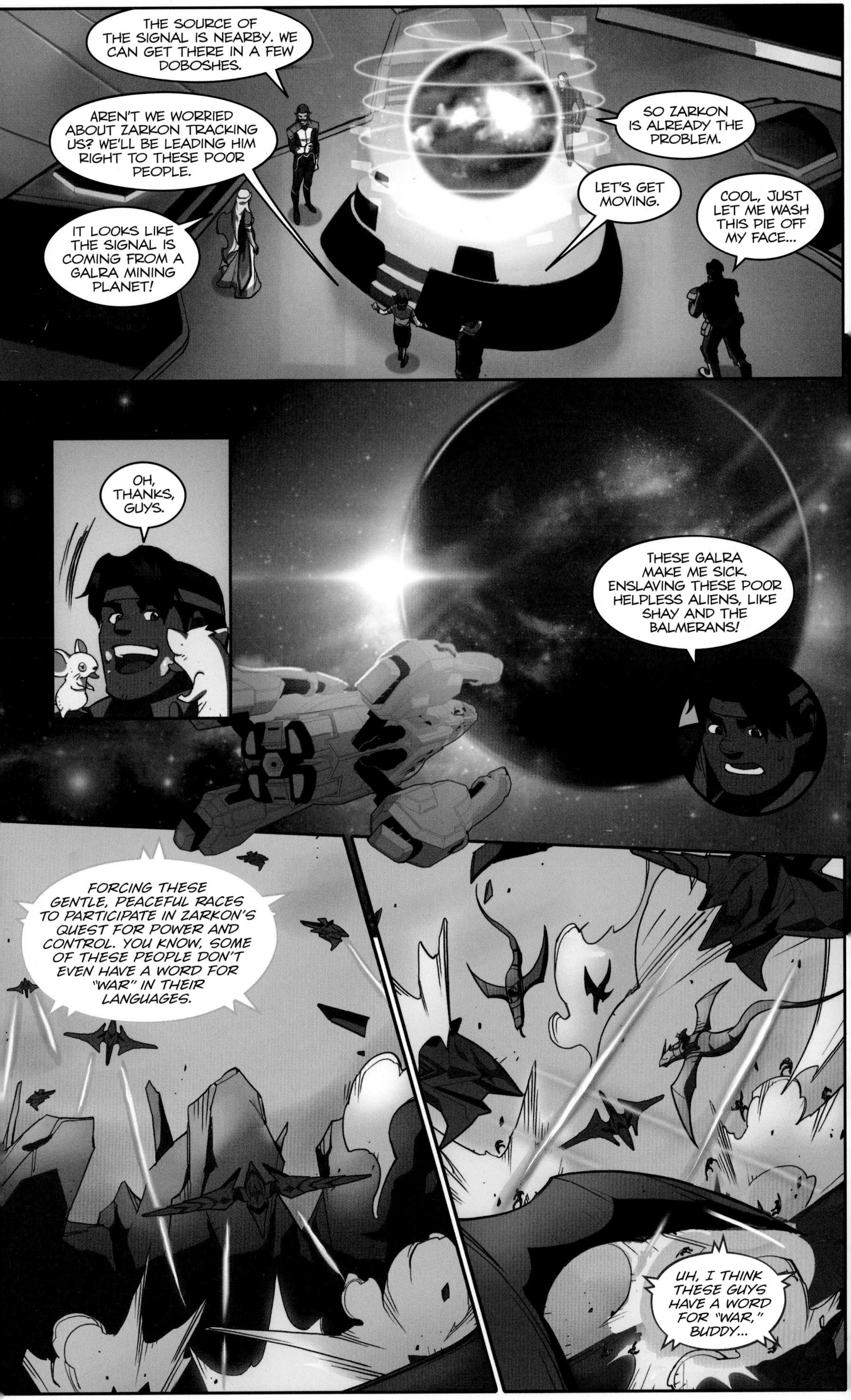
THE SOURCE OF THE SIGNAL IS NEARBY. WE CAN GET THERE IN A FEW DOBOSHES.
AREN'T WE WORRIED ABOUT ZARKON TRACKING US? WE'LL BE LEADING HIM RIGHT TO THESE POOR PEOPLE.
IT LOOKS LIKE THE SIGNAL IS COMING FROM A GALRA MINING PLANET!
SO ZARKON IS ALREADY THE PROBLEM.
LET'S GET MOVING.
COOL, JUST LET ME WASH THIS PIE OFF MY FACE...
OH, THANKS, GUYS.
THESE GALRA MAKE ME SICK. ENSLAVING THESE POOR HELPLESS ALIENS, LIKE SHAY AND THE BALMERANS!
FORCING THESE GENTLE, PEACEFUL RACES TO PARTICIPATE IN ZARKON'S QUEST FOR POWER AND CONTROL. YOU KNOW, SOME OF THESE PEOPLE DON'T EVEN HAVE A WORD FOR "WAR" IN THEIR LANGUAGES.
UH, I THINK THESE GUYS HAVE A WORD FOR "WAR," BUDDY...